FROM INTERNATIONAL RELATIONS TO RELATIONS INTERNATIONAL

This book brings postcolonial critique directly to bear on established ways of theorizing international relations. Its primary concern is with the non-European world and its relations with the North. In advancing an alternative conception of 'relations international', the book draws on alternative source material and different forms of writing. It also features short stories, an interview and explores the role of poetics and performance.

The suzerainty of the disciplinary writ is challenged on three primary grounds. First on its Eurocentrism, which leads the discipline to pass lightly over the distinctive life experiences of most of the world's people. Second, on the discipline's failure to engage in any systematic way with other bodies of knowledge about the international, as for example international political economy, postcolonialism and development. Last, it confronts the 'top down' nature of the politics of the discipline, that seldom addresses everyday life.

From squatter towns to the evasions of the poor, from law through to literature, this work raises a number of problems for international relations. It challenges a colonial mindset, de-centres the West and opens the field to new approaches that are far more inter-disciplinary than international relations generally allows. It is a provocative contribution for students and scholars of IR and postcolonial studies alike.

Phillip Darby is Director of the independent Institute of Postcolonial Studies based in Melbourne and is a Principal Fellow in the School of Social and Political Sciences at the University of Melbourne, Australia.

Postcolonial Politics

Edited by:

Pal Ahluwalia, *University of South Australia*

Michael Dutton, Goldsmiths, *University of London*

Leela Gandhi, *University of Chicago*

Sanjay Seth, Goldsmiths, *University of London*

'Postcolonial Politics' is a series that publishes books that lie at the intersection of politics and postcolonial theory. That point of intersection once barely existed; its recent emergence is enabled, first, because a new form of 'politics' is beginning to make its appearance. Intellectual concerns that began life as a (yet unnamed) set of theoretical interventions from scholars largely working within the 'New Humanities' have now begun to migrate into the realm of politics. The result is politics with a difference, with a concern for the everyday, the ephemeral, the serendipitous and the unworldly. Second, postcolonial theory has raised a new set of concerns in relation to understandings of the non-West. At first these concerns and these questions found their home in literary studies, but they were also, always, political. Edward Said's binary of 'Europe and its other' introduced us to a 'style of thought' that was as much political as it was cultural, as much about the politics of knowledge as the production of knowledge, and as much about life on the street as about a philosophy of being, A new, broader and more reflexive understanding of politics, and a new style of thinking about the non-Western world, make it possible to 'think' politics through postcolonial theory, and to 'do' postcolonial theory in a fashion which picks up on its political implications.

Postcolonial Politics attempts to pick up on these myriad trails and disruptive practices. The series aims to help us read culture politically, read 'difference' concretely, and to problematise our ideas of the modern, the rational and the scientific by working at the margins of a knowledge system that is still logocentric and Eurocentric. This is where a postcolonial politics hopes to offer new and fresh visions of both the postcolonial and the political.

Subseries: Writing Past Colonialism

The Institute of Postcolonial Studies (IPCS)

Edited by:

Phillip Darby, *University of Melbourne, Director of the IPCS*

Writing Past Colonialism is the signature series of the Institute of Postcolonial Studies, based in Melbourne, Australia. By postcolonialism we understand modes of writing and artistic production that critically engage with the ideological legacy and continuing practices of colonialism, and provoke debate about the processes of globalisation. The series is committed to publishing works that break fresh ground in postcolonial studies and seek to make a difference both in the academy and outside it. By way of illustration, our schedule includes books that address:

- grounded issues such as nature and the environment, activist politics and indigenous peoples' struggles
- cultural writing that pays attention to the politics of literary forms
- experimental approaches that produce new postcolonial imaginaries by bringing together different forms of documentation or combinations of theory, performance and practice.

The Postcolonial Politics of Development
Ilan Kapoor

Out of Africa
Post-structuralism's colonial roots
Pal Ahluwalia

The Everyday Practice of Race in America
Ambiguous privilege
Utz McKnight

The City as Target
Edited by Ryan Bishop, Gregory K. Clancy and John Phillips

China and Orientalism
Western knowledge production and the PRC
Daniel F. Vukovich

Reconciliation and Pedagogy
Edited by Pal Ahluwalia, Stephen Atkinson, Peter Bishop, Pam Christie, Robert Hattam and Julie Matthews

From International Relations to Relations International
Postcolonial essays
Edited by Phillip Darby

FROM INTERNATIONAL RELATIONS TO RELATIONS INTERNATIONAL

Postcolonial essays

Edited by Phillip Darby

Routledge
Taylor & Francis Group

LONDON AND NEW YORK

First published 2016
by Routledge
2 Park Square, Milton Park, Abingdon, Oxon OX14 4RN

and by Routledge
711 Third Avenue, New York, NY 10017

Routledge is an imprint of the Taylor & Francis Group, an informa business

British Library Cataloguing in Publication Data
A catalogue record for this book is available from the British Library

Library of Congress Cataloging in Publication Data
A catalog record for this book has been requested.

ISBN: 978-1-138-95848-7 (hbk)
ISBN: 978-1-138-95849-4 (pbk)
ISBN: 978-1-315-66118-6 (ebk)

Typeset in Bembo
by HWA Text and Data Management, London

To the memory of Devika Goonewardene

CONTENTS

CONTRIBUTORS

Tony Anghie received his SJD from Harvard Law School and is Professor of Law at the S.J. Quinney School of Law, University of Utah. He is the author of *Imperialism, Sovereignty and the Making of International Law* (Cambridge University Press, 2005).

Paul Carter's recent books include *Ground Truthing* (2010), *Dark Writing* (2008), and *Meeting Place: the Encounter and Challenge of Coexistence* (2013). He lives in Melbourne where he is Professor of Design, Urbanism at RMIT University.

Phillip Darby is Director of the Institute of Postcolonial Studies and a principal fellow in the School of Political and Social Sciences at the University of Melbourne.

Christine Deftereos is a social theorist based in Melbourne, where she also taught international relations. She is the author of *Ashis Nandy and the Cultural Politics of Selfhood* (Sage, 2013).

Devika Goonewardene taught international relations at the University of Melbourne and was for some time executive officer of the Institute of Postcolonial Studies. Her PhD thesis was on the intersection of international relations and postcolonialism in south Asia. It remained uncompleted on her death in 2009 but a number of extracts and essays have been published posthumously.

David L. Martin taught international relations and postcolonial studies at the University of Melbourne and now teaches at the Politics Department at Goldsmiths College, University of London. He is the author of *Curious Visions of Modernity: Enchantment, Magic and the Sacred* (MIT Press, 2011).

Carlos Eduardo Morreo is a graduate researcher in the School of Politics and International Relations at the Australian National University. Prior to ANU, he was a researcher at the Centro de Estudios Latinoamericanos 'Rómulo Gallegos' and a lecturer at the Universidad Central de Venezuela and the Universidad Católica Andrés Bello.

Ashis Nandy is Honorary Fellow at the Centre for the Study of Developing Societies in Delhi and Distinguished Fellow of the Institute of Postcolonial Studies. He is one of India's foremost public intellectuals and in 2007 was awarded the Fukuoka Grand Prize for his work in support of Asian cultures.

Sekai Nzenza took her PhD in international relations at the University of Melbourne. She held senior positions with World Vision both in Melbourne and Los Angeles. She is now a full-time writer based in Zimbabwe. Her first book, *Zimbabwean Woman: My Own Story* was published in London in 1988, *Songs to an African Sunset* was published by Lonely Planet in 1997, and her fiction has been included in the short story collections *Daughters of Africa* and *Images of the West*.

INTRODUCTION

Phillip Darby

This book invites readers to think about how we might rework our knowledge conventions relating to international politics which contribute to the neglect of perspectives from the South and the marginalisation of most of the world's people. To this end, it extends the critique of disciplinary international relations developed by postcolonial scholars over the past two decades. At the same time it reaches out to other disciplinary formations concerned with the international and to grounded knowledges focused on lived experience to develop a more broadly based platform of global change. It also reflects back on postcolonial studies, arguing that the discourse needs to engage directly with the contemporary politics of the international.

The title of the book flags our commitment to work with a more inclusive understanding of the international than traditionally has been the practice. The phrase "relations international" was coined by Christine Sylvester. On her reading, it conveys "the myriad positions that groups assume toward one another across the many boundaries and identities that defy field-invented parameters". She adds that it is about "inters" of all kinds and that it puts the emphasis on varieties of connection.[1] All this is grist to our mill.

For most of its history IR has been primarily concerned with the view from the top, with the thinking of statespersons, and the logic of power politics or the rationality of liberal theorists, as understood from on high. In such readings, the modern nation-state is invariably taken as foundational. We are now becoming aware that the apparent "naturalness" of the territorial state and the division of space between nation-states screens from view a politics of domination and subordination. Indubitably, the face of politics that shows reflects the kind of knowledge that is valorized. And this, in part, depends upon location. Knowledge of the everyday sheds a different light on the accommodations of diplomacy from the transcripts of officialdom. Thus a Muslim survivor of the communal violence in the Indian subcontinent in 1947 could observe: "To tell you the truth, it was only in the bloodshed of Partition that ordinary people saw the shape of Independence."[2] Sankaran Krishna introduces us to another facet of the nation-building project when he argues: "The making of the nation serves as universal alibi for the violent unmaking of all alternative forms of community."[3]

Whether the advent of international institutions has made all that much difference is open to doubt. Usually such institutions have worked in tandem with powerful states. Despite the hopes pinned on the League of Nations, Antony Anghie writes that all the major developments of the inter-war period "could be seen as creations of sovereignty, as increasingly sophisticated exercises of the powers of sovereignty".[4] Notwithstanding the positive measures that came with the internationalisation of trusteeship, the Mandate System was inseparable from "the creation of new systems of subordination and control administered by international institutions".[5] A broadly similar argument will be developed in later sections of the book with respect to the contemporary United Nations system. Again, it is the view from above which is privileged. The hierarchical structure of many of the UN agencies meshes with that of the international system. Akin to the practice of most Western states, the agendas imposed on non-European societies are essentially determined by the agencies themselves. Moreover, the heavy reliance on expert knowledge rather than local knowledge mostly reinforces First World prescriptions and has the effect of depoliticising the issues at stake. The World Bank's discourse and practice is a striking case in point.

The other side of the story – and the one we wish to bring to the fore – is about how international processes are seen from the ground, from below as it were. It has become customary in the period of neoliberalism to position civil society in this space. Civil society, the argument runs, will give voice to ordinary people and fill the vacuum left by the slimmed-down state. Critics, however, tell a very different story. In the non-European context, civil society mainly consists of middle class groups committed to political and economic development along Western lines. Partha Chatterjee, for instance, argues that in ex-colonial countries such as India, civil society is the closed association of modern elite groups, sequestered from the popular life of communities.[6] Mahmood Mamdani writes of the division between citizen and subject in contemporary Africa inherited from colonial rule. On the one side, small urban elites speaking the language of rights and civil society; on the other, rural people cut off from modernist politics and governed through customary authority. He concludes: "[c]onfined to civil society, democratization is both superficial and explosive".[7]

Looking more closely at the experiences of people in squatter settlements or struggling in the countryside, at people on the move attempting to evade established authority, knowledges that speak to the political simply do not fit the categories of most social science scholarship. Indeed, they may not be recognized as knowledge at all. For one thing, they are not the product of book learning; rather they respond to the exigencies of ordinary life. Often they are embodied and performative – or perhaps one should say performative in a different way from knowledge in the First World. In a track-breaking analysis, Ranabir Samaddar argues that what is needed is a discourse of actions that captures practices such as resisting, organizing, mobilizing as well as developing friendships and making connections. On his account, these practices are essentially collective.[8] We are thus led to bring into reckoning knowledges relating to the social, often associated with traditional religious belief or cultural practice. One thinks immediately of the *Mahabharata* and other Hindu epics, in which sociality features so strongly not only in their content but in the telling. So also the principles of relatedness and practices of care on Aboriginal people in Australia or the senses of community in Ubuntu spirituality that draw on indigenous African religious practices as well as Christianity.

Why does material of this nature need to be brought into international discourses? This is a question that many of the essays in this book will take up, but by way of an opening bid three propositions in capsule form carry the burden of argument. First, it challenges the colonial mindset that permeates so much of First World thinking and policy about the former colonial world, the processes of intervention and the assumption that the West is the model for the rest of humankind. Second, it opens new horizons to better understand why non-European people might choose to author their own politics and to countenance alternative futures. Third, it provided opportunities to rethink established approaches to order, violence and change, and to experiment with other ways of proceeding drawn from the different cultural traditions and political experiences of non-European societies. A few examples may be helpful here. In critical security studies there is a growing interest in exploring the relationship between security and insecurity in Third World contexts, the politics of non-violence and alternative approaches to conflict resolution. If we are to break through the spatial division of the world, it would be productive to reflect on the practices and conventions that enabled traders, pilgrims and others to travel widely before the territoriality of the modern state was extended throughout the world. The concern with the social in some non-European societies could serve as an antidote to its neglect in dominant discourses of the international today. IR, for instance, has much to tell about deterrence, the politics of power including soft power, and what we might call conversion through coercion, but little to say about building relationships across difference.

It is as well to briefly touch on some of the difficulties associated with the retrieval and use of the kind of material mentioned above. Other people's knowledge can no longer be regarded as common property, available to all to be freely used. Sometimes encoded in works of art that cannot be viewed publicly or passed on orally only to a restricted circle, it may not be accessible. Even where it is, conventions about representations, ownership and repatriation must now guide what is said and done in all disciplinary fields and domains of action. At times there may be a problem about identifying the politics in the mix of material because it fails to fly a familiar flag. Silence, taking different forms in different cultures, can carry its own politics. Imperial history abounds with figures such as the "mad mullah", whose "insanity" supposedly takes him out of the realm of politics. Nor can the apparent rejection of politics be taken at face value. The Gaza Youth's Manifesto for Change of December 2010 that begins "Fuck Hamas. Fuck Israel. Fuck Fatah", vents the anger and frustration of young Palestinian cyber-activists about their situation.[9] One member of the group explained: "Politics is bollocks, it is screwing our lives up."[10] Arguably, however, in its rejection of the politics of the states, would-be states and the UN, the manifesto expresses a politics of its own.

And now a caveat of a kind. Earlier I highlighted the potential significance of some of the conventions of stateless societies and of cultural patterns that endured through the colonial period. No one, however, would imagine that traditional practices, customs and rituals could somehow be transposed to the globalized world of today. Rather, the hope is that knowledges we in the West have mostly bypassed might yet unlock our thinking about modern statecraft through a mixture of analogy and imaginative reach. The process, as I see it, is first to privilege the non-European material and then to work through the connections and parallels with recessive traditions in the West. We have much to learn from Gandhi in this regard.

Implicit in the argument thus far is the need to turn to a wider spectrum of ideas and evidence than is usually relied upon in studies of international relations. For starters, there is much to be learnt from other members of the family of disciplinary formations addressing the international such as development, international political economy and international law. The problem is that this family is little inclined to converse, with the result that important lines of thought remain confined within disciplinary enclosures. We therefore engage in border crossing as a means of mutual enrichment. On another plane, and close to the heart of the book, we seek to capture something of the texture of ordinary people's lives, their understanding of and emotional responses to external intervention. Here we look to anthropological and ethnological accounts, literary narratives and visual culture to give insights seldom found in writing about international affairs. Why such sources are enabling will be discussed in individual chapters. At this point I wish to reflect a little more on the task of working across knowledges that appear to be of such a different nature.

The differences we have to negotiate include between the written and the oral, the word and the picture, the scholarly and the popular or everyday, the social sciences and the humanities – though the categories overlap and blur. As we know, bridging these divides is not easy and some strict disciplinarians say they are unbridgeable at least for the purpose of rigorous analysis. Yet we also know that much of the compartmentalization of knowledge was coextensive with the emergence of modernity and that it has been accentuated by the processes of specialization and professionalization over the past two decades. Bearing this in mind and taking heed of David Turnbull's argument that the construction of knowledge is invariably messy,[11] I wish to suggest that the divides may not be as solid as is often thought. Take the text and the visual. When I first studied IR at the University of Melbourne, I was deeply influenced by Reinbold Niebuhr, especially his insistence on the brutality and collective egoism of international politics as well as by the masterly lectures of W. Macmahon Ball, a doyen of international affairs in Australia. Although I am not a visually inclined person, in my mind's eye I had a clear picture of IR as a world cut off from ordinary life, so dark and brooding that we could be on another planet. (Given the literature on anarchy and the state of nature, one can't help wondering if others had an even grimmer picture of a world without IR.) Later at Oxford I became interested in liberalism and empire and I listened to the exchanges between the remarkable characters who presided over the Friday afternoon Commonwealth history seminar. One could not help but have a highly personalized picture of how the spirit of progress shaped the Great Commercial Republic of the World: "Social energy appeared to flow from the happy play of free minds, free markets and Christian morality".[12] (A visual representation of the contemporary liberal trading order might still feature the light of progress but institutions would figure larger and the colour would not be so vivid.)

In a recent book Paul Carter seeks to reconnect the world of ideas and the world of pictures by drawing on his work on spatial history, his artistic interests and collaborations, and his practices of place-making. The root of the problem he locates in the Enlightenment tradition that continues to shape the line of disembodied reasoning that mediates our design upon the world. His solution is to go both above and below this line, bringing bodies into the picture and capturing the traces of movement, interaction and exchange concealed by our representations. By working imaginatively both to recover lost passages of our history and to develop practices that make room for things to happen, the line can be reconfigured as a meeting place and humankind and the environment be seen as unified through movement form. Carter concludes by observing that René Descartes called his work of logic a *discourse*, a running hither and thither, because the right way only emerges after trying unknown paths and blundering along. "Even the most influential philosopher of linear thinking was first of all a cryptographer of the dark and the crooked."[13]

If we are to draw on different source materials it follows that we need to be open to writing differently. Clearly, trafficking with other discourses of the international requires us so far as possible to avoid disciplinary jargon and in-house concepts that display a "keep out" sign to those not in the know. I have argued elsewhere that some scholarly conventions stand in the way of breaking from disciplinary moorings and taking a chance with the unorthodox. To give a few examples, the insistence on proceeding from established disciplinary reference-points (still characteristic of most IR journals), the stamp of authority supposedly conferred by excessive footnoting and the concern with ironing out apparent inconsistencies.[14] On the last point, a colleague recently took me to task for failing to practise what I preach, adding that a seamless narrative is a colonial construction. Here I am reminded that Iris Murdoch once observed that stories "are almost always a bit or very false", but she goes on to suggest that "[i]t may be that the best model for all thought is the creative imagination".[15] Language and style have an intimate relationship with content. Language can tell a story in its own right, especially important if we are to catch something of the rhythm of everyday life. Then there is the role of poetics in extending our imaginative reach. In his preface to *Dark Writing*, Paul Carter urges his readers to trust the poetic logic of the argument: "It provides the ground of the landscape even where you do not recognize the local features."[16] I cannot say that in this book we have got the balance right but we have tried to write in plain English, to vary the narrative form through the inclusion of interviews and short stories, as well as to extend material discussed in individual chapters by the insertion of fragments on related issues in various parts of the text. We have also endeavoured to develop elements of a conversation between the contributors.

A few words are perhaps needed about the understanding of postcolonialism that informs the book. Our emphasis is placed firmly on the grounded practices of assertion and struggle against the hold of the centre, in the hope that new forms of the political may be discerned that speak to the distinctiveness of non-European experience. In short, we are more interested in postcolonialism applied than postcolonialism as high theory. Necessarily, this requires a sustained engagement with IR, development studies, international law and international political economy. Over the past few years postcolonialism has been sharply censured for its silence on many of the most pressing issues of international politics. In a special issue of *New Formations* in 2006, the editors argue that the invasion and occupation of Iraq represents a watershed for postcolonial studies, requiring a fundamental change in the framing assumptions, organizing principles and intellectual habits of the field. What Iraq shows is that the world hasn't change; imperialism remains a deep structural dimension of the world system. The central task enforced on postcolonial scholars is "to work towards the production of a new 'history of the present'".[17] This call for a redirection of postcolonial criticism connects with earlier complaints that postcolonialism has lost its radical edge and that it principally addresses the needs of the Western academy. We aim to contribute to the rethinking of the postcolonial that is now taking place.

One other feature of the book should be noted before moving on. Interwoven in the book's narrative is an account of an IR course that many of us taught at the University of Melbourne which told the story of IR by beginning in Asia and Africa instead of in Europe. I would like to think that this is not some conceit on my part – and indeed the idea of doing so was not my own – but a contribution to the intellectual work of the book. I have often reflected that we need to know much more than we do about how international politics is taught because it so directly shapes the ideas that go out into the world. (And think of the harm that many of them do!) Some work is now being done in this area but little that I have read breathes life into courses.[18] It is our hope that the vignettes included in this collection might help generate debate about what is taught and how.

A few words about how the book unfolds. I have always taken the view that an introduction should avoid a potted summary of the contents of individual chapters. Nonetheless readers may find it helpful to have a brief account of the intellectual work of the various chapters and how they are positioned in relation to the major themes of the book.

The first chapter by Devika Goonewardene sets the scene by looking at how knowledges of the international that fall outside the disciplinary writ figured in the IR course mentioned above. Dipping into the history and politics of the Indian subcontinent and the rich archive of literary narratives, she reflects on the student response to a decidedly postcolonial take on international relations. One of the strengths of this approach, Devika suggests, is that the encounter with a different society encourages students to think about their own society in terms of similarity rather than difference. This line of thought, in many ways pioneered by Ashis Nandy, is taken up by Ashis himself in Chapter 2. In a wide-ranging conversation, he canvasses the possibilities of making connections with others – in several registers – through the cultures of the everyday. Along the way, we gain insights into how he came to resist the rule of experts and the compartmentalization of knowledge, as well as to use (and misuse) scholarly conventions to advance a progressive politics.

Chapter 3 by Antony Anghie takes up problems associated with the nation-state as they manifest themselves in international law – a discourse which in some key respects runs in parallel with IR. How, Antony asks, can the wishes of "a people" be accommodated when sovereignty is vested in the state. In its most acute form, what is to be done about minorities and secession? Antony raises the question of alternatives to the nation-state but he acknowledges that the very idea of alternatives undermines the foundations of international law as we know it. The work of Chapter 4 is to bring the debates about development into the mainstream of international politics. Curiously, disciplinary IR has had little sustained engagement with the development project despite the part it has played in structuring North–South relations. Picking up on lines of thought articulated in the previous chapter, development is shown to have colonial roots and to help underwrite the existing international order. In line with one of the book's major themes, a case is made for doing development differently by a selective engagement with the everyday.

The next two chapters speak to African and Latin American knowledges of the international. In some ways akin to Devika's study of Indian knowledges in Chapter 1, readers may find it useful to bracket together the three essays and to reflect on what they mean for teaching and research. Sekai Nzenza's chapter comprises two short stories about African everyday life, one set in the village and the other in the city. Neither story directly engages with IR but both capture something of African knowledges of the world and how the external filters into everyday life.

The two stories stand in their own right. They are open to multiple interpretations and the work of the book would not be advanced by suggesting how they should be read. Nonetheless, a few words are appropriate about the particular value of literature – and one could add other branches of the creative and performative arts – to an understanding of African politics. The fact is that Africa has fared badly in IR and other discourses of the international. Mostly it has been seen as "the sign of the exception" or more recently, in some quarters, that it is doing better because it is following the prescriptions of the West. Now, of course, Africa has many voices. There is also the historical divergence between north and south. But I think it can be said that most African literature serves to connect across difference and it is also an antidote to analyses focused on the wheeling and dealing of national elites and the institutional structures of states. We may thus be led to see more in the way of exchanges between rulers and ruled. Arguably, this links up with Achille Mbembe's writing on the intimacy and conviviality between the brokers of power and ordinary people.[19] African literature is justly famed for its recovery of the past but, associated, we should also note its concern for more enabling futures. Think of Chinua Achebe's novel *Anthills of the Savannah* or the work of Wole Soyinka.

Chapter 6 by Carlos Morreo examines the case of Latin America. Although a companion piece to Sekai's chapter, this essay takes its lead from the heritage of regional critical and social theory. Carlos argues in forthright manner that IR is misplaced in the Latin American context because it disregards the region's long-time search for some kind of emancipatory sociality. He extends his analysis to recent attempts by the Venezuelan state to develop a people's diplomacy and the contradictions involved in this venture.

The remaining three essays take up areas of concern to international studies which disciplinary IR ignores or short-changes. In Chapter 7 David Martin brings a searching eye to the supposed aesthetic turn in IR and finds it wanting. Why, he asks, has the aesthetic as represented lost the power to make us think afresh? In keeping with its content, the chapter is presented as an experiment in writing – and one that engages with the performative as well. Chapter 8 by Christine Deftereos explores the way the discipline has disavowed a theory of the self or when pressed has offered only a very limited reading of the self. It is Christine's view that postcolonial analysis can function as a tool of disruption. Drawing on the work of postcolonial scholars, in particular Ashis Nandy, she argues that people's everyday experience can challenge the global culture of commonsense and thereby our understanding of the international self.

In the final chapter of the book Paul Carter urges the IR constituency to rethink its political geography in the interests of imagining more enabling international governance. Paul takes the discipline to task for its preoccupation with land masses – that he associates with certitude and fixity – at the expense of the sea – which is conducive to meeting and exchange. What is needed is not technocratic knowhow but poetic logic. Hence his insistence on the significance of language and the processes of naming.

This book is dedicated to the memory of Devika Goonewardene who died in 2009 at the age of thirty-four. Devika taught in our IR course at the University of

Melbourne and was deeply involved in the Institute of Postcolonial Studies. She was also my PhD student. All the contributors to the book have fond memories of Devika and some were her close friends. Several write in their essays of her work or tell anecdotes of shared experiences. We hope that recalling something of her life will personalize the book and serve as an added link between the chapters. Mostly, however, our recollections are intended as a tribute to Devika.

Notes

1 Christine Sylvester, *Feminist Theory and International Relations in a Postmodern Era*, 1994, Cambridge, Cambridge University Press, p.219.
2 Gyanendra Pandey, *Remembering Partition*, 2001, Cambridge, Cambridge University Press, p.125.
3 Sankaran Krisha, *Postcolonial Insecurities: India, Sri Lanka, and the Question of Nationhood*, 1999, Minneapolis, University of Minnesota Press, p.20.
4 Antony Anghie, *Imperialism, Sovereignty and the Making of International Law*, 2004, Cambridge, Cambridge University Press, p.132.
5 Ibid, p.179.
6 Partha Chatterjee, *The Politics of the Governed: Reflections on Popular Protest in Most of the World*, 2004, New York, Columbia University Press, pp.35–42.
7 Mahmood Mamdani, *Citizen and Subject: Contemporary Africa and the Legacy of Late Colonialism*, 1996, Princeton, Princeton University Press, p.289.
8 Ranabir Samaddar, *Emergence of the Political Subject*, 2010, New Delhi, Sage, pp.xxiii–xxv.
9 "Fuck Hamas. Fuck Israel", *Guardian Weekly*, 7 January 2011.
10 Gazan youth issue manifesto, *The Observer*, 2 January 2011.
11 David Turnbull, *Masons, Tricksters and Cartographers: Comparative Studies in the Sociology of Scientific and Indigenous Knowledge*, 2000, Amsterdam, Harwood Academic Knowledges.
12 Ronald Robinson and John Gallagher with Alice Denny, *Africa and the Victorians: The Official Mind of Imperialism*, 1961, London, Macmillan, p.1. Ronald Robinson and John Gallagher were two of the key players in the Commonwealth history re-enactments.
13 Paul Carter, *Dark Writing: Geography, Performance, Design*, 2009, Honolulu, University of Haiwai'i Press, p.227.
14 Phillip Darby, "Reconfiguring 'the International': Knowledge Machines, Boundaries, and Exclusions", *Alternatives*, 2003, vol.28, pp.141–166 at p.164, footnote 23.
15 Iris Murdoch, *Metaphysics as a Guide to Morals*, 1992, London, Chatto and Windus, pp.105 and 169.
16 Carter, *op.cit.*, p.xv.
17 Priyamvada Gopal and Neil Lazarus, "Editorial", *New Formations*, 59, 2006, pp.7–9 at p.9.
18 I am thinking here particularly of quantitative work. See, for instance, "International relations scholarship around the world", edited by Arlene B. Tickner and Ole Weaver, Institute for the Theory and Practice of IR, College of William and Mary. http://irtheoryandpractice.wm.edu/projects/trip/Final_Trip_Report.2009.pdf
19 Achille Mbembe, *On the Postcolony*, Berkeley, University of California Press, 2001, pp.104 and 128.

1

TEACHING AN UNORTHODOX IR COURSE

Devika Goonewardene

This essay reflects on some of the challenges and satisfactions of teaching an alternative IR course foregrounding the non-European world. It focuses primarily on indigenous knowledges of the international and what they can contribute to non-disciplinary ways of seeing the world. It is informed throughout by postcolonial perspectives. It proceeds on the assumption that neither IR nor postcolonialism can by itself offer a compelling agenda for rethinking the nature of the international in the twenty-first century. Indeed, especially in the case of the non-European world it has become increasingly clear that other discourses must be brought into the mix if teaching programmes are to embrace the need for change.

The course of which I speak – which was in its latter days called "International Relations (and Its Others)" – had to constantly affirm its right to be called thus, both by colleagues within the department in which it was taught (Political Science) as well as to our students. Indeed, the "(and Its Others)" part of the title was added at the insistence of those who claimed that we were misleading them by naming what we were doing international relations. The reason for this is quite simple. The course took as its main aim "the possibilities of rethinking the processes of international change and exchange as they affect Third World peoples".[1] The pursuit of this aim required the taking of two fundamental steps. First, an opening-up or decolonising of the discipline which took the realm of the international as its province. Second, looking for a reworked understanding of the international in different places, using different sources.[2]

The problem with proceeding in this way was that it challenged the banner of universality and generality that disciplinary IR proclaims as its special provenance what one critic once called "a view from afar, from up high".[3] Of course this seemingly Olympian view is in and of itself one vested with power and interest. In the words of Edward Said, it brings to mind the various kinds of power – political, intellectual, cultural and moral – wielded by the Occident to attain a positional superiority over the Orient.[4] In this instance, we were faced with the view that the non-Western world could not be the source of meanings, traditions and categories that would help us understand how political collectivities are constituted, interact and relate internationally. The argument that Dipesh Chakrabarty has famously made in regard to history, that the West produced universally applicable theory whilst the non-West only had empirical practice, also dominates in the field of IR.[5] The weight of modernity, especially as it is manifested in IR's reliance on the categories and concepts of nation-state, order, history and public and private all pointed to an idea of the international that rendered the non-West in Orientalised terms as being outside, other, feminine and foe to the West's inside, its masculine and rational self. To again echo Chakrabarty, the non-West was about lack, absence and failure, its subjectivity could only be construed as being present, if at all, in incomplete form.[6] African and Asian nation-states, institutions and peoples mainly figured in proper IR courses as failing, corruption and poverty-ridden basket cases which should be chastised for their inability to meet and match the cultural and military clout of their Euro-Atlantic cousins. Rarely, if ever, can such polities, personages and communities take centre stage and set the terms of the discourse, be the point of view as it were from which the world "out there" is constituted. This perception was not only prevalent among our colleagues and in the disciplinary literature but also seemed to be a part of the popular consciousness of our students.

How is a course that attempts to foreground the Third World and show how its distinctive experience can enrich our approach to the international meant to proceed in the face of such disciplinary abjection? For us the answer lay in engaging with modernity, being aware of its protocols of knowledge-making and using this self-awareness to speak truth to power.[7] By redefining modernity's construction of the international through a principled and selective engagement with discourses of globalisation, and by always keeping an eye on the view from above as it affected those on the ground. Most of all, we set up the oppositional thrust of the course by starting with a figure well known for his pursuit of dissenting knowledges and critique of the dictates that modernity imposes on that which is not or like itself, Ashis Nandy.

The first reading in the course that students encountered was a cartoon rendition of Ashis Nandy, picturing him as an approachable avuncular figure and providing an introduction to arguments he put forward in *The Intimate Enemy* on colonialism's effects on both the coloniser and the colonised.[8] Through this easily accessible depiction of Nandy's work we launched our first volley in unsettling students' understandings of what would be the stereotypical self and other. By speaking of multiple forms of selfhood, the culturally incommunicable nature of some colonised selves, and the shared victimhood – from conceptual to physical oppression – of peoples from the West and non-West alike, we attempted to establish an ethical relationship between self and other as being the foundation upon which to study and ultimately participate in the international.

We also set up the self as being a crucial part of the object of study. This is in contrast to many prevailing conceptions of the international, both popular and disciplinary, that see the international as "out there", somehow disconnected from the observer and his/her culture. The action is across a national border, it does not involve an interrogation of one's own selfhood.[9] The self in this context is taken as a given, to be studied elsewhere – in area studies, history or literature. Thus, what one journalist said of her obsession with India can often be said of our novice IR student:

> Reading about, writing about, trying to understand India allows me not to read about, write about or understand Australia…Easier, perhaps, to worry about poverty overseas than down the road.[10]

Yet through Nandy's work – and later on through Partha Chatterjee's as well – we are asking our students to put themselves (as individuals, as Australians) into the picture, to write about and understand the relationship between India and Australia, which necessarily involves coming to terms with both as self (same) and other (different). I should pause at this point to say that whilst we sought ways of claiming a stake for the non-Western world in the field of the international, we did not specifically set out to Indianise it. What I have termed Indian knowledges, did, instead become the means to enter into other forms of engagement with various parts of the non-West, from Africa and South America through to Australia's immediate backyard of the Pacific and Asia.

At this early stage we sought to find the larger theoretical relevance of Nandy's work on colonialism to the postcolonial present without immersing students in empirical details. Two examples of the sorts of connections being made through our deployment of Nandy might illustrate our simultaneous engagement with and critique of dominant conceptions of the international. First, looking externally, take Australia's tendency to criticise its Asian neighbours for not being culturally, politically, legally and morally like themselves. Instead of divorcing such external posturing from practices at home, we have used Nandy's work to make students think of the Australian side of its international engagement. This in turn leads to the second level of connection, that of reconfiguring what are termed domestic matters regarding indigenous peoples, migrants, refugees and terrorists by the Australian Federal Government, as international ones as well. Instead of hiding behind cries of "national security" or looking to build solidarity across borders through a victorious "coalition of the willing" that stamps out dissent of every stripe, a turn to Nandy sees solidarity being fashioned through a non-pejorative notion of shared victimhood that observes no cultural or economic divides occasioned by the politics of geography.

Whilst their first encounter with Nandy is through the entertaining and comparatively slight format of a cartoon, the second engages with his critique of history, and its consequences for those on the ground who do not necessarily see their pasts through such a lens. In addition to sharing a national day –

Australia Day and Republic Day on January 26th – both Australia and India are in the midst of what has been called history wars. Both countries have their conservative elements, although they manifest themselves somewhat differently within the larger global context of neoliberalism. Thus, the Indian response has been seen in terms of religious fundamentalism, whilst the Australian one reeks of a racial insularity propped up by cultural conservatism. In both instances, the past is a battlefield, mined by politicians and historians to fashion singular conceptions of national identity to which people then have to swear allegiance. Historiography thus carries a politics in both countries.

In a classically provocative piece Nandy makes a strong case for the ahistorical, for mythic ways of organising the past. He contrasts the operation of principled forgetfulness in myth – where what is important is "a refusal to separate the remembered past from its ethical meaning in the present" – to that of disciplinary history, whose enterprise is to bare the past completely, remembering (or rather reconstructing) it objectively in its entirety.[11] For the operation of myth in practice and for the interventions of historians trying to stay true to history and simultaneously debunk politicians and groups who are utilising myth as a justification for violence in the name of capturing the state for themselves, Nandy turns to an examination of the violence at Ayodhya in 1992. His concluding characterisation shows how the European concept of history has marginalised the many mythic pasts of India and left us with a Mahabharatic battle between two sets of illegitimate children, fathered by nineteenth-century Europe and the colonial empires, who have escaped from the orphanage of history.[12]

Whilst the Indian historical specificities are alien to our students, I have found the extensive amount of Indian historiography we teach – from Nandy's ahistoricism, through to the *Subaltern Studies* work of Partha Chatterjee, Dipesh Chakrabarty and Gyanendra Pandey – provide a useful means of addressing similar issues in Australian historiography. There is, thus, the introduction of a dose of Australian history and the ways in which national identity is being fashioned and projected to cohere, inwards for the citizens and outwards in terms of Australia's status of deputy-sheriff to the United States, all being made possible despite our theoretical points of reference being drawn from the particular history of the Indian nation-state.

Another illustration of Indian specificity leading back to reflections on how the inside and outside of the international work in Australia, is achieved through the teaching of extracts from two of Partha Chatterjee's seminal texts on Indian nationalism, *Nationalist Thought and The Colonial World: A Derivative Discourse?*, and his most recent book, *The Politics of the Governed*. Between these two texts, we chart the journey of India from colonial to postcolonial polity. The promises of modernity, the cultural work that needed to be done to turn colonial India into independent India, and the stock-taking of the ways in which the concepts of nation and nationalism have not been able to deliver the benefits of modernity are traversed in these two books. Theoretically, the historical stomping ground ranges from the very nature of what constitutes knowledge under modernity, and the problem of culturally different knowledges ever being able to make the grade as "knowledge", through to liberal and Marxist conceptions of nationalism in India, with specific reference to Bengal.[13] We pick up the story of Indian nationalism in present-day Bengal, when Chatterjee revisits how concepts of civil society, state, citizenship, rights, universal affiliation and particular identities are actually manifested on the ground, operating in a way that renders the theory unable to account for the practice.

Whilst nationalism in the previous book was about achieving subjectivity and recognition through the guise of nation and citizenship, with such attainment being seen as the natural endpoint of political decolonisation through independence from Britain, *The Politics of the Governed* identifies and attends to the split in modern politics between those who occupy civil society and those who are a part of political society. Political society, the arena of the politics of the governed as opposed to those who govern, is simultaneously the object of governmentality, exists in dense and heterogeneous time as opposed to the empty homogenous time of modernity, and makes contradictory demands on the state, at once asking for admission into civil society and at the same time demanding differential treatment of groups suffering from disadvantage or vulnerability because of past injustice.[14] Chatterjee gives us vignettes of people and groups, sponsored by the state, creating their own solutions to the problems they face by redefining the political terrain, even though, on the face of it, their activities fall outside the boundaries of both civil society and legally-sanctioned behaviour.

Seeing the way Chatterjee uses Bengal as a fertile source of everyday practice, the ground from which he redefines the very nature of what constitutes the political, enables us to look differently at both what could be considered political in other societies, as well as seeing in a similar light the differential access given to the indigent and indigenous peoples in a settler society such as Australia. I found it especially revealing to find that what struck students most about Chatterjee's *The Politics of the Governed*, was the parallels with the ways in which the institutions of government and civil society in Australia treated both the poor and Aboriginal peoples as second class citizens, possessing the rights of citizenship in theory, not in practice. The manner in which the Australian Federal Government manages Aboriginal peoples, laying down the ways in which they need to act, politically and culturally, to be considered on a par with other Australians, is not a parallel that needed to be brought to the attention of students, but one they picked up for themselves.

Thus far, you have been regaled with what could be considered a narcissistic form of navel-gazing, with Australian students turning Indian thinkers, examples, events and even the everyday of the political society of Bengal into a means of directing their attention back, with a critical edge, to themselves, their country and their politicians and institutions. To a certain degree, you would be right. One of the complaints I frequently get is that there was too much of

Australia in the course! Another complaint is that it was all about India, and, for our more attentive or Indian students, it was about Bengal in particular standing in for and claiming to be representative of the whole of India. An extension of this argument lay in our, to use the language of Arif Dirlik in his now infamous critique of postcolonialism, apparent conflation of specific problems in Indian historiography and general problems of a global condition and then projecting them globally as representative of a postcolonial sensibility shared by the Third World as a whole.[15]

Such complaints can be countered and contextualised by shedding a little more light on the methodology we adopted as well as delineating the kind of postcolonial pedagogy that was pursued. In the first place, we were heavily influenced by Gyanendra Pandey's "In Defense of the Fragment", where he proposed looking at historical totalities like nationalist histories as being historical fragments.

> [W]hat the historians call a "fragment" – a weaver's diary, a collection of poems by an unknown poet (and to these we might add all those literatures of India that Macaulay condemned, creation myths and women's songs, family genealogies, and local traditions of history) – is of central importance in challenging the state's construction of history, in thinking other histories and marking those contested spaces through which particular unities are sought to be constituted and others broken up.[16]

The resonances between what we were trying to do, decolonising the international by looking for it in knowledges that had not been recognised as such, and what Pandey outlines above should be evident, but bears elaboration. Although billed very much as a discipline concerned with the present and the future, historical knowledges and narratives are the bedrock on which IR is built. That foundation is passed off as an unquestioned master narrative and not, to echo Pandey, as a particular fragment masquerading as a totality. By unseating that master narrative we would, in the words of Sankaran Krishna, ,draw attention to "the political entailments of the specific forms of abstraction" that the discipline of IR expects us to unquestioningly uphold and valorise.[17] We undermined the seemingly universal categories of the discipline that claimed to be above the messiness of the political melee that constituted international practice by situating it back *into* the particular historical practice from whence it came, by turning it into a fragment of the international as opposed to the means of speaking for an international that encompassed all. We gave credence to Krishna's appropriation of Ranajit Guha's labelling of colonial historical discourse as a prose of counterinsurgency to recognise its continuance in the present, with "the narration of international relations [becoming]… the quintessential 'prose of counterinsurgency' – on the side of the state against non-national ways of being".[18]

To this point, the sorts of postcolonial writing I have been discussing are acknowledged canonical texts in the field of postcolonial studies, by authors – Nandy and Chatterjee – whose credentials extend beyond the postcolonial. Each has disciplinary groundings in, respectively, political psychology, history and political science. The penetration of postcolonial writing (and its accompanying epistemological critique) into the social sciences is of a different, more limited degree than its presence and influence in the humanities. The case for the necessity of literature in re-imagining and reconfiguring the international was strongly made by Phillip Darby in his *The Fiction of Imperialism*.[19] Although we live in a globalised age where many of our students have the opportunity and means to travel to other countries and thus have practical experience of cultural exchange, this is still an experience of the international that is not available to all and contains its own limitations. The commonest and most affordable way of experiencing another country is the long-standing one of reading the literature of that country. Much of this course takes Darby's book as an essential background against which we proceed, and that background sees literary engagement as an essential component of a postcolonial international education. Indeed, the course is such that students have two mediums through which to engage with Darby's invocation of postcolonial literature, through reading his book and listening to his lectures. The latter has been dubbed "story-time" by our more receptive students. I have discovered that the different skills needed to appreciate the two Darbys do, in fact, attest to the need for a postcolonial pedagogy. So what does our postcolonial pedagogy look like?

In the first instance we affirm the need to read, both broadly and closely, yet always critically. We package the knowledge that we present in the form of course readers as deliberately simultaneously canonical – in the sense that it has to be read and engaged with – and fragmentary, as *not*, cumulatively, adding up to a storehouse of knowledge, a new master narrative to replace the old one that needs to be reproduced in exams. We highlight that there are particular reasons for including the readings we deem essential, thereby demystifying the process of knowledge production, and in our bid to involve the student we use illustrative fiction as part of our arsenal. You may have noticed a few problems with this, especially if I add that the bait being used was non-compulsory. The students did not have to go off and read Rudyard Kipling, Salman Rushdie, E.M. Forster, Vikram Seth or Amitav Ghosh. It was just made clear that they would benefit from doing so, that there were multiple forms of story-telling being utilised in the course, and that some prose would help people the landscape that IR frequently denuded and depopulated. Along with the peopling that would come with reading fiction, would be that old colonial trick of self-fashioning through literature; as well as trying to inhabit other people's skins, to try and bring about that shock of recognition of sameness even when encountering difference. While such aims may be laudatory, getting undergraduates to read has become harder and harder in the political and economic climates within which Australian universities exist. Practical and professional knowledge have more market value to our students – some of whom insist on taking their position as consumers in a neoliberal educational marketplace to the extreme – than what, under the traditional system of liberal education, was about self-discovery and learning to become a productive member of society. In some corners of disciplinary IR, the university has been recognised as being the site for critical knowledge production about the international, an act in and of itself which is a part of the practical space of the international, as well as its purpose being the education of democratic citizens in a globalised world.[20] But none of this carries much persuasive weight with the student who wants to get into the Department of Foreign Affairs or join an international non-governmental organisation.

It is within such a context that I want to take a brief look at how we used Amitav Ghosh's *The Shadow Lines* in the course. Further to the critiques of history and nationalism raised thus far, we are able to denaturalise the ways in which IR, or what Ghosh calls "the logic of states" manages to lose its "monopoly of all relationships between people" when faced with "the pathological inversion" of a riot.[21] The communal riots in Dhaka and Calcutta in 1964 in response to the theft of a sacred relic in Srinager, brought the two cities together in united horror. The partition of colonial India into independent India and East and West Pakistan was a harsh subcontinental introduction into the realm of the international proper, where nation-statehood bequeathed international standing. Although partition was meant to give territorial expression to differences of various kinds, it is the remaining similarities with which this part of the novel is concerned. Ghosh characterises that similarity as "an indivisible sanity that binds people" across the borders of India and what was then Pakistan in the instance of these particular riots.[22] And it is precisely because of this similarity that such examples of disorder, contesting the regime of internal order of the state, cannot be a part of the historical record, but "had dropped out of memory into the crater of a volcano of silence".[23]

The consequence of such silencing – of aberrant violence – is one that Pandey deals with in his "In Defense of the Fragment", although the register of the riot is different, for it is against both the state as well as the nation and thus an internal conflict at many levels.[24] This does not negate the colonial and international roots of such conflict, nor does it remove the experience of partition, the division of selfhood, that continues to haunt India in its dealings with Pakistan. The little bit of *The Shadow Lines* used here shows how a novel of such complexity as regards its exploration of Indian subjectivity from the colonial to the modern period can be reduced to make a singular point. Much more can, and has, been made of the novel, but it is important to note that the sort of literary interpretation and criticism used in the social sciences is necessarily of the sort to whet the appetite rather than to satiate it. I have yet to encounter a student who took the bait and went off and read *The Shadow Lines*, but we have had some conversions to Rushdie's *Midnight's Children*.

The final writer I wish to look at is Nabaneeta Dev Sen. A much-loved figure who needs no introduction to a Bengali audience; in an IR course, however, it is her very life story, as well as the breadth and range of her creative output, that form the basis of her inclusion. Dev Sen encapsulates the essence of what the course is about by living a life that has been an example of decolonisation. She breaks down the boundary between public and private, between what falls into the realm of the political proper and that part of politics which has yet to be recognised as being political. Is this another expression of what Chatterjee has called political society? It is difficult for a non-Bengali reader to make that judgement, since we only have access to the work she has done in English. What is important though, is to make the point that politics and knowledge can be construed in non-English idioms. Despite its claim to universality, English is the unquestioned language of the international, and the particular kind of English that dominates is the one found in American journals. This is a language that, in the eyes of our students and critics like Dirlik, is like certain strands of postcolonial writing in deliberately courting a kind of complex incomprehensibility. In the absence of knowing the codes, as it were, both discourses have the same tendency to alienate the reader from the social, cultural and political life with which engagement is actually called for as *being* the international, global and postcolonial.

Although only a small selection of Dev Sen's work is available in English, through magazines like *Manushi*, *Outlook India* and *The Little Magazine*, it is possible for Western audiences to read her poem about her relationship to Calcutta, or to see her retell *The Ramayana* in ways that show how women from various parts of India appropriate it for themselves. Thus

> [t]hey call it the *Ramayana* but it is of Sita that they sing…they are not interested in the heroic epic cycle, which has no relevance to their lives. If what they create is fragmentary, it is because their lives are fragmentary. For them, it is the whole story. It reflects a woman's world in its entirety.[25]

Aside from the reappearance of the now familiar fragment, if you keep in mind that students' only exposure to *The Ramayana* thus far has been in terms of how its incorporation into the historical features in the outbreak of violence at Ayodhya in 1992 and Gujarat in 2002, then through Dev Sen, students are exposed to many different *Ramayanas*. Although not evoking Nandy, Dev Sen here can be used to illustrate much of what Nandy had to say about the malleability of myth for those who live in and with the ahistorical.

> But there are always alternative ways of using a myth. If patriarchy has used the Sita myth to silence women, the village women have picked up the Sita myth to give themselves a voice. They have found a suitable mask in the myth of Sita, a persona through which they can express themselves, speak of their day-to-day problems, and critique patriarchy in their own fashion. In the women's retellings, the Brahminical Rama myth is blasted automatically though, probably, unwittingly.[26]

Like the village women here, Dev Sen also contributes significantly to what one scholar in another context has called "the dismantling of the unitary Indian subject".[27] Through her autobiographical and biographical accounts of herself, her mother, grandmother and daughters, we are treated to what it means to be a Bengali female writer across four generations.[28] To approach issues of gender and sexuality – that quintessential inside which the international can usually approach only through metaphor or as objects of pity in need of salvation from non-Western forms of patriarchy – through situated personal narrative is not new to IR. Whilst there is a great deal of literature from Western feminists in IR attempting to de-masculinise the field, Third World feminism and its narratives have yet to get a foot in the door. Dev Sen's life narratives take readers into not just their lives but the worlds they inhabit, from colonial Bengal to a modern Calcutta, criss-crossed by personal and professional engagements in various parts of Europe and the United States.

At the risk of essentialising and totalising the myriad fragments of Australian and Indian self and other presented in this paper, cumulatively, the effect of such work on students has been to direct attention to the normative dimension of IR. Thus, not just what is IR and how do we study it, but the all-important question of why, of reconciling or eradicating the tension between what is and what should be. In this respect I would like to conclude with Ashis Nandy's clarion call to dissenters the world over:

> The recovery of the other selves of cultures and communities, selves not defined by the dominant global consciousness, may turn out to be the first task of social criticism and political activism and the first responsibility of intellectual stock-taking in the first decades of the coming century.[29]

Whilst the magnitude of that task is not something that can be achieved in the course of the single note in search of a symphony that is one university subject, I think a small step in that direction is achieved when you have a student saying at the end of this course that, instead of feeling like a general directing the action, he felt like a fallen soldier on the battlefield.

Notes

1 Phillip Darby, Course guide for 'International Relations (And Its Others)', Political Science Department, University of Melbourne, 2008.
2 *Ibid.*
3 Sankaran Krishna quoting Richard Ashley's 'The Geopolitics of Geopolitical Space: Toward a Critical Social Theory of International Politics', *Alternatives*, Vol.12, 1987, p.408 in Krishan's *Postcolonial Insecurities: India, Sri Lanka, and the Question of Nationhood* (Oxford University Press, New Delhi edn, 2000), p.xxxii.
4 Edward Said, *Orientalism* (Penguin, Harmondsworth, 1991), pp.7 and 12.
5 Dipesh Chakrabarty, 'Postcoloniality and the Artifice of History: Who Speaks for "Indian" Pasts?', *Representations*, Vol. 37, Winter 1992, p.3.
6 Chakrabarty, *passim.*

7   This manoeuvre is famously associated with Edward Said. For his appropriation of Foucault's discussion of the relationship between power and knowledge and Said's extension of Foucault to show how the power of disciplinary and cultural representation lay with the west, see his *Orientalism*.

8   Ziauddin Sardar and Borin Van Loon, *Introducing Cultural Studies* (Icon, Trumpington, 1999), pp.84–89.

9   Kanti Bajpai, 'International Studies in India: Bringing Theory (Back) Home' in Kanti Bajpai and Siddharth Mallavarapu (eds), *International Relations in India: Bringing Theory Back Home* (Orient Longman, New Delhi, 2005), p.19.

10   Sophie Cunningham, 'Mad in India', *Meanjin*, Vol.63, No.2, 2004, p.60.

11   Ashis Nandy, 'History's Forgotten Doubles', *History and* Theory, Theme Issue 34, May 1995, p.47.

12   *Ibid.*, p.65.

13   Partha Chatterjee, *Nationalist Thought and the Colonial World: A Derivative Discourse?* (Zed Books, New Delhi, 1985), pp.1–35.

14   Partha Chatterjee, *The Politics of the Governed: Reflections on Popular Politics in Most of the World* (Columbia University Press, New York, 2004), pp.3–8.

15   Arif Dirlik, 'The Postcolonial Aura: Third World Criticism in the Age of Global Capitalism', *Critical Inquiry*, Vol. 20, Winter 1994, pp.339–341.

16   Gyanendra Pandey, 'In Defense of the Fragment: Writing About Hindu–Muslim Riots in India Today', *Representations*, Vol. 37, Winter 1992, p.50.

17   Sankaran Krishna, 'Race, Amnesia and the Education of International Relations', *Alternatives*, Vol. 26, 2001, p.420.

18   *Ibid.*, p.421.

19   Phillip Darby, *The Fiction of Imperialism: Reading Between International Relations and Postcolonialism* (Cassell, London, 1998).

20   See *International Relations,* Vol. 18, No. 2, June 2004, special issue 'Teaching IR: Critical Knowledge in the Corporate University', edited by Stephen J. Rosow.

21   Amitav Ghosh, *The Shadow Lines* (Oxford University Press educational edition, Delhi, 1995), p.230.

22   *Ibid.*

23   *Ibid.*

24   Pandey, 'In Defense of the Fragment: Writing About Hindu–Muslim Riots in India Today', *passim.*

25   Nabaneeta Dev Sen, 'Lady Sings the Blues: When Women Retell *The Ramayana*', *Manushi*, Vol. 108, September–October 1998, available online at http://indiatogether. org/manushi/issue108/nabaneeta.htm (last accessed 6th February 2006).

26   *Ibid.*

27   Arun Mukherjee, 'The Challenge of Reading Dalit Literature', *West Coast Line*, Nos. 26 & 27, Fall–Winter 1998–99, p.59.

28   Nabaneeta Dev Sen, 'The Wind Beneath My Wings', *Indian Journal of Gender Studies*, Vol. 6, No. 2, 1999, pp.221–239.

29   Ashis Nandy, 'Shamans, Savages and the Wilderness: On the Audibility of Dissent and the Future of Civilizations', *Alternatives*, Vol. 14, No. 3, 1989, pp.264–265.

2

REWORKING THE RULING KNOWLEDGE BANK ABOUT INTERNATIONAL POLITICS

Ashis Nandy in conversation with Phillip Darby

Phillip Darby: Ashis, you have chosen to locate yourself in between the academy and the wider world. On the one hand, your work has been taken very seriously within the academy, despite the fact that it defies many of the conventions of the academy. On the other hand, you reach out to a very broad constituency of people and intervene in the politics of the time. And on that side, you have been widely cited as a leading public intellectual in south Asia, the conscience of India and so on. How do you see being in that in-between position? And how did you get there?

Ashis Nandy: It is difficult to say how I got there, for the simple reason I didn't self-consciously take a position at that location. But if you force me to spell out where I stand, I might say that it followed from my attempt to be an intellectual, rather than an academic. I don't think any intellectual, even the most reclusive one, can be anything but a public intellectual, because the intellectual's response is to the wider world. An intellectual is one who cannot keep quiet when seeing a genocide or ethnic cleansing taking place, even when genocide or ethnic cleansing is not his or her area of specialisation. Even if you are a lonely artist or a poet, you cannot but be sensitive to the ethical demands – *yugadharma* is the term used in Sanskrit and in many South Asian languages – of your times. Otherwise, in some sense I do not have a very well thought out position or design in my life. But I do retain the right to at least scream at the violence and the exploitation I see around me.

PD: I wonder if that says something about place and time. That is to say, in India at least, when you did your doctorate the academy was I suspect less narrow than it is now and there was a broader intellectual tradition outside as well.

AN: Yes, perhaps. Perhaps things were less defined then. In our Centre – the Centre for the Study of Developing Societies – the founding director was Rajni

Kothari, who didn't have a master's degree or a doctorate but he could get away with that. He was one of the most respected social scientists of India. Nobody held the absence of a higher degree against him or against D.L. Sheth, whose intellectual and institutional contributions to the Centre were enormous, or against Bashiruddin Ahmed, who pioneered large-scale empirical studies of Indian democracy. These would all be quite unthinkable today. Things have become more formal and rigid.

PD: And I suppose, in the same vein, much more bounded by disciplinary enclosures. When I think of the early period of the Centre – what I remember of it and have read about it – the thing that most strikes me is the breadth of people's horizons.

AN: You are absolutely right. But in addition I would say that it has now become more difficult to break out of the standard format of a university-based research agenda. This is so even at the Centre. Academic and disciplinary borders always have corresponding borderlines of mind. The latter are more difficult to cross; even when you try to defy the borders outside, the inner borders restrain you. Your education and socialisation rebel at every step.

Everything said, there has been a growing tendency to privilege university-based concepts of proper knowledge and proper dissent. And I fear to look at the future because I suspect that we have moved towards a global culture of the knowledge industry, which is formidable and which you can fight only by being outside it. It is no longer easy, as it once was, for me to say that I must respond like an intellectual, not like an academic on specific issues, because even the concept of the intellectual has changed. It is not an accident that, after World War II, only one or two of the best known French intellectuals who could be called public intellectuals were academics. Indeed, almost none of them were. Today it is impossible to think of public intellectuals who don't have some connection with academe. Probably Susan Sontag was one of the last. At best, we can now think of Woody Allen. That is how far things have gone. I guess we are living in different times and we now have to fight different battles. In any case, in the Southern societies some of the most interesting works are still being done outside the universities. Here, we have to walk a different path.

PD: I am inclined to think you are right. But there are two things that you have done which might hold out hope for the younger generation. Maybe I will mention them in turn. The first is your reliance on different source materials. From your very early writings you have used literature, films, myths, and subsequently the degree to which you have tapped diverse forms of knowledge including activist knowledge. The second thing is your remarkable self-assurance when crossing boundaries; you don't confine your focus to something within a single register.

AN: You are being kind. Frankly, I don't think anybody dealing with a social or political problem can afford to say that this part of the problem falls outside my field, whether that field is economics, politics, or anthropology. After all, such distinctions don't 'naturally' exist in life; they are human constructions and all human constructions are fallible and transient. I was willy-nilly pushed towards the position I took, because I too was a stray, badly trained, conventional psychologist and sociologist. Perhaps the absence of a proper training and the absence of a record of thoroughgoing academic apprenticeship helped me. Also helpful was the fact that there were no figures around me representing exclusionary knowledge in the places I worked. In the psychoanalytic clinic where I was trained we functioned partly as clinicians, and the clinic is a good corrective to grand theories. Because the moment you think that you have firmed up the diagnosis and you know how the disease is going to behave, the patient defies your prognosis and does something very different. Whether this is in a psychiatric clinic or an ordinary hospital, the patient is a corrective, critic and a lively contrarian. Unlike the anthropologist's informants, who are thousands of miles away, or the historian's subjects, who are mostly dead, the patients in a clinic constantly pose a challenge to you and your certitudes. I think the only one other discipline which may have this kind of built-in mechanism for self-correction is political science. Politics is a notoriously unpredictable process. Just when you think that you have understood a situation perfectly, things take a different turn and you are forced to renegotiate your ideas.

PD: That's interesting, Ashis. But I wonder if it is as true of the discipline of politics as of the practice of politics. I have heard several people, including my old supervisor at Oxford, Max Beloff, say that politics doesn't attract the bright students it once did. And personally I find it difficult to associate the discipline with imaginative thought.

AN: That's perhaps true. It's also perhaps true, for example, of academic psychology. I was attending a meeting before I came here. They were talking about the discipline, and they got so caught up in the disciplinary constructions of issues and problems that life experiences hardly entered the picture. In a sense, in academe you operate in a rarefied atmosphere. Everything comes filtered through the dominant categories. You are never really hands-on, so to speak.

PD: That being so, I suppose your wayward education has served you well because it has enabled you to challenge the rule of experts.

AN: Perhaps. You can take the position of somebody like George Bernard Shaw who claimed that every profession was a conspiracy against the laity. Or you can take the position that you have to somehow learn to learn. You have to learn to learn from the subjects of your study. I have been studying the genocide that took place at the time of the partition of India and Pakistan. None of the people involved had the benefit of the services of any psychiatrist, psychologist, psychiatric social worker or psychotherapist. Yet, amazingly, these people *have* grappled with their experiences, however daunting they might have been. They did so at a time when the term post-traumatic stress disorder was not in the textbooks and when nobody advised them to take specialist help to grapple with this or that aspect of their psychological health.

Today we see that in any large-scale massacre, whether it's in Rwanda or in Bosnia, you immediately talk of a traumatised community. And professional mental health experts and aid agencies conjure up a situation where communities, families and individual victims themselves, lose all agency. They become persons, groups or populations that cannot take care of themselves. They are persuaded to believe that specialised knowledge vendors such as psychologists will come in and put their lives together. I find that obscene. Maybe at times it is useful. But that does not mean that you create a situation of dependency where you infantilise entire communities and cultures.

PD: Absolutely. What you say about partition connects very much with what Veena Das had to say about the Bhopal disaster in 1985. In her view, the discourses of professionals took over the suffering of the victims, thus robbing them of their voice.

AN: Yes. Veena's work is particularly relevant in this context. Even the suffering is no longer autonomous suffering. It is not a suffering which you share with your family, your community or your friends. Suffering also has to be public, and it has to be shared with the state, with experts and with international aid agencies specialising in disaster management. Even disaster management has become a discipline and a science.

PD: It has. What you say brings up broader questions about the role of the NGO sector, UN agencies and, of course, the nation state. You have written a lot about the modern state, about how its reach has been enormously extended. Can we talk a little about the dangers you see in this romance of the state?

AN: There is a particular problem in the South where the European idea of the nation-state has been lovingly embraced, in part because the nation-state is seen as the key to the West's economic success and political dominance. As a result, everywhere the business of the state has expanded greatly. Once, the state's core business was national security. Those days are past. Now the state also has to be the dispenser of scientific rationality and the pace-setter in matters of development, progress, education and socialisation. It even has to act occasionally as a psychotherapist to define the norms of child-rearing and set the parameters of normality. A psychotherapeutic state is not unimaginable today. And these new reasons of state, so to speak, have given the state even greater powers vis-à-vis the citizen. It has also allowed the state to increasingly depoliticize the citizenry and take away some of the powers which legislatures previously enjoyed. Partly as a result of changes associated with globalisation, the responsibility for large areas of life has been given away to specialists and experts. Development, for instance, is now mainly the prerogative of the development community, development experts and development economists. So, on the one side, the citizenry are expected to sit in front of the television to see what the politicians do and to vote ritually every fourth or fifth year to give their verdict on governance. On the other hand, you have empowered new groups of people who know only a very small slice of life but have all the technical details that should go into policy formation and political choices. They have no capacity to bring in the available wisdom in society to bear upon policy decisions.

PD: You mentioned a moment ago the professionalisation of development. Might we talk for a bit about the case of development, which I know has been a particular concern of yours?

AN: Development has had a long relationship with national security states, particularly spectacular development. I can think of no country that has shown what we may call spectacular development which did not concurrently show a strong authoritarian streak in its politics. This relationship between speedy development and political authoritarianism is an old one, extending back long before the term development was popularised in 1949 by President Truman. I am talking of the period when countries developed without calling themselves underdeveloped or developing. That earlier phase of development too was associated with authoritarianism of other kinds, in the form of organised, intercontinental, slave trade or imperialism. Development has always had this dark side to it. One of the reasons why development is so important is that it enables states to legitimise things like cruelty, torture, censorship, surveillance in the name of development.

PD: We might take a slight turn here and look at another aspect of development to which you have given much thought. And that is urbanisation. Do you see the city as emblematic of development?

AN: In a sense yes. But it is a different idea of the city that development pursues. It is not the traditional idea of the city, ancient or medieval, European or South Asian or Afro-Asian, with their own distinctive versions of cosmopolitanism. It is a city organised around theories of efficiency, productivity, predictability and nineteenth-century scientific rationality, seeking to exclude or shrink the domains of community, conviviality and eco-sensitivity. In practice, it usually turned out to be a slums-studded, smog-ridden, crime-infected, Victorian city bearing the ugly marks of early industrialisation.

These new cities induce and thrive on massive uprooting and displacement. That price had to be paid because development is by definition contextualised by urban-industrial growth. The 'hard reality' or geo-technology of modernisation consists of urbanisation and industrialisation and the concurrent social changes brought about in human relations, family, individuality, work patterns and vocations. Development takes place within that context.

PD: In your search for alternatives to the kind of development that has been occurring in India, the rise of an aggressive materialism in the middle class and so on, you have gone to a city like Cochin and identified certain things in the traditional rhythm of life that act as a brake on violence, disconnection and similar. I would like to talk about that for a moment. Are there real prospects of holding back the urbanisation process?

AN: I don't see it. You might see a certain tiredness with urbanisation in some of the old urbanised societies like the United States where urbanisation has reached its limits, where not even a genuine village is left. There urbanisation has lost its charm because it is triumphant, everybody is urbanised. But that's not the case in societies like India, Brazil or China. In these societies, the dream of urbanising the entire society and declaring the rural section of the society as obsolete or anachronistic survives. Herman Kahn predicted thirty years ago that within a few more decades the United States would have mainly three large cities. Remember that? He even gave them their names – Boswash (Boston to Washington), and Chicpitt (Chicago to Pittsburgh), and Sansan (San Francesco to San Diego). It has not happened that way, partly because the American imagination is now a bit tired of such extensive, unlimited and uncritical urbanisation. But that tiredness has not set in in countries like China or India, exactly as they are still not tired of pizzas, hamburgers and cola drinks. We will see urbanisation growing in these countries, until the village is rendered supine, or at least politically castrated and non-influential. Personally I have learnt from Jane Jacobs and others like her, and from the Indian case that cities are as old as villages. Some of the oldest archaeological finds are cities. The city is not the next stage of the village nor is the village an earlier stage of the city. The two have co-existed for millennia. One suspects that these two ways of living, two ways of defining one's habitat, have always served, psychologically speaking, as each other's corrective. Neither is complete without the other. For the city, the imagination of the village is vital. For the village too, the city is a corrective – the anonymity, the individuality, the specific kind of solitude a city can offer. These are fantastic counterpoints of the concept of the community in a village: the close-knit living, with face-to-face contacts and the established identities, with the unequal but shared roles in the community. In a village, you don't need to wear a T-shirt to proclaim that you are part of a movement or have an ideology; everybody knows who you are. In a city you have to wear an imaginative T-shirt to flaunt your ideology.

PD: Earlier you spoke of partition, I wonder if we could turn to your partition project. It is interesting that the violence and indeed the whole experience of partition seems pretty much a lost chapter in the writing about the international. And even in India until recently it was a kind of a non-topic. Could you tell us a little about the project? What has emerged from it? What are the things that might be relevant not only to India but to the rest of the world?

AN: There is a mass of data from surveys and interviews and some material has come from archival research, newspaper clippings and so on. The project was a fragmented, decentralised venture. I have not tried to put all this material together because I want to give a chance to those who collected the data to do that first. However, some things are becoming increasingly clear. First, as compared with other genocides, probably this genocide saw more spirited ground-level resistance than previously imagined – resistance not only by the victims, but also by people of the same faith as the perpetrators – Muslims who helped Hindus to escape or to survive attacks and vice versa.

Second, perhaps because the violence was two-sided, the victims tended to be less bitter than those in other, more one-sided genocides. One of the most surprising parts of the violence was the immense sense of nostalgia virtually every victim had about the place where they spent their childhood, especially the memories of the 'perfect' inter-religious harmony and bonhomie they had seen. This may be partly a retrospective secondary elaboration but our findings in this respect are consistent with those of many others. We sometimes found that the sons and daughters of the victims were more venomous than the victims themselves.

In a few places in Punjab the violence sometimes acquired the qualities of a minor battle. At least some participants and victims thought of the violence in that vein and believed themselves to be victims of collateral damage. And because there was this perception and memory of two groups of armed people clashing and fighting, there was an attenuated sense of being hapless victims. Finally, there also was a sizeable proportion of victims who believed that their own community was not innocent. Many of them had actually seen what their own community did to the others; they knew that both sides were hurt and both were culpable.

PD: And in some sense people were participants themselves?

AN: People were often participants themselves. Mahmood Mamdani's formulation that it was a popular genocide is correct. But the diagnosis will remain incomplete unless we recognise that the resistance to the violence too was popular; that communities had not become ineffective or dysfunctional, especially in the villages. A very large section of the victims came to feel that the violence came like a natural calamity, something like a flood, earthquake or epidemic. Indeed, many said that the violence broke out like a psychopathological epidemic in which people lost their humanity. That's also the reason why many didn't want to talk about it. They believed that as with ghosts and snakes, if one remembered those days, the days would come back. They felt that the massive, all-round loss of humanity was like a seizure or a possession by evil spirits and if they talked about these spirits, they would return.

For example, when entire families and villages trudged to their new countries, some of them gave the family jewels and cash to the younger, male members, thinking that they would protect them better from the marauding gangs during the journey. Sometimes some of these young men would run away with the jewellery and the cash, to start a new, more comfortable life by shedding their families. Also, a very large section of the refugees took shelter with near and distant relatives after reaching their destination. After the first few days or weeks, they were often not treated very well by their hosts, particularly if the hosts were economically disadvantaged. Quite a few victims have talked about their elderly women relatives being used as domestic helps and children being prematurely pushed into the job market by the hosts trying to get rid of them. The brutalisation in some sections of the affected communities among the perpetrators was almost complete.

We also had the chance to interview a few perpetrators. In their old age, they certainly did not look like courageous retired warriors, though some of them tried to project themselves as persons who had fought for an ethno-nationalist cause and for their community. In most cases, they came off as pathetic remnants of a mythic army – tired, bent by their own memories and frozen in time. Until now, I have not come across a happy killer at peace with himself. Most of the perpetrators were temporarily mobilised either by their inner demons and sense of self-preservation or by fear, panic and ideology. Once they returned to something approaching a normal life, they began to look back on their 'days of glory' with a peculiar mix of overt pride and covert but easily detectable loathing, tinged with a deep sense of moral discomfort and self-hatred. Those who did not show any discomfort were often worse off; they suffered from psychosomatic symptoms and showed more signs of mental ill-health. They had not been able to live down their past. All this, I guess, has something to do with the trajectory of genocide in a society based on communities, where there is no centralised 'machine' presiding over the killing fields. That's basically the story.

PD: It might be revealing to compare what you are recounting now with the killing of the Sikhs in Delhi in 1984 and also the violence against the Muslims in Bombay in 2001…

AN: It might be. However, compared with the violence of partition, the Delhi and Bombay riots were more organised affairs. Political gains, pillage and gentrification of slums were some of the main motives and to that extent the pogroms at Delhi, Bombay and in Gujarat in 2002 are more typical of riots of independent India. In them, the role of politics was larger, the organisers more identifiably middle-class, and the riots more professionally organised. The killers were anonymous, floating mobs. In all of them politicians who specialised in instigating or precipitating riots played a major role. They used the riots as a pathway to political prominence and access to state power and as a way of establishing their street power. In that sense they were conventional riots; they were electioneering through other means. Partition violence was a different story. It was much larger in scale, more decentralised, the issues were not clear-cut and the borderlines between communities less clearly defined. For example, we found out that in some cases the Muslim marauding mobs that attacked the Hindus in West Punjab included lower-caste Hindus. The violence was an opportunity and a profitable career.

PD: I have not heard of that before. But in many liberation struggles the violence was not simply between colonial and anti-colonial forces but between different tribal groups. I am thinking for example of Mozambique and the antagonism between the Makonde and the Macua or in Rhodesia the score-settling between the Shona and the Ndebele. In both these instances of violence, there of course was a colonial dimension.

I wonder can we change tack after this talk of partition and violence, and talk about non-violence and the Gandhian tradition, which seems to have very little pull outside India? I am thinking in terms of international politics. Even in India it seems less and less relevant – which is surprising in a way when one reflects on the extraordinary change that was wrought among the peasants by Gandhi, and how his kind of politics was so located in everyday life. I have just been reading your former colleague Sudhir Karkar's *Mira and the Mahatma*. I had never appreciated how, when Gandhi was changing the face of Indian and Indo-British politics, three-quarters of his energies were directed to sorting out things in the ashram, battling problems of sexuality, health and so on. Now this is clearly a remarkable chapter. What is your sense of its legacy?

AN: I guess we are living in a time when Gandhi has begun to haunt international relations and political theory from his grave. From Martin Luther King to Nelson Mandela, and from the Dalai Lama to Aung Sang Suu Kyi, the story of the success of militant non-violence is the story of the changing definition of political realism and the return of political ethics as part of normal politics. It is no accident that even when individuals who have nothing to do with Gandhi, have never read Gandhi and have never claimed to be Gandhians, begin to act like non-violent political activists they open up the idea of militant, non-violent resistance and begin to be called Gandhians. That was the case of the Polish trade unionist Lech Walesa and the Philippino political leader Benito Aqino. They did not come to Gandhism through Gandhi. The Dalai Lama, for instance, came through Buddhism – that was his way to non-violent politics. That now seems to be an important watershed in international politics. Gandhi has become a symbol; Gandhism has become a movement.

PD: How does this connect with the extraordinary synergy between Gandhi and ordinary villagers?

AN: That synergy is an affirmation of the potentialities inherent in everyday life and in the ordinary citizen. Democracy is important, but its values are even more important. When they get entrenched in a polity, whether due to enduring traditions of cultural diversity or long exposure to democratic governance, these values ensure that if the democratic system for some reason collapses, it retains the capacity to bounce back. There has always been the fear that without the constraints put in place by the educated elite and enlightened statecraft, democracy would amount to either majoritarianism or technocracy. Yet, here was a man who challenged that and opened up the potentialities of democratic politics in a different way. Nowadays there is much talk of a pre-existing, deep contradiction between Islam and democracy, which subverts the prospects of non-violence. Yet, when Gandhi developed the theory and practice of non-violence in South Africa, his two closest associates were Muslims. And it is no accident that Gandhi said more than once that the Pathans, who have produced the Taliban and hosted Osama bin Laden, were the best non-violent freedom fighters in India.

PD: This was about self-discipline, wasn't it?

AN: It was. In many ways when we talk about Gandhi, we talk not about one person or a particular culture, we talk about human potentiality and how it unfolds in different societies at different times. And I think that Gandhi's time has come. He has returned to disturb conventional political science, conventional international relations and conventional concepts of statecraft, so much so that people are afraid of non-violence, lest it succeeds.

PD: There are other things that are so significant about Gandhi that are associated with non-violence. I am thinking of the brilliance of using salt as a symbol. Also the way he conducted himself in his trial for treason in 1922 – the simplicity of his theatrics, yet the shrewdness of his politics.

AN: And the provocation, the idea of provocation. Think of the moment when Gandhi went to negotiate with the Viceroy after his highly successful Salt Satyagraha, and he carried his illegal, handmade salt with him. When offered snacks with his tea, he took out a pouch to sprinkle his illegal salt on the snacks.

PD: What you are saying, Ashis, is very thought-provoking and encouraging. Still, I cannot help but reflect that so much of our modern culture, so much of the direction of our thinking, points in the opposite direction – coercion, deterrence, pressures to make one think according to the ruling precepts. I have in mind the concepts and ideas that inform state action. I am struck by how little serious investment there is in international relations in pursuing the potentialities of non-violence. Indeed there is not much about relationships in the discipline. That's the paradox about international relations, it is mostly about non-relationships, you might say.

AN: I agree. That's a nice formulation. It is uncritically accepted that violence is foundational, because we are dealing with power as the pivot of political knowledge. Non-violence is seen to work in some countries and under some conditions that are exceptional. That's what I was trying to convey to you when I talked about Gandhi in South Africa and his Muslim associates. I was suggesting that he actually had a much wider base in human nature than is apparent. Also, non-violence often does work. Look at the way the Israeli state has treated Palestinian dissenters. You would find it has always been careful to ensure that those who talked of non-violent protest were first picked up and politically neutralised, because the fear is that non-violence might work. A state like Israel that claims to survive on a moral principle is seriously challenged when a non-violent struggle breaks out. I do suspect that one of the anxieties about non-violence is that it might work.

PD: I find that very compelling...

AN: Nirmala Deshpande, the well-known Gandhian who recently died, once told me that she mentioned to a retired commander-in-chief of the Indian army that she was going to Kashmir to tell the militants to turn to non-violence. She went on to ask him whether he thought non-violence would succeed, because she did not want to give Kashmiris false hope. He didn't reply for some seconds and then said, "I hope you will be patriotic enough not to tell them to turn to non-violent struggle." The general's answer to the question is implicit but clear.

PD: I wonder whether we can bring together many of the things we have been talking about by addressing the present world order. As you know, in international relations, there is a tradition of thinking about world order in terms of a society of states. Your thinking has been in a very different register. I wonder whether you might give us a few glimpses of your own approach to world order.

AN: This approach has some vague similarities with the visions of Raimundo Panikkar and Ali Mazrui, however different they may at first seem. Both make a tacit plea for a dialogue of civilisations and cultures where that dialogue becomes a building block or learning process on the way towards a loosely structured, global fraternity to parallel and correct for the formal, impersonal, nation-state-based international arrangements. Mazrui's world federation of cultures and Panikkar's more open-ended philosophical invitation to what could be called a global ecology of cultures may become at an opportune moment a less ambitious and hence less threatening decentralised venture – perhaps a movement or a moment of transition – in a world that has been so dazzled by power-backed state-centric efforts that it has forgotten the possibilities that lie hidden in the multiverse of culture. The problem with an assembly of nation-states is that it pushes centre-stage the entire baggage of power politics and political history. All cross-national conversation always comes to approximate some variant of bargaining. I have nothing against bargaining; bargaining is better than sullen withdrawal, penal isolation or going to war. It is also a part of normal politics. But it will be another kind of normal politics if we can bypass the present stalemate in many crucial domains like global ecology including climate change, organised terrorism and de-nuclearisation.

However, we must also admit that we cannot ignore or jettison the state system in the short run. The anarchist dream of the nineteenth century survives in the interstices of our public awareness because of a number of colourful figures like Pyotr Kropotkin, Emma Goldman, Leo Tolstoy and Mohandas Gandhi in our times and as a reaction to the illustrious role the nation-state has played in human violence in the last century. (A majority of the victims of genocide in the twentieth century, for instance, were victims of their own state.)

But it is also true that over the last 150 years, so many people in the world have learnt to look at world affairs only through the lens of the nation-states that the category called state has become a common currency for many of us. We cannot just wipe the past clean and talk of cultures and civilisations as the most significant players in the field. Any alternative democratic order we imagine will have to have a place for some version of the state. For a long while, we shall have to see the domain of the state and that of culture as two parallel, complementary and often-antagonistic domains.

PD: It seems to me, Ashis, that if a dialogue between cultures and civilisations is going to be productive, it would need to do more than pick up on what are taken to be dominant themes in different cultures and civilisations. It would also need to bring out the internal differences and recessive traditions within these constraints. Would you agree?

AN: Fully. A civilisation itself is usually an immensely diverse confederation or coalition of cultures. What look like the dominant strains of a civilisation are often an impermanent centrality of cultures thrown into salience by the experiences of the carriers of the civilisation. Alternative and even contrarian possibilities may be recessive and only waiting for their day.

PD: One last point. In your early work you wrote about suffering in an international context. If I remember correctly, you saw man-made suffering as having given the Third World something of its uniqueness but you went on to suggest that it must become representative of suffering everywhere. Now I think that is a really important idea. And it is one that links up with dialogue – relating to or empathising with the other through suffering – but I don't think it has been pursued. There are recent suggestive leads from Judith Butler and Veena Das about how vulnerability and loss might serve to connect people across cultural distance. Would you care to comment?

AN: Human beings have learnt to confront suffering by setting up demonic others. But I have also learnt from my work on violence that it does not mean that they have forgotten how to confront suffering without setting up demonic others. They have also learnt to face suffering with some degree of equanimity and without losing faith in their neighbours even after going through life-altering cruelties. It does not mean that they have developed a common approach to man-made suffering. This is understandable. Each society and each community mobilises its inner resources to cope with trauma, depression and rage. Each community also finds its own way of fighting the demon of brutalisation to restore its moral universe, the success of which depends partly on circumstances, partly on the psychological resources available to the community.

The lessons of the past are clear, to me at least. I would be inclined to think along the lines of how, for example, the metaphors of masculinity and adulthood to legitimise colonialism in the tropics froze the gender roles and affected child socialisation in Victorian Europe. Or how the way Britain first tried out and built a rational-legal, colonial bureaucracy in British India and then imported the system lock stock and barrel to Britain, not perhaps with the best of results, I like to believe. Did cheap slave labour and indentured labour have something to do with large-scale production and popularisation of tobacco and refined sugar in the New World and the later emergence of cancer and cardiovascular diseases as major killers? I like to believe so. I think ultimately what we are saying is that exactly as there can be a shared culture of co-operation and mutual learning not recognised by either side, there can be a shared culture of violence and oppression. Nature, including human nature and biology, exacts a heavy toll for excesses. In the very long run, there is no impunity.

Perhaps the issue of correcting or undoing historical wrongs begins to become much less sharp-edged when we look at it this way. So the slave trade, which I mentioned last time, not only led to devastation in Africa – with millions of unnecessary deaths – but also served as a means of sustaining, among other things, two new agricultural ventures – sugar and tobacco. Together they might have taken a larger toll of life among the progenies of the slavers. You do to yourself what you do unto others, as ancient wisdom and ancient faiths affirm all over the world.

3

NARRATING THE NATION AND INTERNATIONAL LAW

Antony Anghie

The ultimate purpose of the nationalist struggle is for the nation to establish itself as a sovereign entity in the community of nations. Nationalism and international relations are in this way intimately connected. As Phillip Darby puts it in his introduction, 'the modern nation-state is invariably taken as foundational in conventional approaches to international relations'. Given this observation, complex and enduring questions are raised about the relationship between the 'nation' and the 'state', the 'nation-state' and 'the international'. The nation-state is the foundation of the international system; and yet, the international system, through various mechanisms such as international law, plays a role in the creation of nation-states. One of the purposes of this chapter is to explore this oscillating and ambivalent relationship.[1] How does international law attempt to engage with, shape, manage and sometimes even create the nation? And, inversely, how does the character of the nation-state affect the character of international relations? Is it possible to conceive of an international system based on another entity – and what would be the character of such a system? How would it deal with crucial issues of identity and violence and the distribution of resources, for instance?

Devika Goonewardene's BA Honours thesis, titled 'Freedom at Midnight Becomes Darkness at Dawn'[2] focuses on the central and inescapable phenomenon of nationalism and raises and explores a number of issues that have been crucial to the whole project of Subaltern Studies. In her thesis she describes how nationalism strives to manifest itself as 'the material reality of the sovereign nation-state' and, more crucially, how the compulsions of the 'nationalist' narrative characterize the 'people'. One of the principal goals of Subaltern Studies has been to question and rewrite this narrative.

As she argues:

The need to identify the history of a nation with that of its 'people' is a requirement of modernity for a concept and practice that has its origins and earliest applications in Europe. Yet, having identified 'the people' how do we give body and voice to them? How do we construct or produce 'the people' and detect and represent them in all their polyphonic individuality and diversity?

A number of questions are raised by her exploration: in what ways are 'the people' characterized by the nationalist narrative, are there alternative ways of presenting 'the people' and their own understandings of their actions? The questions are in many ways similar to those addressed – not so much answered but somehow vividly presented – by great novels. How are the lives and fates of individuals and communities connected with broad historical events and forces? Perhaps it is the novel, or else drama, that is uniquely capable of exploring these issues.[3] Devika's thesis closely studies the conventional narrative, the traditional historiography that focuses on the 'constitutionality that led to the "transfer of power" and the violence that was emblematic of partition'.[4] She concludes that, within this historiography, 'the subaltern cannot be written into traditional categories, and any approach that adopts these categories can only note the way in which the subaltern is othered'.[5] Subaltern groups, broadly understood as subordinated groups,[6] as opposed to the elites that are the focus of traditional histories, exist only as the 'other' within such histories. In her work, Devika, in addition to showing how traditional categories of history cannot address the problem of the subaltern, suggests some of the political consequences that follow from this failure.

In this essay, I attempt to engage with Devika's work by exploring concerns very similar to hers regarding the nation, from the perspective not so much of the writing of history, but of the discipline of international law. What are the narrative structures used within the discipline of international law to comprehend the phenomenon of nationalism, to characterize 'the people', and indeed, to develop the doctrines and techniques that are fundamental to historical attempts to address the many complications generated by the issue of nationalism? What space, furthermore, is left for the subaltern minority in this discourse?

How then does international law deal with the phenomenon of nationalism? What is the relationship between the 'people' and sovereignty? How does international law characterize 'the people' who are the central actors in the nationalist narrative? In addressing these issues I have attempted to sketch the history of the ways in which international law has attempted to deal with nationalism. My broad argument is that, as in the case of the historical narratives analysed by Devika, international law, by seeking to recognize and give legal status to 'the nation', during the time of the League of Nations, inevitably also created 'the other' of the nation, the 'minority'. This 'other' poses profound challenges to monolithic ideas of 'the nation-state' since it could itself make nationalist claims that could result in secession. Since the time of the League, then, international law has attempted to manage this 'other', and the many threats it poses to the nation-state, by a variety of techniques that are presented in the form of broader narratives such as 'international human rights law' and 'development'. These attempts to manage the subaltern minority continue to face challenges, however, and the question then emerges as to whether it is the conception of the nation-state itself, rather than the 'problem of minorities' that must be interrogated. It is in this way that I hope to engage with one of the major concerns of this volume, the question of the relationship between the nation-state and 'international' relations.

Nationalism and international law: the League of Nations period

The Treaty of Westphalia, asserted to be the foundation of the modern concept of sovereignty, could be viewed, I have argued, as a particular means of resolving the issue of violent religious differences in the seventeenth century. Religious difference, more particularly the claim that a war against a state that practised a different religion would be inherently just, was the cause of ongoing conflict in sixteenth- and seventeenth-century Europe. One of the basic elements of Westphalian sovereignty, the proposition that each state was entitled to adopt whatever religion it chose, providing that minorities within the territory of a state were adequately protected, served to diminish the grounds for making war.[7] From those beginnings has emerged the popular vision of Westphalian sovereignty as holding that a state is entitled to do whatever it pleases within its own territory with regard to its own citizens, and that the international system has no right to interfere with activities confined within such a scope.

Westphalian sovereignty was articulated at a time when kings and queens ruled. It was only later, due to political developments in the eighteenth and nineteenth centuries that theorists postulated what we would regard as modern versions of nationalism as a sociological basis for the juridical form of the state. Under this view, sovereignty was vested in the 'nation' rather than some monarch. Nationalism became a major issue at the end of the nineteenth century as nationalist groups in Eastern Europe and elsewhere sought to liberate their peoples from imperial rule. Nationalism was thought to have contributed to the beginning of the First World War, the 'War to End All Wars'. Understandably then, the League of Nations and the new system of international law and organization it attempted to inaugurate, sought to address directly 'the problem of nationalities'. This was in a context where President Wilson, much to the horror of his advisors, asserted the principle of self-determination, the principle that every distinct people or nation should have its own state. Wilson saw this as a means of reducing the sorts of inter-ethnic tensions that were a prominent part of the lead up to the War. Ethnic groups throughout Europe and leaders of the colonized world immediately seized upon this principle to justify their claims to statehood. The League of Nations, however, only attempted to apply this principle to European and Balkan territories that had been governed by the defeated powers. Thus international law, the post-war settlement, made a deliberate and sustained attempt to create a set of regimes, institutions and norms devised to make nation-states in which 'the nation' would correspond to a 'sovereign state'. The map of Eastern Europe and the Balkans was redrawn in an effort to realize this principle.

Different ethnic groups inhabited the same territory; inevitably then, despite the best efforts of the League, minority ethnic groups remained in the new states thus created. Indeed, it could be argued that these minorities were created by the way in which boundaries were drawn. Equally predictably, these minorities themselves had nationalist aspirations and claimed to have the same right to self-determination that would enable them to become a sovereign state. This would have meant secession from the newly established states. Other newly created ethnic minorities asserted their wish to be part of the larger state from which they were detached. This, for instance, was the wish of many of the Germans who found themselves now to be inhabitants of Poland. A complex legal regime was established to protect such minorities. Under this system, all minorities were guaranteed 'full and complete protection of life and liberty' without any distinction as to 'birth, nationality, language, race or religion'.[8] Further, all Polish nationals enjoyed equality before the law and the same civil and political rights.[9] This was elaborated further, such that minorities were not to be prejudiced in relation to 'admission to public employments, functions and honours, or the exercise of professions and industries'.[10] It is clear then that the idea of non-discrimination played a crucial role in this scheme. A more ambiguous provision of the Treaty required Poland to ensure minorities 'the same security in law and in fact as the other Polish nationals'.[11] Further, it was recognized even within the one treaty that different regimes would have to be devised for different sorts of minorities. Thus, in Article 9 of the treaty, Poland was required, in its public education system, to provide the children belonging to minorities with primary education in their own minority language. This provision applied in towns and districts where the minorities constituted a 'considerable proportion'. Most crucially, Article 12 of the Treaty made it explicit that these provisions regarding the protection of minorities 'constitute obligations of international concern' and that any member of the Council of the League of Nations could basically institute action against Poland claiming that it had violated the provisions of the Treaty.[12] This action could result in the Permanent Court of International Justice, established by the League of Nations, assessing whether Poland had violated the rights of minorities under the Treaty.

Poland was understandably opposed to the Treaty but felt it had no option but to enter into it. The great Polish pianist Jan Paderewski was one of the signatories of the Treaty in his capacity as President of the Council of Ministers and Polish Minister of Foreign Affairs. Poland and other states subject to these treaties regarded them as unfair, as embodying an inferior, subordinate form of sovereignty. None of the victorious Allied States, for instance, would have tolerated such an intrusion into their sovereign affairs.

Simply put, this was a situation in which the very sovereignty of Poland had been in effect *created* by the arrangements inaugurated and administered by the League of Nations. In the classic understanding of international law and international relations, sovereign states precede the international system and serve as its foundation. In this radical case, however, the relationship was reversed: the international system created sovereign Poland, and could therefore establish the terms under which it was created. The significance of this regime was immense. Firstly, and most immediately, it served as the prototype for other minority protection arrangements supervised by the League throughout Europe and extended out to the protection of minorities in Iraq, administered by the Mandate System of the League. Most importantly, it challenged Westphalian concepts of sovereignty by making it explicit that the manner in which a country treated its own nationals, if they belonged to minority groups protected by the Treaties, could be the subject of international concern and indeed of international action and adjudication. Minorities arguably had special rights because they were protected by international mechanisms, whereas Polish nationals who did not belong to such groups lacked such recourse. The Minority Treaty system was, in these vital respects, an important predecessor of the international human rights system. Indeed, the League was in many respects more advanced than most human rights systems, in that an alleged violation of the Treaty could be referred to an international Tribunal, the Permanent Court of International Justice. For our purposes, what is especially significant is the fact that we see in this case study a situation where the attempt to give effect to the nationalist project, to create an ethnically homogenous state, inevitably confronts, if not creates, its other, the 'minority'. And, furthermore, it is this minority that provides a basis for external intervention, in this case, in a juridical form, in the activities of a sovereign state. The protection of minorities, the League declared, is a matter of international concern; it is placed under the 'guarantee of the League'. Under the League's approach to the problem of nationalities then, creation of the national state can only occur through the creation of its other, the 'minority'; the creation of the sovereign states is coeval with the compromise of sovereignty.

The legal technologies developed by the League in the Minority Treaty System were not its only contribution to the issue of addressing the problem of nationalism – a problem that was already threatening to be far more overwhelming – because it was clear by the 1920s that nationalism had become a much broader international issue as colonized peoples sought their own form of self-determination, seeing no reason why the doctrine should be confined to Europe.[13] The League also held plebiscites in disputed areas such as Upper Silesia in attempts to decide territorial disputes. Further, and ominously, the League adopted the mechanism of 'population exchanges' in an attempt to achieve a sort of 'ethnic homogeneity' that would result, it was hoped, in ethnic peace. The 'Greek–Turkish' population exchange managed by the League after the conflict between these two countries, for instance, led to the displacement of more than a million people[14] and was in many ways a harbinger of the tragic events to later take place in India and Pakistan.

The crucial question of whether a nation was entitled to secede under international law was discussed somewhat indirectly in the League period as a result of the matter of the Aaland Islands. The Aaland islanders, who had their own distinctive culture, sought to secede from the new state of Finland once it became independent of Russia in the midst of the turmoil following the Revolution of 1917. The League treated the issue with great delicacy, taking pains to carefully consider the preliminary question of whether international law or an international institution such as the League could even exercise jurisdiction over a matter which went to the very heart of the sovereign state – the claims of a party within it to secede. In addressing the matter before it, the League jurists who considered the issue basically asserted that the issue of secession did not arise for the Aalanders – a 'gallant little race' – as long as their cultural identity was properly protected by Finland. The implication of this decision was that if minority rights were not protected, then it would be open for a group such as the Aalanders to claim a right to self-determination.

While this matter was not before the Permanent Court of International Justice (PCIJ), the Court did hear a number of significant cases that arose from disputes regarding the meaning and application of the minority treaty system. The Court produced an impressive and wide-ranging jurisprudence on issues such as the meaning of the phrase 'equality in law and fact' and the vexed question of the basis on which a person could be said to be a member of a minority or not – was this an 'objective' matter or a 'subjective' matter? Dissenting opinions were a common feature of these judgements. An examination of the reasoning of the judges suggests that the dissents occurred not only because of technical, legal reasons, but because of a larger issue that remained unresolved even amongst the authors of the minority regime. What, in essence, was the purpose of the regime? Did it seek to ensure the preservation of minorities? In such a case, the regime was viewed, by the states subject to it, as fostering an entity that posed a continuing threat to the very integrity of the state. Alternatively, was the real purpose of the regime to facilitate the slow, unforced assimilation of minorities into the larger society? These issues remained unsettled.[15] The tensions and ambiguities of the minority system remained unresolved.

Self-determination and the United Nations period

Following the Second World War, the Minority Treaty System was regarded as a failure. The language of 'nationalism' had served as a justification for Hitler's attempt to create a 'Grossraum' for the German people. Further, the policy of imposing minority treaties on only a particular set of states appeared clearly discriminatory and unacceptable. International law therefore sought to manage the problem of nationalism by using the new techniques of international human rights law, as they emerged in the period to provide minorities with international protection. The Universal Declaration of Human Rights (UDHR) in 1948, set out to articulate a set of Universal Rights applicable to all states. In these circumstances, the UDHR and the International Covenant of Civil and Political Rights (ICCPR), which transformed certain provisions in the UDHR into binding obligations of states that entered into the ICCPR, focused again, principally, on the concept of non-discrimination as a means of protecting minorities. Discrimination was prohibited by the ICCPR and other important treaties such as the Convention Eliminating All Forms of Racial Discrimination, which elaborated on this basic principle. The ICCPR contained a specific provision dealing with minorities; Article 27 read:

> In those states in which ethnic, religious or linguistic minorities exist, persons belonging to such minorities shall not be denied the right, in community with the other members of their group, to enjoy their own culture, to profess and practice their own religion, or to use their own language.

A number of unresolved issues were raised once again. The term 'minority' has not been authoritatively defined in legal terms for the purposes of this Article; instead, several definitions have been offered and have served as 'working definitions'. Equally, perhaps more importantly, Article 27, while it implicitly acknowledges the inescapably collective nature of minority rights, nevertheless confers rights on *individuals* belonging to minorities rather than onto the collective entity, the 'minority'. Human rights were to be based on a liberal concept of society, one in which the only relevant actors were the 'state' on the one hand, and the 'individual' on the other. To advocates of minority rights, such a scheme seriously undermined the political status of minorities and compromised their ability to protect their rights effectively. The League system was more sympathetic to collective rights. For states, on the other hand, the emergence of individual rights already compromised their sovereignty; the acknowledgement of another entity, a minority, particularly if it possessed not only a sociological but also a juridical form that could evolve into a potential rival to the state itself, was unacceptable. Thus, whereas the League system had been animated by the idea of 'nations', the United Nations' system attempted to manage nationalism by refusing to recognize any such entity, and instead conceptualizing political systems in terms of two entities, the 'state' and the 'individual', thus presenting a liberal understanding of 'nationhood' based on the protection of individual rights.

Many of the most brutal forms of violence suffered by minorities would result in violations of classic civil and political rights, such as the right to life, the right to a free and fair trial and the right to equality. Nevertheless, returning to the basic issue raised initially by the Aaland Islands case, the question emerged as to what 'equality' and 'non-discrimination' mean with respect to language policy and other cultural rights of ethnic minorities. Was a state required to provide education in the language of the minority, for instance? Up to what level of education – high school, university? More broadly, was the duty of the state to simply not interfere with minorities who could then practice and develop their culture on their own initiative – for instance by establishing and funding their own schools? Or was there a broader duty on the part of the state to positively support minorities in their efforts to preserve their culture by providing financial assistance and resources? This is an issue that has haunted many of the developments in the field of minority rights. Some authorities have argued that minority cultures can only be effectively protected if states actively and positively support minority cultures. If this view is correct, then an interpretation of non-discrimination to simply require non-interference by the state would result in the erosion of minority cultures. Human rights is classically seen as protecting the individual against the state. But a system of rights that fails to protect the collective aspect of minority rights could be regarded as colluding with the state to undermine minority rights.

Thus, in more recent times, the expert bodies established under the human rights treaties to monitor their operations, have increasingly tended towards expanding the right to non-discrimination to mean that states are under an obligation to affirmatively protect minority cultures. And scholars have argued that an increasing number of multi-ethnic states are extending autonomy rights to minorities; this intensifying practice of devolution suggests an emerging 'right to autonomy'. Difficult questions remain, however, as to whether autonomy based on ethnicity is in keeping with liberal-individual ideals, which would favour autonomy, but not on the basis of ethnicity. The issue then is whether autonomy rights can be normatively justified as being in keeping with the ideals of human rights law, or whether, rather, they are seen as pragmatic responses to the difficult problems caused by ethnic tensions. Integral to these issues are further debates about the relationship between autonomy and democracy, the importance of 'cultural identity' to the wellbeing of individuals and communities, and the effectiveness of autonomy in protecting such identities. The broad argument advanced for a right to autonomy, however, is that it is essential to ensure the overarching goal of equality for ethnic minorities.

Nationalism in the post-colonial world

The League of Nations discussed nationalism, not so much in relation to nationalism in the colonial world, but nationalism in Europe. It was clear, even during this time, however, that the international system would have to devise a way of addressing the many challenges of third world nationalism, and decolonization became a crucial issue for the United Nations. The language of self-determination now became the basis of a legal doctrine that was devised for the purpose of bringing about decolonization. Article 1 of the Charter, outlining the Purposes of the United Nations, referred to the 'self-determination of peoples'. Chapter XI of the UN Charter, replicating some of the language found in Article 22 of the

League of Nations, outlined a series of provisions designed to protect the rights of the inhabitants of 'Non-Self Governing Territories'. These colonial powers, furthermore, were charged with the task of developing self-government in those territories.[16] The somewhat open and ambiguous language of 'self-government' was soon translated into more emphatic language in subsequent actions in the United Nations, particularly through a series of General Assembly Resolutions which culminated in General Assembly Resolution 1514 (1960) which condemned the 'subjection of peoples to alien subjugation' as contrary to the UN Charter, and as a violation of human rights, and which further and crucially asserted that 'All peoples have the right to self-determination'.

A number of difficult issues had to be addressed by the legal system devised to facilitate decolonization. Firstly, it had to take the unprecedented step of recognizing a non-state, pre-state entity that would provide the foundation of the state that was to come into existence. This was another version of the problem that emerged in various ways during the League of Nations period: what was the sociological entity that had to be both recognized and shaped by legal doctrine as a precursor to the state? Could international law, a product of sovereignty, look into the origins of sovereignty and indeed, play a role in its creation? Second and related, the League of Nations in the Aaland Islands case had attempted to negate the destabilizing character of Wilson's articulation of the 'right to self-determination' by asserting that this was a 'political' and not 'legal' principle. The United Nations, however, had embraced self-determination as a *legal* doctrine that would juridically account for and enable the complex political process of decolonization. Many international lawyers argued that the doctrine was dangerous and incoherent: what was the 'self' that was to be determined? How was a 'people' to be defined? This was precisely the question that pre-occupied Third World leaders themselves. One obvious answer that was in keeping with Wilson's vision, was to equate the 'people' with the 'nation'. The problem was that many colonial states were artificial creations of imperial power and bartering with no regard to the communities living within them. The map of Africa was notoriously drawn up by European statesmen following negotiations at the Berlin Conference of 1884–85 and subsequent, often secret, agreements. As a consequence, very often, the boundaries of particular colonies contained many different ethnic communities, each of which claimed to be a 'nation' harbouring its own ambitions to becoming a sovereign state. Such nations could otherwise be reduced to a 'minority group' ruled by a rival majority community whose powers would only be expanded once they acquired control over the extraordinarily intrusive and far-reaching apparatus, the colonial state. The introduction of democratic politics into this scenario exacerbated the situation, as it almost inevitably encouraged a politics of ethnic rivalry and competition.

Ironically then, it was Third World states themselves that emphatically attempted to limit the scope of the concept of 'self-determination' by insisting that the 'people' that enjoyed the right to self-determination were the inhabitants of colonially defined territories. Thus the imprimatur of colonialism was ineffably inscribed into the very being and existence of the supposedly post-colonial, post-imperial state. Scholars still debate whether the map of Africa, for instance, should be redrawn to reflect the realities of ethnicity. The principle of *uti possidetis*, which had developed in South America, was extended globally; the principle basically held that colonial boundaries were decisive and could not be changed without the agreement of the relevant parties. The threat of secession was contained in all these different ways. A further important General Assembly Resolution declared that 'Every state shall refrain from any action aimed at the partial or total disruption of the national unity and territorial integrity of any other State or country.'[17] Importantly, however, the Resolution made it clear that the states that deserved this protection were states that were 'possessed of a government representing the whole people belonging to the territory without distinction as to race, creed, or colour'.[18] As in the case of the Aaland Island decision, there was a suggestion here that any state which did not protect its minorities, or which did not allow them to participate effectively in the political system, could be vulnerable to secession. Importantly, then, the effective participation by minorities in the system of government became one means of furthering minority protection. Equally important was the suggestion that states that failed to protect their minorities undermined their own legitimacy as a result.

Put simply then, the United Nations regime for minority protection was universalized; Article 27 of the ICCPR, which purported to protect the rights of minorities, focused on the rights of individuals; and the right to self-determination, which was developed as the legal doctrine that would facilitate and account for the acquisition of sovereignty by the colonial states, was confined in various ways to peoples inhabiting defined territories. As a result of the last principle, in effect, the right of self-determination was bestowed upon territories rather than peoples. The territory defined the people, rather than a situation where the people defined a territory. This approach was understandable in the light of the problems encountered by the Wilsonian project of providing each 'nation' or 'people' with its own territory. But this point was of little comfort to ethnic groups in post-colonial states that now had to prepare for life under a new regime which would in all likelihood be dominated by the ethnic majority.

The paradoxes of nationalism as it emerged in the post-colonial state have been well documented by scholars such as Clifford Geertz. Nationalism demanded the re-assertion of an authentic, autochthonous self that pre-existed colonialism. But nationalism, although it could be connected with many other political movements based on religion and ethnicity, was in many ways a Western political movement whose origins could be traced to the eighteenth and nineteenth centuries. Nationalism could be conceptualized as the attempt to provide a political and sociological foundation for the juridicial form of the Westphalian state once the king ceased to be a legitimate source of authority; the 'people' were sovereign, but those people, in the case of many European states, were not just any people, but those bound to each other by a common history, or language or religion, or by a shared consciousness.[19] The paradox then, and it is one which is a prominent feature of the whole process of decolonization and indeed its aftermath, was that indigenous authenticity had to express itself in accordance with a script written by the West in order to achieve a political form that was created by the West and that was the only means by which an entity could assert itself in the international realm as a full, sovereign state. It has been powerfully argued that Third World nationalism developed its own distinctive forms and strategies.[20] Nevertheless, to the extent that nationalism was based on a distinctive ethnicity or language, it could only exacerbate tensions in colonies that were multi-ethnic (and this was the case in the overwhelming majority of colonies).[21] Thus, even as Third World nationalism succeeded in winning sovereignty for the formerly colonized countries, its furtherance contained within itself the possibility of future division because the very form of the nation-state inevitably created its 'other', the minority which would experience itself as subordinated because it was denied the status of sovereignty that the international system presented as the ultimate power. And international human rights often failed to provide the protection it promised.

Development as nationalism

The development project offered an alternative political vocabulary and political vision which could have served the purpose of providing direction and identity to the post-colonial state while diminishing the dangers of ethnic conflict and secessionism. Poverty and deprivation were the greatest problems facing the states and peoples of the Third World; 'development' was the overwhelming compulsion of the time, and it was understandable then that the new states which emerged from decolonization termed themselves, precisely 'developing countries'. I have argued elsewhere that it was in the creation and operation of the Mandate System of the League of Nations that many of the most crucial elements of what we now recognize as 'development' came into existence.[22] For the administrators of the Mandate System, the promotion of the 'well being and development' of the peoples of the mandate territory would result in all those peoples relating to each other through the structures and demands of a system of political economy. Ethnicity would consequently become a less significant feature of their identities. The post-colonial state, then, attempted to foster something akin to 'development nationalism'; the 'nation' was to be defined as the people of the new state, bound together, whatever their ethnic and cultural differences, in a united effort to achieve development. The grand project of development, which was ideally devised to benefit all the inhabitants of a country, could unify different ethnic groups, indeed, undermine ethnic identification by presenting a compelling idea of citizenship based on development promoted through a neutral state, and also justify government intervention in areas of activity that had previously been within the control of somewhat autonomous groups, many of them ethnically based. As Chatterjee argues about development,

It was premised…upon a *rational* consciousness and will, and insofar as 'development' was thought of as a process affecting the whole of society, it was also premised on *one* consciousness and will, that of the whole. Particular interests needed to be subsumed within the whole and made consistent with the general interest.[23]

Most prominently, this was the process by which the 'development state' emerged, together with all the ideologies, disciplines and structures that gave it legitimacy and enabled its expansion. International law, and indeed law itself more broadly as a modernizing, rational force, was adopted by many post-colonial states as a means of achieving development. The new discipline of 'Law and Development' emerged in the 1960s as a result. The goal of 'Law and Development' practitioners and scholars was to devise means by which development could be achieved by the creation of legal systems and law reform. As one of its principal exponents put it:

The rise of modern law supplants local, 'particularistic' and traditional forces, and is thus the vehicle through which the state replaces communal or traditional authority. As national law grants men rights and immunities they escape from the hold of the village and tribe. Similarly, modern law's rationality and universality strengthens the state.[24]

Tragically, the ambitions of development nationalism were rarely met, either in terms of achieving development or reducing ethnic tension. Simply, in many cases, rather than development controlling ethnicity, ethnicity controlled development. That is, the ethnic groups that seized control of the state used those unprecedented state powers to enrich themselves at the expense of minorities. In some cases, as with the Ogoni in Nigeria, the resources that were found in the lands inhabited by the minority were exploited to the benefit of the majority. The minority were not only deprived of their wealth and livelihoods, but they often suffered intensely as a result of the environmental and social devastation that often accompanied these forms of development. The question then arose: to what extent did international law and in particular, international human rights law, provide minorities with a vocabulary with which to assert their claims?

Development, then, rather than reducing ethnic tensions 'tends to sharpen religious, interregional and ethnic tensions by "pitting" traditional communities against each other'.[25] Having in some ways exacerbated ethnic tensions, the state then intervenes further in the guise of attempting to resolve them. But it does so by invoking rationalities of economics and development which emerge as some sort of 'master narrative', an objective scientific reality that determines all politics. Lost in all this is the politics of negotiation and accommodation among ethnic groups which, whatever their differences, share an understanding of the importance of what might only be termed, crudely, 'cultural identity'. As Nandy argues, 'What was once a complex encounter of cultures becomes, thus, a hard-eyed battle for "concrete" development-related gains.'[26] Worse, in many cases, these supposed 'development gains' really further benefit particular ethnic groups or elites. The ostensibly neutral and scientific language of 'development' could easily become another weapon of ethnic conflict. The modern liberal state – and it is that state which is the model of international human rights law – presents itself, particularly through human rights law, as a protector of tolerance and cultural diversity. Nandy argues, however, that this idea of the state is both modern and far from universal; there is another tradition which 'refuses to accept the modern idea of the nation-state as the only genuine version of state'.[27]

What scholars such as Nandy have been outlining are the tensions and violence associated with the emergence of the modern nation-state. The legitimacy of the state, which effects this widespread dispossession, deracination, and displacement in the name of 'development', then becomes inexorably connected with the actual achievement of such development. It is hardly surprising then, that the survival of the state in countries such as China and India is largely dependent on ensuring impressive growth rates, some as high as 7 or 8 per cent.

The 'nation-state' and the 'international system'

Since the time of Wilson at least, international law has had to grapple with the powerful idea that each nation should have its own state. In the course of constructing itself, the nation-state based on this idea constructs its other, the cultural minority within. The emergence of sovereignty is coeval with the emergence of the minority, the entity that has been the focus of international protection and concern, ever since the creation of Westphalian sovereignty. Westphalian sovereignty is popularly understood to propound that the sovereign state has absolute right over its own territory and with respect to its own citizens – authorities such as Leo Gross have pointed out, however, that this is not the case. Minorities, even if they were technically citizens of the sovereign state, were objects of international protection.[28] Given that very few 'nation-states' meet the demands of purity postulated by the classic idea, it is virtually inevitable that disastrous attempts at population exchanges, ethnic cleansing and indeed genocide have been resorted to by those obsessed by making this vision of the nation-state a reality. Perhaps then, as Ashis Nandy claims, genocide – the elimination of an entire ethnicity – is the foundation of sovereignty.[29] Correspondingly, it seems, in recent times, the international community has sought to provide the survivors of massive ethnic violence with a sovereign state by way, possibly, of reparations, or protection. We may interpret the creation of Israel, South Sudan, Bosnia, Timor, in this way. International lawyers have begun to discuss the concept of 'remedial secession'.

We may interpret international law and its many attempts to resolve the problem of ethnic conflict – through the formulation of new and expansive definitions of minority rights, of autonomy rights, by peace building and, more recently, post-conflict constitution making – as increasingly sophisticated attempts to provide an adequate and humane response to the problems of nationalism. But they may also be regarded as ineffectual and doomed endeavours that are misplaced because they do not sufficiently appreciate the underlying problem – the very concept of the nation-state that is the basis of international law and that has been promoted as such. Despite the attempts of international law to assert the concept of liberal nationhood based on individual rights, the older idea of the ethnically based nation endures, and indeed is furthered by the politics of ethnicity that has riven many post-colonial societies.[30] In this situation, the international legal protections offered by sovereignty are used as a means to further the project of the ethnically based nation – one in which minorities, if not killed or cleansed, are supposed to be entirely subordinate. The further difficulty is that the international system, even as it claims the 'end of the nation-state' and the 'erosion of sovereignty', contains within it the enduringly powerful idea that the nation-state is the ultimate form of political authority, the entity which enjoys the monopoly on legitimate violence (an idea that is distorted to mean that any violence committed by the state in defence of itself is legitimate). Violence becomes inherent in the idea of the nation-state as nationalism constitutes its adversary, the minority, even as it constitutes itself. And, further, in this era of globalization and intensified migrations, new issues arise as to how the purity of the nation-state – this idea, although dormant, is a powerful one even in the most liberal democratic states – is to be preserved against external contamination and threat. This is suggested by the responses of several European states to the 'threat of the veil'.[31]

Seen in this way, the challenge, as Nandy suggests, is to conceptualize new forms of association. The European Union, with its claims to transcend narrow visions of nationalism, offers itself as one such model – although one doubts whether it is one that Nandy would approve of. For many societies in Asia, it may be a model of tolerance and plurality that had historically existed, but that was distorted by the very technologies of modernity – including human rights law – that grandly proclaimed themselves as vehicles of harmony and mutual understanding. James Scott's recent work on the politics of not being governed may also be useful in this respect. It is interesting to note that the Assyrian minority in mandatory Iraq asked to be ruled by the traditional millet system of the Ottoman Empire rather than the new systems of rights and constitutional protection that the British thought necessary. The question remains – to return to Devika's argument – in what ways does international law, the rules that determine the character of sovereignty, limit our ability to envision different actors, forms of society and freedom? International law can argue that its emphasis on individual rights is directed precisely at the empowerment of the subaltern, the individual. But what is evident is that the other great narratives of nationalism and sovereignty, namely 'self-determination' and 'development' are in tension with such a claim, as both these narratives subordinate the individual and community to some larger abstract entity. Indeed, it is interesting to note in this respect that Third World countries insisted that the 'right to self-determination' is a necessary precondition of individual rights. It remains unclear, further, whether a system of individual rights adequately takes into account the relationship between the individual and his or her community. To raise such criticisms invites the response that critique is based on vague, contradictory and utopian terms, as it seems to demand a system that balances the individual and the community and broader society. But this perhaps is the task of political theorists.

The issue remains of the relationship between the nation-state and the international. The nation-state is the foundation of international law. If we examine the issue of the emergence of the nation-state, however, we see how international law – and international politics – has attempted to develop a systematic approach to this crucial issue. Apart from the doctrine of self-determination discussed here, the doctrine of state 'recognition' also attempts to address this issue in a coherent fashion. The key issue here is when a state can be said to come into existence, and the importance of 'recognition' by established states of the emerging entity asserting itself as a new state. Once again, however, the only answer is irresolute and ambivalent – as suggested by the International Court of Justice which, when asked to rule on the legality of Kosovo's unilateral declaration of independence, simply confined itself to stating that such a declaration was not illegal.[32] What all this might suggest is that a rethinking of nationalism, the foundation of the nation-state, may be a central aspect of rethinking international relations itself.

Towards a conclusion

I have attempted to develop two arguments here: one is the inextricable link between international law and the nation-state, a relationship both related and analogous to the relationship between the discipline of international relations and the nation-state. Modern international law is based on the nation-state. It is thus hardly surprising that classical accounts of the history of international law cite the treaty of Westphalia, the legal arrangements that are said to create the modern nation-state and the enduring model of 'Westphalian sovereignty' as the founding moment of the modern discipline of international law. The concept of Westphalian sovereignty – perceived as the absolute right of the sovereign to do as it wishes with respect to its own citizens within its own territory – creates its own problems. What is the relationship between sovereignty and international law? Does the sovereign state create international law? Does international law govern the creation of sovereign states? These are ongoing issues which have never been decisively resolved. International law has nevertheless flourished and expanded by treating these problems as either already resolved, or else, part of a productive dynamic of inter-dependence that relies precisely on its irresolution for its effectiveness. It is occasionally, in cases such as the Kosovo Decision, however, that the existence of this fundamental problem emerges in a dramatic manner to suggest the very fragile theoretical foundations of international law.

Secondly, I have argued that a study of the treaty of Westphalia suggests a paradox that became exacerbated once 'the nation' was posited as the sociological foundation of the juridical entity, the sovereign state. The Treaty of Westphalia is now being subjected to new historical and theoretical scrutiny. 'Westphalian sovereignty' is commonly taken to mean the exercise of absolute power within a state over its own territory. What a study of the Treaty of Westphalia suggests, however, is that the Treaty characterized religious minorities as the subjects of rights that transcended the sovereign state, and that were to be internationally protected. Indeed, Gross goes further in suggesting that the protection of minority rights was central to the peace established by the Treaties – just as the United Nations Charter suggests that the protection of human rights more generally is central to peace as conceptualized by the system of the United Nations Charter. In brief, Westphalian sovereignty, seen in this way, is a conditional sovereignty; it is conditional upon the protection of the rights of religious minorities. Failure to protect such rights could result in legally justifiable intervention under the scheme of 'collective security' embodied in the Peace of Westphalia. Once this system is studied in the context of the emergence of nationalism several centuries later, we arrive at a situation where a sovereignty based on nationalism almost inevitably creates its other, the minority, whose rights are subject to international protection. As such, minorities have, historically and structurally, challenged and compromised the state's aspirations to absolute sovereignty. The nature of the intervention that the international community can engage in has changed over the years, but in recent times, principles such as the 'Responsibility to Protect' may be adapted to justify such interventions.

The further compelling question arises as to whether there are alternatives to the nation-state that must be considered, given ongoing ethnic violence, and the emergence of a phenomenon labelled 'failed states'.[33] The international community has expended an enormous amount of energy and resources with regard to 'state building' – an activity that has extended from East Timor to Somalia to Afghanistan and Iraq. The ongoing challenges faced by such efforts – which are essentially based on an ideal of the liberal democratic market-oriented nation-state – raises the question of what model of the nation-state or polity animates such efforts, and whether they are inherently incapable of succeeding.

If it is accepted that alternatives to the nation-state must be explored and articulated, then the question arises as to where these may be found or, indeed, how they can be conceptualized at all. R.B.J. Walker, in his difficult and suggestive book, *After the Globe, Before the World*,[34] explores a parallel issue of how and whether it is possible to conceptualize an alternative to the modern sovereign states system based on the broad idea of 'the politics of the world' – by which he seems to mean a cosmopolitan alternative. Walker's argument points to the dangers and difficulties of such a 'move' and in particular, powerfully asserts that many of the 'alternatives' are themselves based on assumptions that are essential to the model of the nation-state that the alternative seeks to transcend.[35] Similarly, I would argue, international law creates a problem – the sovereignty/minority problem – which it then seeks to resolve through mediating mechanisms such as 'minority rights' or 'human rights'. But international law's very existence is premised on the modern nation-state, the maker of international law.[36] More prosaically, only sovereign states make international law – whatever the influence of other actors such as Non-Governmental Organizations. It is hardly likely then that sovereign states would consider alternatives to their own system; it is one thing to consider alternatives such as the European Union or the World Trade Organization, in different ways the most technocratically advanced manifestations of the modern nation-state. But these models, whatever the impact that WTO agreements have on their daily lives, are hardly relevant to many of the people confronting the ongoing problems of ethnic conflict in the Third World. Where then may such alternative models, if they exist, be found?

My argument here is that they are to be found in studying, in detail, what international law has suppressed in a battle that has occurred historically and whose strategies and victories may be clearly articulated. This is what I would term the 'historical' approach. The traces of such challenges to the nation-state model are to be found, for instance, through studying the manner in which European international law – which is based on the European model of the nation-state as the decisive and central actor of the international system – confronted very different types of polities, ranging from 'Amerindian and African kings and chiefs, Muslim sultans, khans and emirs, Hindu princes, and the empires of China and Japan'.[37] The effect of nineteenth-century imperialism, and the European international law which legitimized it, was to render all these complex and unique polities inferior to the idealized European sovereign nation-state which proffered itself as the one model that all societies had to establish if they were to be recognized as sovereign actors in international law. This, then, was the enormous challenge confronted by the colonized states as they struggled to regain their independence. They had to transform their polities into nation-states based on the European model. This was the task that the nationalist elites of these states set themselves.[38] It was hardly an easy task, and it remains in many ways unaccomplished, perhaps inevitably so. But it brought about massive transformations and disruptions. One of the key concerns of Devika's work was to point to the ways in which the subaltern was scripted by official histories. The transformation by overarching invocations of 'the nation' of plural identities lived by people in their everyday lives is a central aspect of this shift. As Geertz points out, in terms of the transformations wrought by nationalism:

> The first formative stage of nationalism consisted essentially of confronting the dense assemblage of cultural, racial, local and linguistic categories of self-identification and social loyalty that centuries of uninstructed history had produced with a simple, abstract, deliberately constructed and almost painfully self-conscious concept of political ethnicity – a proper 'nationality' in the modern manner.[39]

It is easy to see how nationalism distorted and precluded the sorts of practices and accommodations that Nandy speaks of by insisting on the existence of a decisive and abstract whole or entity. It is unsurprising then that scholars have asserted that nationalism is inherently violent.[40] It is as a consequence of this realization that scholars belonging to what might be broadly called the 'Third World Approaches to International Law' tradition have focused increasingly on the plight of minorities within Third World states. Simply, for these scholars, the assertion of post-colonial sovereignty as against imperial powers cannot justify ongoing and systematic violence against minorities by that same post-colonial state. Thus scholars such as Obiora Okafor have written extensively on the issue of minority rights in a post-colonial context.[41] Attempts to extend the doctrine of self-determination to provide for autonomy rights for minorities under the rubric of 'internal self-determination' are also a prominent feature of many contemporary works dealing with the plight of minorities.

In many ways, these initiatives have been an aspect of the discussions of nationalism and minorities since the time of the League of Nations. The more radical and far-reaching question may be whether it is the very idea of the nation-state itself that must be interrogated, and whether alternatives to the nation-state can be articulated. In looking for such alternatives, what we must now be cognizant of is that these alternative polities have not simply disappeared, and that, indeed, the failures of the nationalist project post-independence indicate their powerful presence. International institutions and organizations have expended enormous efforts to recreate nation-states out of 'failed states'; but these efforts themselves have proven unequal to the task they have set themselves. At least two responses to this predicament are evident. First, international institutions could treat these failures as a spur for the development of new institutional techniques and technologies and doctrines directed at achieving better, more improved nation-building. It is in this way that international institutions, such as the World Bank, transform their failures into a compelling reason to expand the range of their own activities. Second, however, is the option that a number of international lawyers are engaged in; questioning the premises of the entire project itself, and focusing most notably in this effort on the idealized notion of the 'nation-state' that animates these projects. Thus Rosa Brooks argues that 'The populations of many failed states might benefit more from living indefinitely in a "nonstate" society than in a dysfunctional state, artificially sustained by international efforts.'[42] In this regard, it is interesting to note that the International Crisis Group, in its recent report on Somalia, has recommended that international efforts should be oriented towards supporting various sub-state actors rather than a centralized state, as the former seem more capable of providing for the needs of the people.[43] The recent work of James Scott and his analysis of people who have fought incorporation into states, and have prevented states from arising among them, may offer another model of a different sort of polity.[44]

We should not be sentimental or romantic about these alternative polities, or overlook the sorts of violence which are often an essential aspect of their existence. But the issue remains of why they persist, why the people who are supposed to be liberated by the modern nation-state resist its encroachments despite all the benefits that are supposed to follow. These, then, are the 'subaltern experiences' that we may draw upon in the ongoing efforts to rethink nationalism and the manner in which it has shaped the modern world and the realm of political imagination.

Acknowledgements

I am very grateful to Phillip Darby for his incisive comments and for making this volume possible in the first place. My thanks also to Edgar Ng for all his work on this volume.

Notes

1 For important examinations of the implications of this, see Nathaniel Berman, 'Sovereignty in Abeyance: Self-Determination and International Law', 7 *Wisconsin Journal of International Law* (1988–1989) p. 51; James Crawford, *The Creation of States in International Law*, 2nd edition (Oxford University Press, 2006).
2 Devika Goonewardene, 'Freedom at Midnight Becomes Darkness at Dawn: the Partition of India' [hereinafter Devika, Thesis]. Thesis submitted in partial fulfilment of the requirements for the degree of Bachelor of Arts (Honours), Departments of Politics and History, Monash University, November 1996.
3 And of course, scholars such as Benedict Anderson have argued that the novel itself plays a key role in the construction of the Nation. And indeed, Devika herself uses the work of the Punjabi writer, Saadat Hasan Manto, to suggest the complexities that the conventional narratives cannot capture. See Devika, Thesis, pp. 62 ff.
4 Devika, Thesis, 79.
5 Devika, Thesis, 79–80.
6 Devika, Thesis, 6.
7 See the classic article on the Peace of Westphalia: Leo Gross, 'The Peace of Westphalia, 1648–1948', *American Journal of International Law*, 42 (1948) p. 20.
8 'The Allies and the Republic of Poland', *39 Minorities Treaty* (June 28, 1919) Article 2. It is interesting to note that 'minorities' were defined in relation to these concepts of 'birth, nationality, language, race or religion'.
9 The Allies and the Republic of Poland, Article 7.
10 Article 7.
11 The Allies and the Republic of Poland, Article 8.
12 The Allies and the Republic of Poland, Article 12.
13 Erez Manela, *The Wilsonian Moment: Self-Determination and the International Origins of Anticolonial Nationalism* (Oxford University Press, 2007).
14 See Omut Oszu, 'Fabricating Fidelity: Nation-Building, International Law, and the Greek–Turkish Population Exchange', *Leiden Journal of International Law,* 24 (2011) pp. 823–847.
15 See Nathaniel Berman, '"But the Alternative is Despair": European Nationalism and the Modernist Renewal of the Interwar Framework', *Harvard L. Rev.*, 106 (1992) pp. 1792–1803.
16 See UN Charter, Article 73(b).
17 'Declaration on Principles of International Law Concerning Friendly Relations and Cooperation Among States in Accordance with the Charter of the United Nations', *GA Res. 2625* (1970) [hereinafter 'Declaration on Friendly Relations'].
18 Declaration on Friendly Relations.
19 The question of 'what is a nation' has been extensively examined: e.g. Ernest Renan, *'What is a Nation.'* http://ucparis.fr/files/9313/6549/9943/What_is_a_Nation.pdf

20 See Partha Chatterjee, *Nationalist Thought and the Colonial World: A Derivative Discourse* (University of Minnesota Press, 1993); Partha Chatterjee, *The Nation and Its Fragments: Colonial and Postcolonial Histories* (Princeton University Press, 1993) pp. 5–6.

21 Chatterjee points out that the colonial administration of India was based on the concept that because India was constituted by various 'communities' and colonial governance, it was inherently ethnically oriented and conducted in part by identifying 'representatives' of these communities. Chatterjee, *Nation and Its Fragments*, p. 224.

22 See Antony Anghie, *Imperialism, Sovereignty and the Making of International Law* (Cambridge University Press, 2005) Chapter 3.

23 Chatterjee, p. 204.

24 David M. Trubek, 'Towards a Social Theory of Law: An Essay of the Study of Law and Development', *Yale L.J.*, 82(1) (1972) 1.

25 Ashis Nandy, *The Romance of the State: And the Fate of Dissent in the Tropics* (Oxford University Press, 2003) p. 180.

26 Nandy, p. 181.

27 Nandy, p. 15.

28 See Leo Gross, 'The Peace of Westphalia'.

29 Ashis Nandy, interview with Phillip Darby.

30 For a powerful analysis of the endurance and return of the model of ethnic nationhood in the post-Cold War world, see Mohammad Shahabuddin, '"Ethnicity" in the International Law of Minority Protection: The Post-Cold War Context in Perspective', *Leiden Journal of International Law*, 25 (2012) pp. 885–907.

31 See Geoffrey Leane 'Rights of Ethnic Minorities in Liberal Democracies: Has France Gone too Far in Banning Muslim Women from Wearing the Burka?', *Human Rights Quarterly*, 33(4) (2011) pp. 1032–1062.

32 Accordance with International Law of the Unilateral Declaration of Independence in Respect of Kosovo, Advisory Opinion, ICJ Reports 2010, p. 403

33 An earlier literature captures elements of such entities as 'quasi states'.

34 R.B.J. Walker, *After the Globe, Before the World*, 1st edn (Routledge, 2010).

35 For a broad-ranging discussion of this central issue, see Jens Bartelson et al., 'Critical Exchanges on R.B.J. Walker's After the Globe, Before the World', *Contemporary Political Theory*, 10(2) (2011) pp. 286–310.

36 Cf. Jens Bartelson, who argues that 'we…are compelled to accept that the sovereign state and the international system are mutually constitutive of the same quintessentially modern order.' See Jens Bartelson, 'What is Wrong with the World' in 'Critical Exchanges on R.B.J. Walker's After the Globe, Before the World', *Contemporary Political Theory*, 10(2) (2011) pp. 286–310 at p. 288.

37 Hedley Bull, 'The Emergence of a Universal International Society', *The Expansion of International Society* (Hedley Bull & Adam Watson eds., Clarendon Press, 1984).

38 See Partha Chatterjee, *Nationalist Thought and the Colonial World: A Derivative Discourse* (University of Minnesota Press, 1993).

39 Clifford Geertz, *The Interpretation of Cultures* (New York: Basic Books, 1973) p. 239.

40 See e.g. Pradeep Jeganathan and Qadri Ismail, *Unmaking the Nation: The Politics of Identity & History in Modern Sri Lanka*, 2nd edn (SSA Sri Lanka, 2009). ('The pursuit of this single minded monolithic object has brought nothing but violence, terror and destruction to us all.')

41 Obiora C. Okafor, *Redefining Legitimate Statehood: International Law and State Fragmentation in Africa*, 1st edn (Springer, 2000).

42 Rosa E. Brooks, 'Failed States, or the State as Failure', *U. Chi. L. Rev.*, 72 (2005) p. 1159. I should add that I do not agree with all Brooks's recommendations as to how this issue should be addressed.

43 International Crisis Group, 'Somalia: An Opportunity that Should Not Be Missed', *Africa Briefing No. 87* (Nairobi/Brussels, 22 February, 2012) pp. 8 ff.

44 James C. Scott, *The Art of Not Being Governed: An Anarchist History of Upland South-East Asia* (Yale University Press, 2009) p. x.

4

DEVELOPMENT AND WORLD ORDER

Phillip Darby

The problem with the idea of development, Ashis Nandy tells us, is not its failure but its success. "Developmentalism has succeeded where Western colonisation and evangelical Christianity failed. It has established itself as one of the few genuine universals of our time."[1] There was a period of vigorous dissent from the late 1960s to the early 1980s in which intellectuals and activists challenged the colonial character of the project. But the ranks of the critics have thinned and their contestations are now mostly confined to the margins of public debate. Development, it seems, has become a good in itself.

This essay is intended as a contribution to reopening the issues and reaching out to new constituencies. Development, I contend, is too important to be cocooned from the broader workings of the international system as a matter left to the development community, however committed it may be to the course of change. Increasingly, the development project has become an integral part of a regularity system for the maintenance of order which consolidates the subordination of the South to the North. As such, it should be of unquestionable concern to students of international relations. Yet mostly the discipline has shied away from an engagement with development because it has not been seen as germane to the ideas that distinguish IR as a distinct domain of political life. The disciplinary gate-keepers have much to answer for in this respect. This chapter sets its sights not only on directing attention to points of intersection between development and IR, the most obvious being the coming together of development and security, but also attempts to show how the historical lineage and internal debates within development discourse can enrich emerging agendas such as the politics of the everyday and the much neglected distinctive perspectives and interests of the non-European world.

Yet so far as facilitating cross-disciplinary debate is concerned, development discourse has problems of its own. Although it is often observed that development studies has been unable to seal its boundaries after the manner of more established disciplines, it has engaged in surprisingly little dialogue with other knowledge formations concerned with the international. Indeed, the argument runs that for some decades development has been becoming more self-enclosed. Henry Bernstein writes of the loss, to a considerable degree, of "the wider intellectual, and political, understanding of development as a process of struggle and conflict, and use of the diverse intellectual resources available to advance such understanding".[2] He goes on to suggest that oppositional thinking thrives outside the institutional spheres and practices of development rather than contributing to its internal debate.[3] Much of this article will be devoted to exploring Bernstein's contention and the impediments within the development establishment which constrain its reach.

In short, we must look within both IR and development studies to explain development's sequestration from broader currents of thought and what this might mean. By proceeding in this way development is seen in relief and we are better positioned to understand why its larger function in relation to the world system has remained hidden from public scrutiny.

The argument goes forward in four sections. We begin by sketching an account of how little disciplinary IR has addressed the question of development and go on to consider why there is this lacuna. Next, looking at the period of neoliberalism, it is argued that development as it is practised works to endorse the existing international system. We then explore how this situation evolved by presenting some vignettes about the colonial experience and the politics of the Cold War. This material also provides leads as to how development might be done differently. This question is taken up in a concluding section which advocates moving towards a politics of the everyday, with the emphasis being placed on the North attending to its own everyday at home.

The occlusions of international relations

As the discipline most concerned with world order, IR might have been expected to engage with development, particularly with regard to its place in structuring the relationship between North and South. For the most part, however, it has not done so. Certainly individual IR scholars have made important contributions to the debate but very often their interventions have been outside the disciplinary fold.[4] Leaving aside those episodes when development has become entangled in the politics of the central balance, the development project has attracted little sustained interest. It is indicative that the *Oxford Handbook of International Relations* has no chapter on development and practically no substantive discussion of the politics of development.[5] Looking at recent publications in two of the most influential IR book series – Cambridge University Press and University of Minnesota Press – one finds that development is missing. The picture is somewhat different when we turn to the IR readers, mostly coming from the United States, which now proliferate. Usually of an encyclopaedic nature, development does rather better, in most cases rating a chapter. Rarely, however, does the treatment reflect back on what is taken to be the hard core of the discipline.[6]

On the journal front, for a regular coverage of development issues it is necessary to go to journals primarily concerned with the South. *Third World Quarterly* is a case in point. It is also of particular interest to IR students because it has attracted scholars at the edge of IR to write pieces that traffic across disciplinary boundaries. One such piece contains a cursory analysis of topics covered by five leading IR journals and it found that very few articles were specifically directed to development.[7] For instance, *Millennium*, which was not included in the survey, might have been expected to do rather better because of its progressive orientation. But it has not. Over the past decade it has published only two articles primarily concerned with development. Yet in the 1990s there was one special issue and one other article that remain required reading for anyone interested in the field.[8]

It is evident that the place of development in the discipline cannot simply be read off surveys of titles or lists of citations. Some of the relevant material may not fly a development flag. Ideas travel, at times having currency in small but strategic locations. Then there is teaching to be taken into account. Teaching matters because it so directly shapes the ideas that go out in the world. Unquestionably, we need to know more than we do about what is taught and how. It may be, of course, that analyses of course structures and reading guides would give a limited and perhaps skewed idea of how development connects with the key postulates of the discipline.[9] Especially in the South, what is thought and said is rather different from what features on the syllabi which tend to follow those in the North. There is also the point then when development surfaces in the discipline it is often in relation to other agendas.

As is well known, during the Cold War development was mainly addressed in terms of foreign aid and its significance was understood in terms of the central balance between the United States and the Soviet Union. In the late 1960s and 1970s the politics of development surfaced because of the growing radicalism of many Third World leaders. The issue was the challenge to development orthodoxy by dependency theory that led into the struggle for the New International Economic Order in the early 1970s. Essentially the dependency theorists repudiated two fundamental presuppositions of development, and they did so with a certain conceptual symmetry. It was their contention that the causes of underdevelopment were external not internal. Associated, rather than there being a complementarity of interest between developed and underdeveloped, the relationship was of a zero sum nature. Dependency was widely criticised in the First World for being ideologically driven, which of course it was (as if development wasn't also). The debate trickled into international relations belatedly and here also dependency was not well received. In retrospect, what stands out is that IR scholars were drawn into the debate because of dependency's claims about the making and nature of the international economic order and the question of development emerged in the slip-stream.

It is useful to put these last remarks in the broader context of IR scholarship. There are, I want to suggest, problems within the house of IR that make it inhospitable to any serious fraternisation with development. For a start, the Eurocentrism that has deeply marked IR at least since the Second World War has not been conducive to an engagement with a project that, despite its origins in Europe, has come to be seen as primarily directed to internal change in the non-European world. As such, development did not appear to connect with the core workings of the international system, all the more so to use another spatial metaphor because it was mostly about 'low politics'. Certainly at times it hit the 'high politics' button, usually in the guise of foreign aid, such as for instance when there were fears about the South using its resources as a bargaining weapon after the Report of the Club of Rome in 1972 and the OPEC crisis of 1973. Interest, however, quickly waned as the threat of resource diplomacy evaporated.

This brings us to a second point, namely that the South has had little visibility in IR because so much of the discipline's concerns have been about the exercise of power. This was the burden of argument in the special issue of *Millennium* on poverty in 1996. As Roger Tooze and Craig Murphy put it: the poor are hidden because they don't have any bargaining power. Hence poverty is a problem that is left for development or Third World studies to handle. The authors go on to argue that visibility is a product of epistemology, and the epistemology of both IR and international political economy is seriously deficient.[10] Writing in the same year, Roxanne Doty takes up the story. Underlying First World representations is a cultural unconscious that we have the capabilities that they lack. Hence the inability of the South to exercise agency in the same manner as the North "is repeatedly inscribed in the identity of the non-Western 'other'".[11] North–South relations, she concludes, "have been constituted as a structure of deferral".[12] Notwithstanding Joseph Nye's ideas about soft power, it is very doubtful whether the intervening years have seen any fundamental change. To redress this situation would require IR to rethink its understanding of what constitutes knowledge about the international and to broaden very substantially its use of source materials.

There are two aspects of the discipline's traditions of knowledge production that stand in need of a major overhaul. The first is the discipline's assurance that the quest for international order can best be pursued from within its own corpus. Except for a selective trafficking with globalisation, this has meant that there has been very little dialogue with outside bodies of thought. It has also involved the loss of insights that might have come from activists and everyday experiences which tell of ordinary people's anxieties and imaginings. Second, there is the problem of the adversarial mode of engagement between the different schools of thought that constitute IR. From the great debates between realists and liberals to the in-house contention between the proliferation of subfields and perspectives of today, knowledge may have been professionalised but at high cost. Think of all the energy expended at the expense of tackling international relationships, the failure to open up lines of communication and to recognise the other in the self. The result has been to compartmentalise knowledge, with IR deploying a 'keep out' sign to would-be intruders and shying away from rethinking the structure of world order. Certainly there are signs of change – the influence of complexity theory, a growing eclecticism, a somewhat more open approach to knowledge – but the discipline has a way of domesticating criticism, of appropriating alternative approaches to established reference points.

Underwriting the world order

In this section I wish to argue that development discourse and practice work to consolidate the existing world order. The main body of writing on order in international politics is not very helpful with regard to this contention because its primary concerns lie elsewhere – the nature of order, the relationship of order to justice, questions about polarity and so on. It is therefore necessary to place development in the wider framework of First World dominance and to take account of how it figures in the regulatory processes of neoliberalism with which we all are familiar. The argument is not that the development establishment is consciously acting to prop up the existing economic and political system, but rather that the project functions to endorse the prevailing international hierarchies and that in large part its politics remain hidden.

The role of development in the neoliberal order cannot be understood apart from the changes in the capitalist system associated with globalisation. The time–space compression of late capitalism, involving accelerated flows of capital, commodities and currencies, and the resistance generated, led to a substantial reshaping of thinking and practice in the political and social spheres. As attention came to focus on the instability and violence in the former colonial empires, development was given more geopolitical significance and the tasks entrusted to it grew substantially. There was, however, remarkably little reflection on how far the difficulties of the time were a legacy of colonial rule and later neo-colonial involvement – or for that matter whether development itself was a colonial venture.[13] When instability became more acute – as it often did – the role of development was enlarged. At the same time development was brought into the family of practices – peace-keeping and conflict resolution to name two – that operated in the same spatial arena and were seen to be mutually reinforcing. But we need to ask what was being reinforced. On one line of argument, a particular kind or order was shaped by Western experience, which mainly furthered Western interests. Writing of the experience of UN peacekeeping interventions, the Indian novelist Amitav Ghosh expressed the fear that a two-tier system of nation-states will emerge, one in the North and the other in the South. The nation-state "so eagerly embraced by the peoples of the colonized world ... will become, effectively, the instrument of their containment".[14]

The extension of development's reach was largely a step-by-step process. The seeds were sown long before, but incrementalism was a response to the uncertainties of the time – certainly about the non-European world. In 1996 Samir Amin could write that "development is off the agenda [since] the governments of the West are preoccupied with crisis management".[15] But a crisis can work to put things on the agenda. In the case of development the word wasn't 'crisis'. It was 'emergency'. The construct of 'emergencies' served to present recurrent breakdowns as exceptional when they were endemic to the system.[16] Mark Duffield writes of "permanent emergency". As he sees it, "states of emergency are essential for the existence of liberal governance, including development".[17]

At this point we need to bring in the moral politics of aid. Tomohisa Hattori is insightful here. Foreign aid, he argues, has the effect of signalling and affirming the status quo, particularly the subjection of the South to the North.[18] A character in the Somali writer, Nurrudin Farah's novel *Gifts* conveys something of the process involved when he writes in a local newspaper:

> Every gift has a personality – that of its giver. On every sack of rice donated by a foreign government to a starving people in Africa, the characteristics and mentality of the donor, name and country, are stamped on its ribs.[19]

What Hattori emphasises, however, is that the politics embedded in the civic virtue attaching to foreign aid help to create a moral distinction across material lines, over and above the imperatives of power politics or market forces.[20] In a companion article, Hattori goes on to consider the ethical justifications and practices of international aid organisations and the way they contribute to the construction of capitalist hegemony.[21] The social relations embedded in the giving and acceptance of a gift that is not reciprocated confirm the virtue of the giver which in turn strengthens the bonds of the donor community. There is little incentive to challenge the underlying material hierarchy and mostly over time the ethics work to endorse it. On the other side, the acceptance of gifts signifies a kind of consent to the neoliberal order. Following George Monbiot, we might retort that "Everything has been globalized except our consent."[22] But Hattori has a point when he concludes that the institutionalisation of gifting is a mechanism of acceptance of the capitalist order.

The duplicity of an implied consent that is forced by dire circumstance is brought home when we examine the programmes of governmentality that are imposed on states, societies and people that are found to be underdeveloped. The push for good governance was put on the agenda by the World Bank's 1989 study of sub-Saharan Africa.[23] The call for good governance became increasingly insistent during the 1990s and since then it has served both as a conditionality of aid and a pretext for much broader intervention in non-European societies. Insensitive to any notion that politics in the non-European world work very differently from in the West,[24] and secure in the conviction that the economics of development are universal, the procedural democracy required is one that facilitates the entry of foreign capital and the processes of privatisation. But invariably there is a tension, and often a contradiction between the strictures of market-led development and the pretence of democratic practice.[25] There is also a contradiction between the call for democracy and transparency on the part of aid recipients and what has been called the 'democratic deficit' of global institutions, which are hierarchical, poorly representative and far from transparent.[26]

We also need to take account of the way democratisation, dealing largely with the state, works in conjunction with the role ascribed to civil society and the initiatives taken to develop more rational economic behaviour on the part of families and individuals. A UN Development Programme publication declared that the cultivation of civil society was necessary "to fill the vacuum left by the slimmed-down state".[27] Exactly. A publication of USAID's Center for Democracy and Governance explained: "It is through the advocacy efforts of civil society organizations (CSOs) that people are given a voice in the process of formulating public policy".[28] Perhaps. The problem with this line of thinking is that the transposition of Western ideas and experience of civil society doesn't mesh well with non-European practice. It is Partha Chatterjee's view that in ex-colonial countries such as India, civil society is cut off from the popular life of communities. The poor engage in political struggle but they are not part of a participating citizenship as supposed by international financial institutions and development agencies.[29]

While there is little to suggest that Chatterjee's argument has had much of a hearing either in aid or IR circles, there is certainly an awareness that often people at the grassroots behave differently towards the market economy from those higher up in the pecking order. In an important contribution to the literature, David Williams has argued that international organisations find it necessary to reshape identities to promote individual autonomy and the ability to calculate, in the process stripping away cultural and social ties such as the family. To this end, and despite professions that economic rationality is 'natural', they are involved in ambitious programmes to inculcate the knowledges and habits required for the market economy to flourish and expand. Williams goes on to show that the training in basic capitalist skills is characteristic of much Western NGO activity as well.[30] The 1998/1999 World Bank report on knowledge is surprisingly revealing about the process. Two kinds of knowledge, it declared, are critical for developing societies: knowledge about technology and knowledge about attributes, "such as the quality of the product, the diligence of a worker, or the creditworthiness of a firm, all crucial to effective markets".[31]

The most recent addition to development's inventory of tasks is its contribution to security. In the course of the 1990s, it became an axiom of Western state policy that development couples with security; that the one cannot be had without the other. At about the same time the idea took root in international organisations and it worked its way down the NGO chain. Again, this was not entirely a new development. It had a long lineage and its immediate precursors were humanitarian intervention in complex political emergencies and relief operations in what Naomi Klein calls "disaster capitalism",[32] a recent example being the role of the US military after the hurricane in Haiti in January 2009.[33] In its contemporary manifestation the linkage between development and security is much broader in ambit, holding out the vision of a new global society in which developed and underdeveloped are brought together in a compact of mutual self-interest.[34] This is not simply the rhetoric of state leaders but it informs the world-view of human security advocates.[35] Development is dependent upon security; fighting poverty overseas enhances security at home.

In summary, the revamped version of development that now prevails functions to consolidate the present world order. Driven by the imperatives of the market economy, the development venture has been extended into the realms of governmentality, civil society and security. Its significance is twofold. First, it has led to a deepening involvement in refashioning the state, remaking societies and recasting the identities of those to be developed. This is interventionism that in some ways goes beyond the dreams of the rulers of empire. Second, development has legitimated the existing global system with its structural inequalities by holding out the prospect that the underdeveloped can join the developed. It might even be argued that without development's promise of redemption, neoliberalism could never have become international ideology.

The evolution of high politics

Development's contemporary predicament did not emerge overnight, as it were, with the globalisation of neoliberalism. While neoliberalism stitched development into the framework of world order, it picked up on earlier processes and currents of thought. In this section I select a few fragments from the evolution of development doctrine and practice to indicate the historical continuities and disjunctions, as well as to enable us better to imagine how development might be done differently.

Over the past decade or so there has been an upsurge of interest in the origins of development in Europe and its projection into the non-European world through the colonial project. How far this early writing related to world order, however, has not been directly addressed. The centrality of the motivated individual in the development process went back to the body of thought that emerged in Great Britain in the late eighteenth century and evolved in the nineteenth century. Stemming from the work of Adam Smith, the classical political economists saw material progress flowing from private individuals maximising their utilities. The pursuit of free trade provided an alternative to the natural economic fluctuations that earlier had been accepted as inevitable. Yet it was understood that the state had a role to play in the process of economic development. A framework of law and order had first to be put in place and at times it would be necessary to help create the social conditions for the market economy to flourish. This beneficent vision, although primarily economic, had a political dimension. In the dictum of the time, the 'Great Commercial Republic of the World' would deliver not only the marvels of the market economy but also a more harmonious world order. This was a pitch to the future. Mostly colonies were required to be self-supporting; in the main development overseas was directed to the needs of home economy and European treasuries were deeply sceptical about colonial development projects.

Michael Cowen and Robert Shenton make the case for a substantially different genealogy of development, one that draws heavily on positivist thought as it emerged on the continent in the course of the nineteenth century.[36] Investing development with a specific meaning of their own, on their reading development came into being not to accelerate economic growth but to establish the political conditions through which order could be imposed on a process of industrialism which otherwise produced disorder. Accordingly, they give pride of place to the Saint-Simonians and Comte as the inventors of development and show how J.S. Mill carried positivist ideas to Britain, and Friedrich List was the unacknowledged progenitor of development planning in the Third World.

Development as it has evolved in practice, however, has not been approached in the very restricted sense of Cowen and Shenton. Rather, it has been understood as the search for some kind of accommodation between promoting economic growth and restraining the destructive and politically destabilising effects of unfettered capitalist development. Perceived thus, it might be said that development has a dual European heritage, but classical political economy provided the primary frame of reference for development as it came to be practised in the non-European world. The continental tradition at times works within the corpus of classical political economy, at others it works against it. Often enough it is absent – even if affinities can be identified between nineteenth-century thought and that of policy-makers and critics in the Third World.[37]

Following the pioneering work of Edward Said and Samir Amin,[38] recent scholarship has established that much that was branded as 'made in Europe' emerged through Europe's relationship with its outside, in particular through the colonial project.[39] So it was with development. In significant ways, colonial difference challenged the hold of European intellectual traditions. Here we are dealing not simply with different circumstances but with all kinds of assumptions, misunderstandings and fictions, and with processes of experimentation on the ground. We cannot, therefore, fix development with a single meaning over time. By way of illustration, let us briefly consider two lines of thought that lost their relevance or were overturned.

In many parts of the colonial world the idea of development was tied to the problem of labour – the myth of the 'lazy native', and of 'races of low social efficiency'. Such representations generated a politics of difference which strengthened the assurance of the metropoles and downgraded the colonial other. At the same time they gestured to a practical problem confronting colonial capitalism. In Africa for much of the colonial period the shortage of labour was held to be a major impediment to tropical development.[40] Forced and immigrant labour was a stopgap measure. The longer-term solution was seen to lie in inducing Africans into 'honourable productive labour' by such means as creating new needs – "so long as the natives have no wants they will not and need not work".[41] Like other features of the development agenda, it was believed that bringing people into the work force – and into the international economy – would break through the barriers that divided the world into the developed and the underdeveloped. Something of the same faith remains with us still but in much more qualified form, except for zealots, because of structural changes in the international economy since the 1970s. Capitalism has not proved as dynamic as earlier had been expected, and the emergence of the informational economy has contributed to the marginalisation of large parts of the South and the need for its labour. On some readings the net result is that hopes for transforming the lot of the world's poorest people have been replaced by strategies of management and containment.[42]

The second area of change relates to the state. Most significantly in the case of Britain, the years between the two world wars saw an expansion of the role of the state within the framework of a more defensive approach to the liberal trading order. Prodded by liberal and radical critics, official thinking moved hesitantly from a series of protective injunctions to a recognition of the need to a more systematic interventionist approach to economic and social advancement. One index of the extent of rethinking was the growing criticism of indirect rule in Nigeria. The welfare of indigenes could not be left to the vagaries of external capitalism and a series of checks on the traditional native administration; it was the task of the colonial state to prise open the doors to development.[43] The full impact of this emphasis on the enabling role of the state was not seen until after the Second World War with the development agenda of the Atlee Labour Government. Influenced by Fabianism, the rejigged colonial state with it, marketing boards and responsibilities for industrialisation became the basis for the strong ex-colonial state after decolonisation. But the strong state turned out to be a problem for Western policy-makers. Beginning in the 1960s and continuing through the structural adjustment programmes of the 1980s, it was cut down to size, giving way to the tamed state that did the bidding of international financial institutions.

The inter-war years also saw a movement away from racialised understandings of the development gap to an emphasis on the West's superior knowledge, technology and skills. Economic expertise was fundamental here. It is Timothy Mitchell's contention that, heavily influenced by work in the colonial laboratory, very significant changes took place in the structure of economic thought that transformed the nature of development strategies. Drawing on the early writing of Keynes (whose first book *Indian Currency and Finance* (1913) was written while he was working at the India Office) and on his own extensive research into colonial Egypt, Mitchell argues that it was in the 1930s that the economy began to be understood in its modern sense as an object rather than as earlier a mode of behaviour involving the exercise of 'thrift'. As he presents it, in large part "the realisation of the economy belongs to the history of colonialism."[44] Moreover, "the economy was the object upon which the new politics of development was built after the 1930s".[45] Thus began the dominance of developmental economics, presented as a specialised knowledge, objective and calculable which could, unlike classical political economy, be separated from the sphere of politics. In addition, this knowledge, configured to fit the space of the nation, worked inexorably to augment the power of the state – in the first instance the colonial state and in due course the ex-colonial developmentalist state.

The entry of the United States into the business of aid-giving outside Europe in 1948 and 1949 added a new dimension to the politics of development. The earlier experience of the European states in the colonial world was an unknown chapter. Starting afresh, one notable feature of America's approach was the belief that Third World societies could be readily transformed with only modest injections of external aid. In Truman's view, America's vast reserves of technical knowledge held the key to solving the problems of want and disease.[46] This faith in expertise had its parallels in earlier European thought but the optimism about what could be accomplished was a testament to America's self-belief. Of more far-reaching significance, the strategic imperative of the Cold War framed thinking about development, very largely determining where aid went, the kind of aid that was given and who benefited. Tellingly, Walt Rostow's text *The Stages of Economic Growth*, so influential at the time, was subtitled *A Non-Communist Manifesto*.[47] The global perspective also contributed to a distinctive universalism in American thinking about development that discounted local knowledge and the politics of place. The modernisation theorist David Apter declared: "The work of modernization is the burden of this age...Modernization, and the desire for it, reaches around the world".[48] It is David Slater's contention that the deployment of modernisation theory was a reflection of a will to spatial power: "It provided a discursive legitimation for a whole series of practical interventions and penetrations that sought to subordinate, contain and assimilate the Third World as other".[49] It needs to be said, however, that the European metropolis never attached the same significance to the geopolitics of the Cold War as did the United States.

The overt racism that characterised both earlier American approaches to Asia and the European development tradition was much less evident in the highwater days of the Cold War. Immutable backwardness now gave way to ideas about historical and social conditioning. The need to win the support of Asia in the struggle against communism required a reworking of orientalist inscriptions and making evident the ways in which development connected with local culture. The work of reclamation is exemplified by the novel *The Ugly American*, written by two American political scientists, William Lederer and Eugene Burdick.[50] *The Ugly American*, which is really a series of linked short stories, was a response to Graham Greene's *The Quiet American* and its sharp critique of American universalism. The main protagonist, Homer Atkins, is shown to be as at home in an Asian village, building and marketing his water pump, as in California. The local peasants think and act like Americans, and respond to economic incentives similarly. In such ways, the novel depoliticises America's problems in Asia by dissolving cultural difference. The novel was a popular success and made an immediate impact. Four public figures – including J.F. Kennedy – sent copies to each member of the United States Senate. Senator William Fulbright critiqued the book from the floor of the Senate. Richard Nixon made use of the novel in a major speech before his presidential nomination.

The latter years of the Cold War saw the internationalisation of ideas and practices that established the rules of engagement between donors and donees. It is worth simply noting two main features of this system-in-the-making because, when reworked by the neoliberal precepts of the 1990s, it morphed into the international development coalition which remains with us today. Foremost was the movement from thinking within the tradition of the political economy of development to the confines of neo-classical economics. The rise to prominence of a macroeconomics valorising the market severely curtailed the interdisciplinary nature and broader reach of development thought. The result was that the models and methodologies of economics came to colonise the space of the social and the political. Reflecting on the early days of British development studies in the period of decolonisation, John Cameron observes that political economy questioned the mainstream claim to be the apolitical handmaiden of developing states.[51] John Harriss' account of these years conveys a similar sense of intellectual excitement, although he concedes that much of the work undertaken inclined towards micro studies rather than the macro.[52] The other development of these years was that the role of the state changed from being understood as the principal agent of change to being an obstacle to change because it interfered with the workings of the market.

The rise of development discourse as a body of specialised expertise went hand-in-hand with changes in the organisations and knowledge machines which implemented and informed the development project. This is what Arturo Escobar called the institutionalisation of development which makes the exercise of power possible.[53] The period from the late 1940s to the late 1980s saw the state joined by a range of institutions and knowledge formations engaged with development. A growing commonality in approach was also evident. Led by the World Bank, UN agencies came to figure much more prominently than before. Increasingly, institutional knowledge became policy oriented and, many argued, less critical as a result. The NGO movement which earlier had a low profile with both policy-makers and researchers gained wider recognition, leading to considerable expansion in the linkages with states and international bodies.[54]

The remarkable growth of the development community and the increasing connection between its various wings occasioned very little interest in IR because they fell outside the main categories of reference within the discipline. Yet they had the potential to galvanise new lines of thought inasmuch as they brought into a single frame development as an international doctrine and development as directly touching the lives of ordinary people. Nor, within the development community, has the institutionalising of development been a subject of public debate. Underlying the reluctance to take up the issues appear to be a shared acceptance of liberalism as an international ideology – or at least a sense that it is better approached as above or outside politics – and an anxiety on the part of non-governmental partners about the risk of losing their classification as charities plus the flow of project finance.

James Ferguson's dictum that development is an "anti-politics machine" enables us to bring home the significance of these changes. This machine, Ferguson elaborated, works by "depoliticizing everything it touches, everywhere whisking political realities out of sight, all the while performing, almost unnoticed, its own pre-eminently political operation of expanding bureaucratic state power".[55] Ferguson was in fact writing about development in Lesotho between 1975 and 1984 and his concern was with how it expanded the exercise of state power. Nonetheless, his argument about depoliticisation applies with equal force to development as an international process. And in this case the beneficiary is the global development coalition, rather than simply the state.

The net result of the processes examined in this section is to screen out or at least to devalue alternative knowledges about development. Three kinds of knowledge are most affected. First, there are the knowledges of local people, the sense of being-in-the-world of those who are to be developed. Second, there is the marginalisation of knowledges about the world system that do not mesh with the liberal agenda, including international political economy, the radical strands in international law and world systems theory. Significantly, statist knowledges about world order find a place in the development lexicon because of their currency with policy-makers and their compatibility with liberal orthodoxy. Third, there is the loss of knowledges about the social so influential in many non-European societies. Think, for instance, of the *Mahabharata* in India and its concern with the relationship of people to each other, or the centrality of the kinship connection in many Australian Aboriginal communities. The significance of such knowledges was underlined by the development economist Kari Polanyi Levitt when she stated that she no longer believed in the complicated development plans she once made. She went on: "I believe development has to do with how people relate to each other, whether co-operatively and with synergy or competitively, with conflict. The one will produce development, the other will produce conflict".[56]

Devolving development to the everyday

If development is to be done differently, a first move might be to look to the everyday. This would address many of the problems associated with development being delivered from the top and the outside. Escobar has pointed to the importance of the everyday in the Latin American experience and suggested that it could be the site from which a new understanding of social practice in the Third World emerges.[57] More recently, he has argued that cyberspace and complexity theory strengthen the credentials of self-organisation so much so that in the long run it "may amount to re-inventing the dynamics of social emancipation itself".[58] Robert Cox also sees complexity theory as facilitating purposive change in world politics. The task, as he puts it, is to be alert to and to work with movements of self-organisation in social and political relations that have been created collectively.[59]

No one, of course, imagines that the everyday and the principle of self-organisation could somehow dislodge the existing hierarchical structure of the development project plus its ancillary bodies of expertise. The hope is rather that these twin concepts might take root in some quarters of the development consortium and come to represent an alternative mode of knowledge; one that can inform policy-making in attempts to harness the social and a politics embedded in lived experience. More than this, that the everyday so long neglected in international relations and security studies might become a reference point for thought and research about a broader politics of change.

Despite the impressive lineage of writing on the everyday,[60] the concept has its difficulties particularly as a guide to action by outsiders, whether they be scholars, development professionals or concerned ordinary people. For one thing, the everyday is by no means always progressive. Because the literature has focused on the patterns of resistance to established authority, we tend not to enquire too deeply into the interests and values that are to be protected – at times uneven development, tribalism, patriarchy, even violence. Consider for instance the position of women in some everydays. Rowena Robinson writes of the "tenuousness and fragility of the boundary between the violence of everyday life and extraordinary violence".[61] Taking a more holistic view, we may be led to the position that the everyday needs to be approached selectively – perhaps after the manner of Nandy's approach to the past.[62] We also need to recognise that the everyday is everywhere penetrated by the state, as Veena Das and Arthur Kleinman put it "through the soft knife of policies that severely disrupt the life worlds of people".[63] At times, however, the state will be absent and this also can be a problem.[64] Another issue that must be addressed is the ethics of intervention into the life-worlds of the everyday by outsiders. The everyday in other societies, and in certain aspects our own, can no longer be regarded as an open book, available to all as a kind of global property. Stemming from concerns in and relating to anthropology and ethnology, normative conventions about representations, knowledge ownership and repatriation, and responsibility to the people who are the subject of investigation, must now guide what is said and done in all disciplinary fields and domains of action.[65]

There is a more fundamental reason why we in the North should be wary of becoming directly involved in the politics of the everyday in the non-European world, namely that it can stand in the way of local people authoring their own political subjectivity, of becoming political in their own way. Here I would like to bring in a recent study of the emergence of the political subject by Ranabir Samaddar.[66] Although Samaddar nowhere refers to 'the everyday', his work speaks to it in a distinctive way. His concern is to show that politics in former colonial countries such as India is a discourse of actions rather than one of philosophical reflection as understood in the European tradition. He proceeds by focusing on 'situations' and 'positions', perhaps 'daily and ordinary', which help shape the emergence of the political subject. His next step is to examine this subject not only theoretically but in relation to a set of practices such as agitating, mobilising, claiming rights and identity, as well as practices of friendship. Restated in terms of the politics of knowledge, the process is one of 'unlearning' established knowledge and learning new things about society and power relations – which lead to new practices of a collective nature.

Samaddar's analysis is applicable to the subject of development. The rhetoric of many development organisations about connecting to the everyday holds out the prospect of somehow enabling the underdeveloped to be brought into political selfhood. What is significant, of course, is that it is a different kind of subjecthood from that envisaged by Samaddar and that the strategies pursued to bring it about have led to ever-deeper intervention into Third World societies. Samaddar's work, taken in conjunction with the caveats presented two paragraphs back, serves to warn of the risks of transposing Western theorising about the self – not to mention ideas about self-interest – to non-European societies.

The conclusion I draw is that development would be best advanced by the First World maintaining a certain distance from other people's everydays and concentrating on working with its own. The temptation to colonise other people's everydays is built into liberal theorising and has deeply marked the history of Western involvement in non-European societies. For so long the problem of underdevelopment has been located in the otherness of 'out there'. As has often been observed, what stands out is the various 'lacks' of the peoples and societies in the South, exemplified by the case of indigenous people. From the lack of cultivation and the lack of a work ethic we have moved to the lack of good governance and the lack of attributes relevant to the market. Often enough the knowledge gained on the ground has been used – at times with the best intentions – to wipe the slate clean for a new regime, not only of theoretical knowledge but of applied politics. Think of the role of missionaries in the expansion of empire: Livingstone, for instance, whose understanding of central African society was remarkable for his time. Yet, convinced that Christianity would never prosper unless tribal society was undermined, he wrote of "the advance of ruthless colonists" as a "terrible necessity".[67]

None of this is to suggest that external initiatives and support for strengthening the everyday and its standing in relation to national and global politics have no place in a postcolonial agenda. International networks and linkages are becoming more important in place-based struggles, and we should be thinking of development agencies as junior partners in a mutual endeavour. This, however, would involve a sea-change in First World approaches to project evaluation that presently constitute a compulsion 'to do it my way'.

The other side of my argument is that much more attention needs to be paid to the work of development in the North, particularly with regard to advocacy and education. In part, the neglect of the task at home is a function of the preoccupation with knowledge transfer, not exchange; with changing the behaviour of others but not ourselves. Think of the aid personnel spread across the former colonial world shedding the light of development in a manner reminiscent of the missionaries shedding the light of the gospels. The mindset that sees the South as the site for action helps to shield from view deeply troubling aspects of the politics of home which need to be confronted. One is the historical role of the First World in contributing to the poverty, instability and violence in the non-European world through the appropriation of resources, uneven development, the strengthening of ethnic identifications and so on. There are continuities today but there is a widespread refusal to acknowledge them in such terms. Another is the part played by the Western powers in determining the structure and workings of the international system – which resulted in the collapse of the scheme for a new international economic order nearly forty years ago. Although there have been some recent moves to accommodate the rise of new powers, the resistance to fundamental change in the contemporary world system is evident in the determination to maintain control of global financial institutions and in the approach adopted in the negotiations about climate change. Taken together, these very negative strands in the West's approach to the Third World cut against the efficacy of the development project. It is a matter of giving with the right hand and taking away with the left hand the opportunity for non-European societies to be self-reliant.

The challenge is now to work with the everyday in the metropoles so that it can connect with the everyday in the non-European worlds. The first requirement is enabling representations of the other to replace the images of victimhood, disease and disaster that have served as the staple in NGO fund-raising campaigns. To this should be added some broader context about how the work of development relates to the existing international order. Given the importance of the mass media,[68] the accent might well be on story-telling but accounts by the grateful recipient hardly fit the bill. Reversing the traditional pattern of movement, bringing people from non-European societies to speak of their experiences and ideas would seem a productive move, but perhaps not if they come from a local arm of an international NGO. The difficulties are, of course, formidable. Pictures of starving children and schemes of child sponsorship are very effective in raising funds. The political may have to be approached indirectly for fear of losing charitable status and tax deductibility. Grants to Northern NGOs for educational and promotional work are likely to get a bad press because they may be seen as political sleight of hand as well as money lost to the immediate needs of the poor.

Attempting to change what is done in the name of development within the metropolis should involve reviewing the teaching of development studies and, where appropriate, presenting a case for revision. This is overdue in any case. There is much to suggest that with the academy increasingly dependent on the market economy, courses have become oriented to career prospects and to skills such as project evaluation at the expense of critical thought.[69] It has been argued throughout this chapter that development cannot be abstracted from the wider politics of the international, from the workings of cultural difference and from the life worlds and political subjectivity of ordinary people. It seems highly unlikely that many development studies courses would clear the bar in these respects. While no doubt there are numerous people both in the academy and outside who would welcome opening up courses in this way, institutional resistance can be expected. One would like to draw heart from a recent article by a member of the World Bank's Development Research Group in which it was suggested that students possessing "technocratic skills alone risk ... becoming part of the problem rather than the solution". However, the 'core competencies' spelled out only touched on the political at one remove.[70] This, taken in conjunction with the World Bank's track record with knowledge management,[71] is hardly very encouraging.

It is not enough to tie the shortcomings of the development project at home to the instrumentality of Western policy-makers. This is part of the story but the development establishment and the everyday cannot be absolved quite so easily. The negativity towards other cultures and the intolerance of difference go back long before neoliberalism became international ideology and was emplaced in the institutional structure of states. What needs to be recognised is that development was part of the orientalist project and it resonated with popular assumptions and sentiments about self and other. As we have seen from the case of *The Ugly American*, these assumptions and sentiments were malleable and could be harnessed for different political purposes such as the struggle against communism. So also in the years that followed – years of widespread prosperity in the West, punctuated by worries about globalisation, and refugees and asylum seekers – the politics of the everyday could be tapped selectively to support supposed national interests and the electoral prospects of politicians. As it has been refracted at the political level, then, the culture of the everyday has not been conducive to taking constructive initiatives with respect to development. Nor, in large part, has the development sector been very active in attempting to turn the situation around. What is required is a geographical re-orientation based on the recognition that much of the work of development should be located in the North.

Early in this chapter I drew attention to IR's failure to engage substantively with development, arguing that in large part this was a function of the disciplinary engrossment with Euro-American theory which relegated the non-European world to a shadow life cast in the image of the First World. I wish to conclude with the thought that bringing development into the disciplinary fold opens up the possibility of IR rethinking disabling aspects of its corpus.

Development could then become a catalyst for moving beyond a preoccupation with an externally imposed or inspired system of stability and security in the formerly colonised world to an engagement with the emancipatory potential of the everyday. This would surely connect with the momentous changes presently taking place in the Middle East and become an integral part of a design for a different world order.

Notes

1 Ashis Nandy, *The Romance of the State: And the Fate of Dissent in the Tropics* (New Delhi: Oxford University Press, 2003), p.171.
2 Henry Bernstein, 'Development Studies and the Marxists', in Uma Kothari (ed.), *A Radical History of Development Studies: Individuals, Institutions and Ideologies* (London and New York: Zed Books, 2005), pp.111–137 at p.119.
3 Ibid., footnote 17, p.134.
4 I have in mind particularly Mark Duffield and Christine Sylvester. There are of course difficulties of categorising where people locate themselves in disciplinary terms and what constitutes disciplinary space.
5 Christian Reus-Smit and Duncan Snidal (eds), *The Oxford Handbook of International Relations* (Oxford: Oxford University Press, 2008).
6 One text that does rather better is John Baylis, Steve Smith and Patricia Owen, *The Globalization of World Politics: An Introduction to IR* (Oxford: Oxford University Press, 4th edition, 2008).
7 Caroline Thomas and Peter Wilkin, 'Still Waiting After All These Years: "The Third World" on the Periphery of International Relations', *British Journal of Politics and International Relations* 6:2 (2004), pp.241–258 at pp.245–246. A similar examination eight years earlier of five major IR journals published in the United States yielded no article that concentrated directly on development. See Mary Durfee and James N. Rosenau, 'Playing Catch-Up: International Relations Theory and Poverty', *Millennium* 25:3 (1996), pp.521–545 at p.524.
8 The special issue was on poverty, *Millennium* 25:3 (1996). The article is David Williams, 'Constructing the Economic Space: The World Bank and the Making of *Homo Oeconomicus*', *Millennium* 28:1 (1999), pp.79–99.
9 See for instance Arlene B. Tickner and Ole Waever (eds), *International Relations Scholarship Around the World* (Abingdon, Oxon; New York, Routledge, 2009).
10 Roger Tooze and Craig N. Murphy, 'The Epistemology of Poverty and the Poverty of Epistemology in IPE', *Millennium: Journal of International Studies*, 26:3 (1996), pp.681–707, see especially p.681.
11 Roxanne Lynn Doty, *Imperial Encounters: The Politics of Representation in North–South Relations* (Minneapolis and London: University of Minnesota Press, 2006), p.162.
12 Ibid., p.170.
13 On the latter see Phillip Darby, 'Rolling Back the Frontiers of Empire: Practising the Postcolonial', *International Peacekeeping* (Special issue on 'Liberal Peacebuilding Reconstructed') 16:5 (2009), pp.699–716.
14 Amitav Ghosh, 'The Global Reservation: Notes towards an Ethnology of International Peacekeeping', *Cultural Anthropology* 9:3 (1994), pp.412–422 at pp.421–422.
15 Samir Amin, *Capitalism in the Age of Globalisation: The Management of Contemporary Society* (London: Zed Books, 1997), p.93.
16 C. Calhoun, 'A World of Emergencies: Fear, Intervention and the Limits of Cosmopolitan Order', *Canadian Review of Sociology and Anthropology* 41:4 (2004), pp.373–395.

17 Mark Duffield, *Development, Security and Unending War: Governing the World of Peoples* (Cambridge: Polity Press, 2007), p.33.
18 Tomohisa Hattori, 'The Moral Politics of Foreign Aid', *Review of International Studies* 29 (2003), pp.229–247 at p.234.
19 Nurrudin Farah, *Gifts* (London: Serif, 1993), p.195. Farah also acknowledges his debt to Marcel Mauss. Earlier in the book (pp.45–47) there is an instructive account of a conversation between a Somali woman, Yussar, and Ingrid, a Danish aid worker about the philosophical and cultural aspects of giving and receiving gifts.
20 Hattori, 'The Moral Politics of Foreign Aid', p.244.
21 Tomohisa Hattori, 'Giving as a Mechanism of Consent: International Aid Organizations and the Ethical Hegemony of Capitalism', *International Relations* 17:2 (2003), pp.153–173.
22 George Monbiot, *Manifesto for a New World Order* (New York and London: The New Press, 2003), p.1.
23 World Bank, *Sub-Saharan Africa: From Crisis to Sustainable Growth* (Washington, DC: World Bank, 1989), p.60.
24 See for example Patrick Chabal and Jean-Pascal Daloz, *Africa Works: Disorder as Political Instrument* (Oxford: International African Institute, James Curry, and Bloomington and Indianapolis: Indiana University Press, 1999).
25 See for instance the Australian White Paper on development assistance published in April 2006 which in the spirit of the times ties development aid to recipient states reworking their economies in the light of neoliberal precepts and the Western security imperative (AusAID, *Australian Aid: Promoting Growth and Stability,* Canberra: AusAID, 2006). Critics allege that although the White Paper associates market-led development with democracy, the model of good governance it advocates is anti-pluralist, attempting to insulate institutions from popular influence. See Toby Carroll and Shahar Hameiri, 'Aid Misses the Mark', *The Age,* 8 June 2006.
26 The phrase comes from Rosemary Foot, 'Introduction' in *Order and Justice in International Relations,* eds, Rosemary Foot, John Gaddis and Andrew Hurrell (Oxford: Oxford University Press, 2003), p.9. For a substantive discussion see Ngaire Woods, 'Order, Justice, the IMF and the World Bank', in Foot, Gaddis and Hurrell, *Order and Justice International Relations,* pp.80–102.
27 *Government for Sustainable Development* (New York: United Nations Development Programme, 1997), p.20.
28 Center for Democracy and Governance, USAID, *Democracy and Governance: A Conceptual Framework,* November 1998, p.15.
29 Partha Chatterjee, *The Politics of the Governed: Reflections on Popular Protest in Most of the World* (New York: Columbia University Press, 2004), pp.35–41.
30 David Williams, 'Constructing the Economic Space: The World Bank and the Making of Homo Oeconomicus', *Millennium* 28:1 (1999), pp.79–99.
31 World Bank, *World Development Report 1998–99* (Washington, DC: World Bank, 1999), p.1.
32 Naomi Klein, 'The Rise of Disaster Capitalism', *The Nation,* 2 May 2005, pp.9–11. See more generally her *The Shock Doctrine: The Rise of Disaster Capitalism* (London: Allen Lane, 2007).
33 The presidents of Venezuela and Bolivia had an alternative nomenclature – an 'American invasion and occupation'.
34 For a very different view see David Chandler, 'The security–development nexus and the rise of "anti-foreign policy"', *Journal of International Relations and Development,* 10 (2007), pp.362–386. It is Chandler's argument that the security–development nexus reveals a lack of policy focus.
35 On this see Duffield, *Development, Security and Unending War: Governing the World of Peoples,* ch.5. The introduction to Duffield's book gives an excellent account of the development–security nexus.

36 M. Cowen and R. Shenton, *Doctrines of Development* (London and New York: Routledge, 1996).

37 This was a theme in Cowen and Shenton's work. They claim, for instance, that the theologian John Henry Newman writing in the 1840s anticipated the idea of underdevelopment as elaborated by Gunder Frank and others in the 1960s. See Cowen and Shenton, *Doctrines of Development*, ch.2.

38 The key works are Edward Said, *Orientalism* (London: Routledge and Kegan Paul, 1978) and Samir Amin, *Eurocentrism*, translated by Russell Moore (London: Zed Books, 1989).

39 See for instance Michael Hardt and Antonio Negri, *Empire* (Cambridge, MA and London: Harvard University Press, 2000), at pp.70, 114 and 115 and Tarak Barkawi and Mark Laffey, 'Retrieving the Imperial: Empire and International Relations', *Millennium Journal of International Studies* 31:1 (2002), pp.109–127.

40 See W.M. Macmillan, *Africa Emergent: A Survey of Social and Economic Trends in British Africa* (London: Hodder and Stoughton, 1938), p.241 and Herbert Frankel, *Capitalist Investment in Africa: Its Course and Effects* (London: Oxford University Press for RIIA, 1938), p.8.

41 Cited in Timothy Burke, *Lifebuoy Men, Lux Women: Commodification, Consumption and Cleanliness in Modern Zimbabwe* (London: Leicester University Press, 1996), p.86.

42 See Mark Duffield, *Development, Security and Unending War*, ch.1; Mark Duffield, *Global Governance and the New Wars: The Merging of Development and Security* (London and New York: Zed Books, 2001); and Ankie Hoogvelt, *Globalisation and the Postcolonial World: The New Political Economy of Development* (Houndmills, Hants, 1997), chs.4 and 8.

43 See Phillip Darby, *Three Faces of Imperialism: British and American Approaches to Asia and Africa 1870–1970* (New Haven and London: Yale University Press, 1987), pp.112–113.

44 Timothy Mitchell, *Rule of Experts: Egypt, Techno-politics, Modernity* (Berkeley and Los Angeles: University of California Press, 2002), p.83.

45 Ibid, p.84.

46 See Harry S. Truman, *Memoirs*, vol.2, *Years of Trial and Hope 1946–53* (New York, Signet Books, 1956), pp.268–276.

47 W.W. Rostow, *The Stages of Economic Growth* (Cambridge: Cambridge University Press, 1960).

48 David Apter, *The Politics of Modernization* (Chicago and London: University of Chicago Press, 1965), p.1.

49 David Slater, 'The geopolitical imagination and the enframing of development theory', *Transactions of the Institute of British Geographers* n.s. 18 (1993), pp.419–437 at p.421.

50 William J. Lederer and Eugene Burdick, *The Ugly American* (London: Corgi Books, 1960 – first published 1958).

51 John Cameron, 'Journeying in radical development studies: a reflection on thirty years of researching pro-poor development', ch.7 in Kothari, *A Radical History of Development Studies: Individuals, institutions, ideologies*, pp.138–156 at p.139.

52 John Harriss, 'Great Promise, hubris and recovery: a participant's history of development studies', ch.2 in ibid, pp.29–30.

53 See Arturo Escobar, 'Power and Visibility: Development and the Invention and Management of the Third World', *Cultural Anthropology*, 4:4 (1988), pp.428–443.

54 On this see David Lewis, 'Individuals, organizations and public action: trajectories of the "non-governmental" in development studies', in Kothari, *A Radical History of Development Studies: Individuals, Institutions and Ideologies*.

55 James Ferguson, *The Anti-Politics Machine: 'Development', Depoliticization, and Bureaucratic Power in Lesotho* (Cambridge: Cambridge University Press, 1990), p.xv.

56 Kari Polanyi Levitt, 'Development, Change and Society: An Interview with Kari Levitt', *Race and Class* 49, no.2 (2007), pp.1–19 at p.5.
57 Arturo Escobar, 'Imagining a Post-Development Era? Critical Thought, Development and Social Movements', *Social Text* 20:2 and 3 (1992), pp.20–57 at pp.30 and 44–45.
58 Arturo Escobar, 'Other Worlds Are (Already) Possible: Self-Organization, Complexity, and Post-Capitalist Cultures', in Jai Sen, Anita Anand, Arturo Escobar and Peter Waterman (eds), *The World Social Forum: Challenging Empires*, 2003, accessed at www.choike.org/neuvo_eng/informes/1557.html, pp.349–358 at p.353.
59 Robert Cox, 'The Point is Not Just to Explain the World but to Change It', ch.4 in Christian Reus-Smit and Duncan Snidal (eds), *The Oxford Handbook of International Relations* (Oxford: Oxford University Press, 2008), pp.84–93 at pp.87–89.
60 The foundational texts include Michel de Certeau, *The Practice of Everyday Life*, trans. Steven Randall (Berkeley: University of California Press, 1984); Henri Lefebvre, *Critique of Everyday Life*, vol.1, trans. J. Moore (London: Verso, 1991); and James C. Scott, *Weapons of the Weak: Everyday Forms of Peasant Resistance* (New Haven: Yale University Press, 1985).
61 Rowena Robinson, *Tremors of Violence: Muslim Survivors of Ethnic Strife in Western India* (New Delhi: Sage, 2005), p.147.
62 Nandy writes of "principled forgetfulness" which involves separating the remembered past from its ethical meaning in the present. Accordingly he declares "it is often important *not* to remember the past objectively, clearly or in its entirety." Ashis Nandy, 'History's Forgotten Doubles', *History and Theory* 34 (1995), pp.44–66 at p.47.
63 In the introduction to Veena Das, Arthur Kleinman, Margaret Lock, Mamphela Ramphele and Pamela Reynolds (eds), *Remaking a World: Violence, Social Suffering, and Recovery* (New Delhi: Oxford University Press, 2001), p.1.
64 Rowena Robinson argues that redress for victims of violence "is never sufficient if it is not state-led or state-legitimized", *Tremors of Violence: Muslim Survivors of Ethnic Strife in Western India*, 40 (note 42).
65 Key texts here include Karena Shaw, 'Whose Knowledge for what Politics?', *Review of International Studies* 29 (2003), pp.199–221; Julian Eckl, 'Responsible Scholarship After Leaving the Veranda: Normative Issues Faced by Field Researchers – and Armchair Scientists', *International Political Sociology* 2 (2008), pp.185–203; and Wanda Vrasti, 'The Strange Case of Ethnography and International Relations', *Millennium: Journal of International Studies* 37:2 (2008), pp.279–301.
66 Ranabir Samaddar, *Emergence of the Political Subject* (New Delhi: Sage Publications, 2010). See especially pp.xi–xxxii.
67 Tim Jeal, *Livingstone* (London: Heinemann, 1973), p.105. See also pp.54–55 and 373–374.
68 A UK survey of people's sources of information about the developing world found that 82% of respondents cited television news and 63% cited newspapers/magazines. *National Statistics Omnibus Survey on Political Attitudes to Development*, July 2003, DFID UK.
69 For a strongly argued piece to this effect, see Frans Schuurman, 'Critical Development Theory: Moving Out of the Twilight Zone', *Third World Quarterly* 30:5 (2009), pp.831–848. See also Andy Sumner and Michael Tribe, 'What Should Development Studies Be', *Development in Practice* 18:6 (2008), pp.755–765.
70 Michael Woolcock, 'Higher Education, Policy Schools and Development Studies: What Should Masters Degree Students Be Taught?', *Journal of International Development* 19 (2007), pp.55–73 at p.62.
71 On this see Robin Broad, '"Knowledge Management": a case study of the World Bank's research department', *Development in Practice* 17:4 & 5 (2007), pp.700–708.

5

GLIMPSES OF AFRICAN LIFE

Two short stories

Sekai Nzenza

The donor's visit

Just after dawn today, Ndodye stood on top of the anthill and woke the whole village up. He was shouting: "A message to old ladies, widows and orphans! *Chiziviso ku chembere, shirikadzi ne nherera!* Today the donor is coming only for you. Get up and go to Simukai Centre for your food handouts. If you do not get up now, you will die of hunger in your hut." Ndodye's voice rules the mornings. Voices travel fast before sunrise.

Every day Ndodye stands on top of the anthill near his compound and announces all the village meetings and events. Last week Ndodye shouted that the donor was coming. Chiyevo and I got up early and started the journey to the food distribution meeting. Halfway there we met Sabhuku, the kraal head. Sabhuku said that was not true. There was no donor coming. Ndodye got the days wrong. We turned and went back home. Ndodye has a big voice. He used to be a soldier. Because his rank in the Rhodesian Army was very low, he never had a chance to shout and order people to do anything. Now his time has come: Ndodye is the village crier, neighbourhood police officer and Zanu PF village chairperson.

I say to Chiyevo, "Ndodye was drinking *chi one day* beer at your mother's house till very late last night. When did he get this message and how do we know it is true that the donor is coming?" Chiyevo tells me: "Last week he called all family heads. Today his message is only for old ladies, widows and orphans. It is a special day for them. Ndodye cannot get the message wrong again."

We get up and start the long walk to meet the donor. Chiyevo walks in front of me. Chiyevo is my granddaughter, *muzukuru wangu*, one of my late son's daughters. She accompanies me on long journeys like this and helps me carry whatever the donor gives us. This year Chiyevo will be turning eighteen. She only passed two subjects in Form Four last year. How could she pass? She missed many days of school because we did not have the money for school fees. I sold my goat, her mother sold two chickens and we made enough money for her term fees, books and uniforms. Then the river was in flood for days and days and Chiyevo stayed home. When she went back to school, the teachers were on strike. "Teaching has no money", they said. "The government is not paying us enough. We are teaching your children only because we are merciful." Chiyevo got her results at the beginning of this year. She passed only two subjects out of eight. Her mother was beside herself and did not know what to do.

"I wanted you to become a teacher or a nurse. But you failed. You only passed Shona and Religious Knowledge. Where does that take you? What will you do next? You want to be someone's maid? You want to be a second or third wife to a sugar daddy?" Chiyevo's mother asked her. As usual, Chiyevo shrugged her shoulders, smiled and said nothing. Her mother shouted at her, called her names and said she had wasted her chickens and her goats paying school fees for a dumb and lazy girl. "You do not have a brain", her mother said in anger, "Your head is full of nothing but water."

Chiyevo cried and I said she should not cry. She was not the only one who did not pass at Simukai Secondary School. Many children failed.

Chiyevo and I stop at the river for a wash. It is still morning but it is already quite hot. Cicadas are singing. They promise good rains, I tell Chiyevo. She laughs and says, "Mbuya, last year you said the same thing. Cicadas mean good rains. And did we get good rains? No. Last year we had the worst drought ever."

Chiyevo is right. Last year was bad. We harvested very little. The donors did not come at all. This is September and our granaries are already empty. The rains will only come at the end of next month. If they come at all.

There were times *muzukuru*, when we were never hungry. We harvested more than we could eat. Even these forests gave us wild fruits and mushrooms, I tell Chiyevo. She gives me one of those smiles that say: I do not believe you. What do they believe, the young people? You tell them that there was a time we sneaked out at night to feed Mugabe's men, the comrades. We risked being killed by Rhodesian soldiers. During the day war planes flew so low that you could see the white soldiers and their helmets. They could have easily thrown a bomb on to our compound and destroyed us all, as they did in some villages. I also tell her that her aunt, my first-born daughter Emma, her husband and two sons were killed in one night and thrown inside a cave. Their bodies stayed there, untouched for several years.

All Chiyevo says is: "I have heard that story before. Is that really true?"

Truth. How much truth and how many times should we tell them what happened? How much truth should we leave out? Some people say Emma and her family were sell-outs and they got killed by Mugabe's soldiers. Others say they belonged to Sithole and they were killed by Muzorewa's forces. All I know is that they were not killed by white soldiers because those who were present at the *pungwe* said they did not see any white men. During the liberation war, more than thirty years ago, I lost a daughter, a son-in-law and two grandsons. They

were singled out from the crowd and shot dead. In public. All in one night. I will
never know who killed them. But what does it matter now? They all died. I can
only thank the ancestors for keeping all their bones safe so we could give them
a proper burial after independence.

Unlike her older sisters and some of her cousins, Chiyevo is a decent girl. She
listens to me and takes advice. One day she will be a good woman to someone.
Chiyevo goes to church and works in the garden. Every day she comes to help
me collect firewood, cook and fetch water from the well. If these were the old
days and men were still strong, I would have gone to look for a husband for
her. But these days, where would I look? Everywhere all you can see are skinny
men. Even those who call themselves bachelors do not look healthy at all. Some
of the widowed men are just looking for a younger woman to care for them
until AIDS snatches them away, as it does. The only healthy men I have seen
are those who work for donors, Zanu PF, MDC, the churches and the Chinese
clothing merchants. Businessmen are also healthy. They drive big cars and they
have big stomachs. These men will take Chiyevo as a second or a third wife. But
I will not let Chiyevo go with these men. They will treat her well at first until
they find another beautiful girl to replace her. I tell Chiyevo that money can
buy beautiful women. She should be patient and avoid situations with men that
will lead to sex. One day a healthy-looking single good man will come along.
Chiyevo does not say anything. All she does is listen to me, nod her head and
do as I tell her.

In times of plenty, *mumaguta*, Chiyevo is normally fat, beautiful and strong.
At present she is skinny. We all are. We are hungry. This is a bad season. When I
was her age, I was fat and already married with two children. My father wanted
more cattle so he married me off to VaMandiya, Chiyevo's grandfather. I was
his third and youngest wife. I came to this village before I had my first period.
I was not a woman yet. *Vahosi*, VaMandiya's senior wife made me sleep behind
VaMandiya's back to keep him warm. After my first period, I became his wife.
He loved me and called me VaNyachide, meaning I was his beloved.

Chiyevo, do not walk so fast. I am not your age, I tell her. She slows down.
I used to be a good walker. Once I accompanied my mother from Hwedza to
Mazowe for a *bira*, the ancestor worship ceremony. We passed through Salisbury
on foot. Then when the liberation war came, the curfew stopped us from going
anywhere far. After the war, the number of buses coming here from Harare
were so many. But everything changed when white farmers were forced to
leave the farms and Tony Blair and George Bush put sanctions on Zimbabwe.
Because of this buses do not come to the village any more due to the shortage
of petrol. These two also made our money very weak. All the money in my clay
pot could not buy me cooking oil. Then Obama said we can use his money
but where do we get it? People say there are no jobs in Harare. That Obama
is just like the rest of those Africans who live overseas and forget where they
came from. Tony Blair, George Bush and Obama have made life very difficult
for us. We have to walk many miles to Simukai Centre to get a bus to Harare.

Everything begins and ends at Simukai Centre – Zanu PF and MDC meetings, burial society, council meetings, agriculture meetings, Chinese herbal tea sellers and now the donor's visit.

Chiyevo increases her pace again and pulls my hand: "Mbuya, if we walk like Kamba the tortoise, by the time we get there, the donor will be gone. Look, Sabhuku's two daughters just passed us. They will be way ahead of us in the queue by the time we get to Simukai Center. Come to think of it, they are not widows, where are they going?"

I will not answer Chiyevo's question about Sabhuku's daughters. Talking while I am walking tires me. The message from Ndodye was an invitation for widows, old ladies and orphans. Sabhuku's daughters should not be going to the donor for food handouts today. But who can stop them? Sabhuku is the kraal head. He writes the names of those who qualify to get food handouts. We all know that Sabhuku's daughters went away to Harare to work as maids. Some years later they came back with five children between them. Who is going to tell the donors that Sabhuku's two daughters are not widows? And his five grandchildren are not orphans? The donors do not know who we are. We do not know who they are. We just know that the donors are merciful white people from overseas. They do not like politics. Every year we get donors with a different name. Most of them say they are Christians. They have plenty of food in their countries and they do not want us to die from hunger. They give us food through their workers – the local donors who live here.

We are at Simukai Centre now. My legs are sore and my back hurts. The donors are already here. So Ndodye was correct. Last time I was here, a year ago, there was one lorry. We waited for a very long time to get one bag of beans per family. One bag of beans. That was all. Today is different. There is a big lorry covered with a tent. Behind the lorry are two trucks. The lorry is full of sacks. Food. There are many people here. People I have not seen since independence! Jakobho, the Anglican pastor from St Peters is here too. We are the same age. He has lost all his teeth and his back is all bent. Madaka, the war veteran who lost his leg when he stepped on a landmine. They gave him an artificial leg and when he is wearing trousers, you cannot even tell that he has one leg. I heard that he married a second wife with his war compensation money. His son is a strong member of the MDC. What a shame to the family that is. MDC did not give us land. Mugabe did. This is why I carry my Zanu PF card and my *chitupa* (identification card) tied at the corner of my headscarf.

When we left home this morning, Chiyevo said, "Mbuya, you only need your *chitupa*, not your Zanu PF card." I told her that you never know when they will ask for the Zanu PF card. I am always ready with it. She laughed and said, "Mbuya, both your cards tell lies about who you are. Your date of birth on both cards say you are sixty years old now. That is not possible because my father would have been fifty now if he were still alive. And he was the last of your eight children. You must be seventy-five or seventy-eight. Also the card says your name is Enifa. Your name is Makumbi."

What does it matter what year I was born? I ask her. Who was writing the time and the day of my birth? Enifa is my Christian English name, given to me when I was baptised as a young girl and I became an Anglican. I kept the same name when Mugabe's men said I should change and support the Catholics during the liberation war. They said Catholics supported the fight for our land. Anglicans did not.

Chiyevo never learns; she leaves home without her Zanu PF card all the time. Last time some youths at Simukai Centre asked her to produce her Zanu PF card. She did not have it so they said she was a Morgan Tsvangirai MDC supporter. It was just luck that Ndodye was getting off the bus when he saw them harassing her. He told them that Chiyevo was from Chimombe kraal and as they very well knew, there is not a single MDC supporter in Chimombe. He, Ndodye, would not allow that to happen. They let Chiyevo go. I keep telling her that she should just keep both cards with her in different pockets. Right pocket for the Zanu PF card and left pocket for the MDC card. That way she will be safe when youths from either political party ask her for a card.

This food distribution centre is noisy and chaotic. A policeman is shouting: "We want order. *Chembere* one line! *Shirikadzi* one line! *Nherera* one line!" My legs are burning. It is hot. The donors are standing further away near the cars. Three men and two young women. One white woman. They are talking and laughing while drinking water from bottles. I am thirsty.

"If you do not stand in line, there will be no food distribution to anyone!" shouts the policeman. Someone needs to tell the policeman that the lines are all confused. Who says an old lady cannot be a widow and a widow cannot be an old lady? I belong to both lines. Orphans cannot stand in line on their own unless an adult stands with them. Some adults accompanying orphans are widows and some of them are old ladies. How do we know which line to go to?

The policeman is getting impatient. He is holding a whip. I think he is close to whipping some people into line. Under the *muchakata* tree, all the headmen are having a meeting. One of them goes to speak to the policeman. After listening to the headman for a short while, the policeman changes his orders: "Everyone must stand according to their kraal!" I am pushed into the Chimombe kraal line together with Sabhuku's two daughters and their five children. Ndodye helps us and within a short time, our line is straight, long and orderly.

We have been standing in line for a long time. Nothing is happening. My back is very sore and my knees are shaking. Chiyevo comes to tell me to go and sit under the shade of a tree. She will stand in line for me. When she gets closer to receiving the food package, she will call me. I rest under the shade and take my snuff. After a while I feel the need to go and pass water. There are Blair toilets here. The rude nurse from the clinic is walking around shouting and telling people to use the public toilets. I have never used public toilets. Never. Who knows what disease you can pick up from those pit toilets? Their smell is worse than a dead skunk. The bush is cleaner than the toilets at Simukai Centre. I disappear behind the bush. The rude nurse sees me. She shouts at me: "*Imi*

Gogo, listen, we do not use the bush here!" I ignore her. I am only passing water. Since when did she start telling people what to do with their private waste? That is not her job. She should be inside the clinic giving injections. She is only shouting like this to get some favours from the donors. Maybe she will get free aspirins to sell once the donors leave.

When I come back from the bush, Chiyevo is nowhere to be seen.

"Have you seen Chiyevo?" I ask Ndodye. He is smartly dressed in a blue jacket, brown trousers, shirt with red and pink flowers, a yellow tie and a big brown hat. On his jacket are several war medals, probably stolen from dead soldiers. He does not stand in line because he is managing security here. Ndodye will get a double food package as reward for his services later on. He tells me that two donor women took Chiyevo away from the line. He points in the direction where he saw them heading. To a car parked under a tree a bit further away from all the activity. I go there to ask Chiyevo why she let them take her away. Now I have missed my place in line. They have given her a chair – the type that can be folded up. Chiyevo is drinking water from a bottle. Two young donor women, one white and one African are talking to her. They are both wearing pants.

"This is my grandmother," Chiyevo tells them. The white woman smiles at me. She extends her hand for me to shake it. The last time I shook a white woman's hand was Mrs Janet Smith, the wife of the Rhodesian Prime Minister, Ian Smith. That was many years ago, long before independence. It was at the Agricultural Show at The Range. My pumpkin won the number two place in the biggest pumpkin competition in Charter district. Mrs Smith wore gloves to greet us, just like the Anglican missionary women. I shake hands with both donor women, the white one and the African. They have soft hands – hands accustomed to holding a pen, not a hoe.

"*Gogo*, we want to interview your granddaughter for a project we are working on with the youth," the African one says, "She will be back in time to get her food handout." I do not know what she means by a project. I thank them and go back to the line. It has moved much closer to the food lorry. Sabhuku's girls and their children allow me to go in front of them. When my turn comes, a young clerk shouts: "Enifa! Enifa Bako! Chimombe Kraal." A boy born only yesterday calling my name as if he is calling a schoolgirl. Ah, how this hunger takes away all respect for age. I get my bag and wait for Chiyevo under the tree. The bag is heavy. Inside is a bottle of cooking oil, a packet of red beans and a big bag of bulgur. I like bulgur because it is like wheat and a bit like rice. It is easy to cook. In 2008, three years ago, when we were very hungry, bulgur saved us. Chiyevo said she read that bulgur came from America and it was meant for horses. But what did it matter? It was food. Starving people ate bulgur and within a couple of weeks they gained weight. Village women's bottoms became prominent again.

The donor women gave Chiyevo a small plastic bag with something. When I saw the bag, I felt happy: at least Chiyevo had not been interviewed for nothing. Sabhuku's daughters look at her with envy. I do not want them to know what gift Chiyevo got from the donor women. I will wait until we get to the river then see the special gift. Maybe they gave Chiyevo biscuits, sweets, a packet of powdered milk or even sugar. Or some US dollars. We need some to pay for the grinding mill services. One dollar per one twenty-litre bucket of maize. Chiyevo carries my food bag on her head and holds the smaller bag with the gift in her hand. I walk behind her. We stop at the river to rest and drink some water.

"Tell me what the donor women wanted", I ask Chiyevo.

"They said they were doing a research, an investigation. They want me to be part of a project to do with measuring the number of girls able to use protection when having sex."

"Sex with a man? What man? You do not have a man."

"That is true Mbuya, I do not have a man."

"So, what do you protect?" I ask. I am puzzled. But I wait. I am expecting her to show me something to eat. Or maybe the gift of money. After all, donor women come here to give.

"They gave me this," she says. Then she pulls out several plastic tubes from the bag. I recognise the tubes immediately. Condoms. I have seen them at the clinic before. They are disgusting. Chiyevo takes another small packet out of the bag. She opens it and says, "And this Mbuya, is a female condom. You put it inside yourself before meeting a man." She hands it to me to have a look.

"Chiyevo, you do not even know what a man feels like. So you want to feel a tube first before you feel a man? And how are you going to have a baby if you put that tube inside you? No, I do not want to touch it", I tell her.

Chiyevo shrugs and smiles. Then she says, "In this packet are thirty condoms for the men and in this other one are thirty female condoms. They are all for the study. The donor women want to know the number of girls able to tell men to use condoms. They also want to know the number of girls able to use the female condom. Once a month I am required to tell the sister at the clinic the number of times I use protection and what type of protection I have used. She will write that number against my name. Mbuya, the donors said I must be prepared to protect myself when I meet a man. A man can't always be in control of what happens."

Chiyevo is smiling. Is this Chiyevo talking? I shake my head. I feel anger rising inside me.

Chiyevo, you disappear from the queue. I stand until my legs and my back hurt so much while you sit in a chair like some educated lady, drinking water from a bottle and talking about sex and condoms with strangers. Do you eat condoms?

"Mbuya, this is just a study. Nothing else," Chiyevo says, shrugging her shoulders at me.

"Instead of asking for sugar, a bar of soap, or just one dollar for the grinding mill, all you do is sit there answering questions about sex. What do you know about sex? Then you walk away with a bag of condoms for men and condoms for women. Can't you see what these women are doing? They hide behind the food truck so they can snatch you from the crowd and give you condoms. They are encouraging you to have sex before you get married."

Chiyevo shrugs her shoulders again, smiles and says nothing. I say to her, "Chiyevo, go back to the donor women and tell them we do not have sex before marriage. Tell them condoms are not food. Tell them only those with full stomachs have time to think about sex. Tell them we want food, not sex. Go back now."

Chiyevo looks at me as if I am mad. I am not mad. Why should the donors visit us and encourage our children to have sex? Even Chiyevo's mother does not tell her anything about sex, I do. It is my job as Chiyevo's grandmother to teach her about sex and marriage. What is the use of age if I cannot teach my grandchildren our culture, *tsika dzedu*? We are hungry, we are poor, but we still have a culture to follow.

Chiyevo walks back. Slowly.

I sit by the river and wait for her. After a very long time, Chiyevo comes back. She is accompanied by Ndodye. And she is still holding on to the packets. "What happened? Why did you not give them back?" I ask her. She says the donor women were already gone when she got there. Ndodye's smile tells me Chiyevo is lying. "So what are you going to do with those?" I ask.

I want to grab the packets of condoms from her and throw them into the river. Ndodye speaks with a soft polite voice: "Mbuya, the donors come to give food and they also give us condoms. We need both to stay alive. You cannot stop change. Let her keep the condoms. It is dangerous without protection out there."

Then Chiyevo nods her head and giggles, "Mbuya, I want to keep them," she says looking at Ndodye. Everyone says this daughter of my son is beautiful. What they do not know is that her head is full of water. Chiyevo's mother is right: this girl does not have any brains. She listens to the donors doing a project on her and accepts what they give her. Now she is listening to Ndodye who wants some of those things for himself. Today the donor's visit has given me food. But it has also taken Chiyevo away from me. I cannot tell Chiyevo what to do any more.

The changing urban market

After Zimbabwe's independence, Pedzanhamo market emerged as the most popular place to buy African artifacts. Situated in the old African suburb of Mbare between the former "whites only" cemetery and the Methodist church, Pedzanhamo was only a few kilometres from Harare's city centre. A busy road separated the rundown colonial cemetery from the noisy crowds in Pedzanhamo market. This was the place where we found things we left back in the village. Drums, clay pots, masks, baskets, spears, bows and arrows, war head dresses, gourds, snuff and cattle tails to ward off bad spirits. Things we never knew were art and could be sold for money. Age-old natural herbs to heal every conceivable ailment. Medicine in all forms – roots, crushed, uncrushed, or powdered, tree barks, fresh or dry herbal leaves, cured, roasted or ground tobacco. There were strong herbs and oils to soothe aching back and joints. Also special concoctions to enhance both male and female sexual libido. Much prized was the wooden replica of the sacred *nyaminyami* snake carved by the displaced Tonga people of the Zambezi river valley. If Tete Maggie, the head of the market women at Pedzanhamo, trusted you not to tell, she would introduce you to the man who sold the most potent marijuana grown locally or imported from Malawi and Mozambique. It was illegal, but here at Pedzanhamo, some people could discretely get high. You could tell by the laughter and the redness of their eyes. In Shona, "pedzanhamo" means "finish all your worries".

When Pedzanhamo first opened, everything made by Zimbabwe's different ethnic groups – Shona, Ndebele, Ndau or Tonga – was cheap and affordable. Brave tourists from all over the world, sometimes accompanied by local guides, ventured through crowds of people looking for authentic drums, wooden giraffes, wire toy cars and other exotic African stuff. For Africans living in the diaspora like me, there was everything at Pedzanhamo to help us maintain the ethnic and exotic look. Beads to add to plaited or dreadlocked hair, copper bracelets for the ankles, Rastafarian woven strings, black power wrist bands and strong snuff our ancestors took during ceremonies back when we lived in the village.

But shopping at Pedzanhamo was always a risk. There were thieves everywhere. I was robbed there twice. The first time I got robbed was fifteen years ago. That was on the day I took my Australian university professor and a fellow student from Hong Kong to Pedzanhamo. I wanted to introduce them to my African roots. A visit to Harare was not complete without a visit to Pedzanhamo market and some exposure to the slums of Mbare. Mbare was not exactly my roots. I grew up in a village 200 kilometres from Harare. I only came to the city for the first time when I was seventeen. But that did not matter. I had enough knowledge of Mbare to educate my visitors. I could go anywhere, even to the former white people only suburbs without being asked for a pass the way the Rhodesian police required of us. President Mugabe freed us from all that. This was my city and my country. Therefore I belonged to Harare and to Pedzanhamo market as much as I belonged to the village.

The professor had my handbag sitting comfortably between his legs, the passenger window wide open. With the casual confidence of a tourist guide, I drove slowly, explaining that Pedzanhamo market was a postcolonial creation and Mbare was the oldest African suburb. This is where the African migrant workers came to live when Cecil John Rhodes claimed Rhodesia for the Queen, I said. "You see those flats with sewage leaking from the exposed drainage pipes? Those flats were originally built for bachelors because the government did not allow African women to come to Salisbury at the onset of urbanisation. Years later you now find two families living in a one-bedroomed flat. There is no privacy as each family is separated by a thin curtain. Poverty has no room for decency." I pointed to the communal toilets and washrooms. They listened, sympathised and nodded. Suddenly a young man came to my window, interrupting my tourist guide speech. His voice breathless and speaking very fast, he told us that there had been an accident ahead of us. He pointed to a big truck in front. We all craned our heads to where the accident was supposed to have happened. Within seconds, my handbag was snatched by another young man from between the professor's legs. I saw it disappearing behind communal toilets in the swift hands of a marathon runner. Professor tried to chase after my bag but it was no use. A woman pedestrian told me to call him back because it was not safe for a white man to chase anyone in the flats. Money, bank cards, licence and other things were gone forever.

The second time I got robbed was not so dramatic. I was coming out of the market with my bag of beads when a man selling cigarettes and matches on a cardboard tray stopped me. He held several five dollar notes and said, "I have too many fives and I do not want to carry them along with me in case I get robbed, can you spare one fifty dollar note?" "Sure, no problem", I said, thinking here was an honest hard-working man making a living from selling cigarettes and matches; it must have taken him days to make fifty dollars. I gave him my fifty dollar note. He counted the fives between his fingers and gave them to me. An ice-cream seller sitting on his trolley watched the whole transaction without saying anything. The cigarette man thanked me and quickly disappeared into Pedzanhamo market crowd. I counted my five dollar notes again. There were only five, not ten. I had just been robbed of twenty-five dollars! The cigarette man had counted the five dollar notes folded double between his fingers. The ice-cream seller laughed at me. He said, "At least here at Pedzanhamo, they do not knife or shoot you for twenty-five dollars as they would do in South Africa. Shona thieves are experts in trickery."

For the past twenty-five years, I lived in Australia, coming back to Zimbabwe once or twice each year. On each visit, at the risk of getting robbed, I never missed a trip to Pedzanhamo market. My supply of African beads needed replenishment. I also went there to get some African art for the house back in Melbourne. My workmates at the Moonee Ponds nursing home always asked me to bring them a small present. Something African, they said; "So long as it is not a skull," one of the old residents once joked. On arrival in Australia, the beads were never a quarantine problem because they were hidden; already adorning my waistline by the time I went through customs. The drums and masks stayed for several weeks in Australian quarantine until they were cleared of anthrax or any horrible African disease. An African party in Melbourne was not a party unless we played a drum from Pedzanhamo market. After midnight, with enough beer and wine circulating, we Africans shared snuff and sneezed the way our elders did to praise and honour our ancestors. We then danced to appease the various ancestral sprits from all over Africa. The sound of the drum told the distant spirits who we were and where we were.

I first met Tete Maggie at Pedzanhamo market more than twenty years ago. She was one of the earliest pioneers of Pedzanhamo. She must have been around fifty then. Out of respect for her age, everyone called her *tete* meaning aunt. She had lived in Harare for many years, from the days when it was still called Salisbury. A village marriage in her younger days had produced no children. Marginalised because of her infertility, Tete Maggie left the village one day and never returned except for immediate family funerals. She counted herself among the very first African women to maintain a secret romance with a white man. "Ralph Bennet was a good old man. A bachelor all his life. I was his maid when he fell in love with me. I would have married him. But the Rhodesian law ruled against mixed race marriages," she told me once. When Ralph Bennet retired back to England during the liberation war, Tete Maggie lost her job as maid and lover. She became a sex worker instead, giving up the trade soon after independence because competition from younger women made the job difficult. Then she became queen of Pedzanhamo market. Her stall was in the far right corner of the market. Among other authentic artifacts, Tete Maggie sold African beads, snuff boxes made from a goat's horn, wooden plates, village clay pots, copper bracelets and wooden earrings. Without her informal consent, nobody could set up a stall at Pedzanhamo. She told new vendors the market rules: you only sell something African. This way, we promote our culture and our traditions. Promises had been made to the traditional ancestral owners of the land at Pedzanhamo and an agreement made never to sell any Western goods. Doing so would definitely bring down the wrath of the ancestors. The place could be hit by lightning or wiped out by a fierce storm. Even ice-cream vendors stayed right outside the market.

Every year around Christmas or Easter time, Tete Maggie knew I would come to buy new beads to replenish my collection. With each string of beads, she told me a story about where they came from: "These colourful red and black ones were worn by our ancestors at Great Zimbabwe, long before the white man came to tell us that waistline beads were primitive and uncivilised," she said. The beads were beautiful and not made of cheap plastic. "And these silver ones came with the Portuguese through Mozambique when they were trading for slaves on the coast," she said. I bought them all, history or no history. With every purchase of the beads, Tete Maggie provided free marriage counselling and advice to all women. Some distressed women sought advice on how to stop their husbands from womanising and setting up "small houses" with second wives elsewhere. Tete Maggie had a recipe to help them: "Find a bitch with several puppies. Choose the one that is likely to die of hunger and kill it gently. Prepare puppy stew. Add the red powder (from crushed roots of a special tree only found in the dry areas along the Limpopo River), add a little chili to mask the taste of the powder and give your unsuspecting husband the stew with sorghum *sadza*. From the moment he finishes eating the puppy stew, he will whine for you like a puppy and want only you. After work he will come straight home to you. No more detours to the pub. When he gets home, he will follow you around lovingly like a puppy looking for milk." Some of the women came back to thank Tete Maggie for the effective results of her recipe. As for those women who did not come back to thank her, Tete Maggie said they were too busy keeping their needy husbands happy. Tete Maggie prided herself in keeping many marriages intact and reducing the number of urban polygamous marriages. She also claimed to know the special root medicine that could help restore virginity to women. Some men discretely came to ask her for the traditional *vhuka vhuka*, "wake up, wake up" African herb she said was more effective than Viagra.

During one of my visits, Tete Maggie suggested that we go into a business partnership that involved shipping African artifacts and traditional medicine to Australia. "I hear Viagra is very expensive overseas? No?" she asked. I said I really did not know as I had not, as yet, been exposed to a situation that required full knowledge of the price of Viagra. "You live with the white people so you must know what they like to buy from Africa," Tete Maggie said. Since access to the African crafts and herbs was not a problem for her, Tete Maggie proposed that she would be the buyer. My job was to ship the goods to Australia (including *vhuka vhuka*) and find venues to sell them. She was convinced that through this proposed partnership, she would make a lot of money. Within a couple of years she was going to leave the one room she rented and become the proud owner of a house in Mbare. I promised to do some market research on the demand for African art from Zimbabwe once I got back to Melbourne.

That was in early 2008, just before the disputed elections between Robert Mugabe and Morgan Tsvangirai. By the time I came back to Harare in November of that year, Zimbabwe's economy had crashed. The Reserve Bank was printing more dollars at a figure value of millions and trillions. No other country in the whole world could print its own currency in such large quantities and circulate it so quickly. Zimbabwe's hyperinflation was international news. Negative images of Zimbabwe were everywhere. George Bush and Tony Blair declared sanctions on Zimbabwe. So did John Howard and various European presidents. Several airlines stopped flying to Zimbabwe. A gallery selling Shona sculptures in Melbourne closed down. 2008 was a bad year. There was nothing to buy on the supermarket shelves. Nothing at all. People in the rural areas starved. Some resorted to eating banana roots, if they could find them. Others survived on *muhacha* fruits, normally a favourite for donkeys. Children died of kwashiorkor and marasmus. Donors provided bulgur, a high protein wheat product some people claimed was meant for American horses. Horse food or not, bulgur saved lives.

At Pedzanhamo market, there was not much buying and selling either. Tete Maggie's proposed joint business venture had to wait. To end the political and economic crisis, President Robert Mugabe and Morgan Tsvangirai agreed to share power in a new Government of National Unity, GNU. The Reserve Bank stopped printing money. The trillions and quintillions of Zimbabwe notes became valueless. Zimbabwe adopted the US dollar as its main currency. There was food on the supermarket shelves. Tete Maggie and all the vendors at Pedzanhamo waited for customers at their stalls. But the Western tourists did not return. Occasionally, one or two inquisitive Chinese people walked through the market.

★ ★ ★

I made the decision to return to Zimbabwe in early 2011. A bad name for a country does not stop it from being your country. I still had my mother and a village to go back to. I had not been to Pedzanhamo market since 2008. But soon the time came to make a visit. Because I need some more beads and something authentically African for my new place in Harare. I am not going to get robbed for a third time. I am wiser now. My cousin who has lived all her life in Mbare gave me some good advice about shopping at Pedzanhamo. She said, "Do not look like those newly arrived Africans of the diaspora. They wear flashy clothes and want to show that they have access to US dollars. Dress like a local and you will not attract attention from the thieves."

I park on the busy road opposite the old "white people only" cemetery. My cousin will guard the car and protect it from a break-in while I shop. I am dressed appropriately. Flat canvas shoes, a long skirt, an African wrapper on top of the skirt, a head scarf covering every single bit of dreadlocks. No earrings, no watch, no rings of any kind. No wallet. No phone either. Some loose US dollars folded nicely inside the cup of my bra. At the entrance to Pedzanhamo, I buy a big "Mbare bag" with pictures of skyscrapers and "Florida" written across it. It costs me one dollar. I squeeze my way through the crowds, heading straight for Tete Maggie's stall, hoping she is still there.

As soon as I pass through the entrance, the sound of people shouting is deafening. It was never this busy or this noisy before. There are tables full of new goods everywhere. I am confronted with loads of colourful plastic flip flops, polyester batteries, radios, phones, fans, colourful trinkets, plastic blonde dolls, toy cars and a whole lot of cheap-looking goods. A woman with a baby on her back shouts: "Children's shoes, five dollars a pair! Slippers! The rains will be here soon; do not step on cow dung. Buy your slippers here. Only two dollars each. Come to my table!" Another voice is competing to be heard nearby: "Dresses! All new! Direct from Dubai! Why buy second hand when you can buy new!" I walk past the cheap and shiny clothes, toys and shoes and continue to the middle of the market. More noise and more activity. Young men stand around pyramids of wrinkled second-hand clothes. Their voices compete to attract customers: "New *bhero*, new *bhero*. New bale! New bale! Straight from the United States of America! Clothes worn by Michelle Obama, Beyonce and shirts from Obama himself, they are all here!" The next pyramid has one young woman shouting: "Two dollars shirt! Two dollars skirts! Dollar for two T-shirts! Best *bhero*, best *bhero*!"

Bales of tracksuit pants squashed in big plastic bags are being pulled out and piled to make yet another pyramid. People everywhere foraging through masses of clothes. Where are they all coming from? Next to the clothes are tables full of sports shoes – all brands, new and old. A young man walks alongside me and gently leads me to a table with shoes. He says, "Mother come here. We talk. You want Michael Jordan's shoes for your husband or for your son? Give me thirty." The shoes are almost new. And they are real. The type that would cost more than a hundred dollars in Australia.

I move on past more bales of second-hand clothes. Some almost new. I stop at the one dollar per T-shirt. The crowd of shoppers here is big and it is too hot to be rubbing shoulders with everyone while bending over. Then I notice one big pyramid with clothes that are not so wrinkled. They look like good quality. Someone is shouting: "Five dollars skirts! New *bhero*. Clean *bhero!*" Several women surround the pyramid and rummage through, picking one skirt, examining it, throwing it back into the pile or keeping one on the side until they are ready to buy. A serious-looking man with a huge stomach sits at one end of the pyramid with a bag of money stuck tightly between his legs. He is taking the money from buyers. Opposite him, sitting in a deckchair is his wife or maybe his girlfriend. She also has a bag of money between her legs and is giving the man loose notes when he needs change. Her straight black wig comes right down to her shoulders, some of the hair resting on a huge cleavage. She has heavy make-up on. Her face is very light, almost yellow. But her arms are the same colour as mine, quite dark. She is obviously using skin-lightening creams to make her face yellow and less dark. A wig and a lighter skin colour speak of more beauty. They are also a sign of more money. New money. The yellow woman turns to me and rudely says, "There is plenty of room, move away from me." I realise that I was standing right behind her looking down at her boobs, wondering if they are real. A little too close for her comfort. I apologise, move away a bit and then I start rummaging through the pyramid of clothes like the other women.

Five dollars for a skirt? I check the brands. They all look familiar. They are all from Australia. I know all the brands. From the cheaper lower end of the market to the upper end of designer clothes. Linen, cotton, silk, polyester, all sizes. Some expensive skirts I would normally find in up-market recycle shops in the affluent suburbs of Toorak and Camberwell, back in Melbourne. I rummage through the pyramid and out comes Australian, New Zealand and American designer labels. Not the fake ones you get in Bangkok or China. Real ones. Some of the skirts are new, never worn, with tags on them. No need to go on eBay to search for a skirt by a designer brand any more. They are all here at Pedzanhamo. A man tells us to move aside so he can reshuffle the clothes. After the reshuffle I find clothes similar to those I used to buy in Opportunity shops in Melbourne. Some of them still have the red shield "Salvation Army" label on them. Memories of my student days flood back.

When I first arrived in Australia in 1985, I was a poor student with no money and plenty of needy relatives back in Zimbabwe. I worked part time in a nursing home and bought clothes in second-hand shops or Opportunity shops. The voluntary ladies in the "Op shops" got to know me well. They called me by name and sometimes they gave me clothes for half the price. They said, "Australia is a lucky country. We get to choose what we want to wear every day. Others can't. Here love, take this one. Your people in Africa sure need these clothes." Throughout the 1990s, I shopped for second-hand clothes and filled up the whole attic. I planned to ship them all to Zimbabwe one day so every one of my relatives would have something to wear. But the clothes never left the attic. Shipping anything to Zimbabwe was going to cost more than the price of the clothes. There was no room for so many old clothes. One day at dawn, without anyone seeing me, I took all the clothes back to the Salvation Army bins. Being seen would present a very bad image to future donors of clothes. An African woman giving away clothes to the Salvation Army would discourage Australians from donating clothes to help recently arrived African migrants.

I find two beautiful designer skirts. One linen and the other a combination of cotton and silk. No room to try the skirts on but I know the designer and I know my size. A wash in cold water and a good iron, and these skirts will be as good as new. I pay ten dollars to the yellow lady. She tucks the money in the bag between her legs. She does not even say thank you.

I move on in search of Tete Maggie's stall. "Do they still sell things African here?" I ask a woman selling several DVDs – all pirated from somewhere. She points to the far left corner, quite the opposite to where Tete Maggie used to be. I am relieved to see Tete Maggie. She has been pushed to the side, together with others still selling African artifacts from the village. Tete Maggie gives me a big hug. On her stall are a few clay pots, some beads, plus dry medicinal twigs and snuff. That's about it. I ask her how she is coping, swamped by goods from China and *mabhero* from all over the world. She says, "Ah, don't worry. I will survive. *Mabhero* are illegal and will not last. Donors ship these bales of clothes to help the poor in Tanzania, Zambia and Mozambique. But every day, bales and bales of clothes are smuggled into Zimbabwe. If people can jump borders, clothes can do the same. I tell you, some people in this country are making money from those donated clothes. But it won't last! After the elections, we will kick all these *mabhero* people from Pedzanhamo. Then everything will be back to normal."

I sit on a wooden stool while Tete Maggie prepares my beads. She tells me that women no longer come to get the puppy recipe from her because one woman reported her to the RSPCA, the animal protection authorities. The police and RSPCA officers came looking for puppies at her stall. "As if I would keep puppies in the market," she laughs.

Tete Maggie then asks if I know any Chinese people in Zimbabwe. I shake my head to say, no, I do not. She looks surprised. "You mean, with so many Chinese people coming into Zimbabwe opening factories, restaurants, shops, building the Defence College, farming, mining; you do not know just one Chinese person?" I shake my head again and tell her that back in Melbourne, I had one Chinese friend from university but that was all. "Why do you need to know Chinese people?" I ask her. Tete Maggie pauses from threading the beads and speaks to me slowly, as if I am deaf: "Because, these days, to make money quickly, you have to be in business with the Chinese. The Chinese know where the money is. Forget the English, the Americans, Australians and all the others. Even the Indians, forget them too. Look East. Think Chinese." Tete Maggie pulls me towards her and whispers into my ear: "Do not tell anyone. But Pedzanhamo market must change with the times. I have rhino horn powder to sell to the Chinese. They also want something African."

6

ON MISPLACED IR / IR *FORA DO LUGAR*

Politics and emancipation in Latin America

Carlos Eduardo Morreo

Politics and international relations in Latin America are misplaced. Though could political discourse somehow be 'properly' Latin American for it to not be 'misplaced'? And has the coming of 'revolution' and 'left' governance in Latin America signalled a displacement of misplaced politics and IR that would have made things right again? May we not see political discourse and IR – and, perhaps, Latin American politics generally – as being properly anomalous, that is, as being 'out of place' in such a way that could only be so for us in Latin America? May we not in their familiar character appreciate the fact that these discourses – misplaced in Latin America – are properly ours in their peculiar failure and misrecognition as regards the political? And, finally, what are we to do with our politics or IR, radical or not, once we come to recognise the proper character of their being out of place and the need for some kind of knowing displacement?

The discussion that follows is an interrogation of Latin American thought and texts that seeks to bring into view our misplaced politics and international relations. In particular, I am interested in discussing the nature of this misplacement as it relates to the politics of the 'left turn'. To approach such an issue, in my view, we might best be served by thinking in terms of a genealogy of Latin American critical perspectives. As regards IR, to be sure, we may wonder what kind of dialogue has taken place between regional critical and social genealogies of thought and what goes under the name of political theory and IR (disciplinary or not) in Latin America. The likely moments of such a critical genealogy – from early Spanish–American ventures towards regional unity or federative government to contemporary postcolonial/decolonial Latin American critiques and socialist projects – all have in common the search for, and espousal of, particular kinds of 'emancipatory sociality'.

Emancipation, without a doubt, speaks through all that is both 'out of place' and 'in place' in Latin America. These critical or political projects require that we grasp their significance and the avenues opened up through them in our effort to overcome a thinking of politics and the international that remains obsequious to the logic of colonial modernity. It is this belief that notions of emancipation and novel forms of sociality are expressed in these historical and contemporary projects that may be seen as the positive moment in my critique of misplaced IR and politics.

In what follows, I am not essentially interested in the workings of mainstream thinking regarding IR in Latin America. It should suffice to say that a certain appropriation of European and mainly Anglo-American IR has been fundamental to all contemporary forms of political envisioning within the Latin American discourse and its projected statecraft throughout the second half of the twentieth century.[1] Thus, as regards specific and contemporary deployments of IR in Latin America, I will only discuss the proposal by Venezuela's self-styled Bolivarian Revolutionary government of what it has termed a 'people's diplomacy' (*la diplomacia de los pueblos*). Accordingly, we pick up on a recent deployment of an emancipatory sociality for the Venezuelan state and its international relations, which, even as it argues for a radical people's diplomacy (or what I occasionally refer to as an 'embodied diplomacy'), it nevertheless remains lacking theoretically and politically. In my reading of the Venezuelan project, I critically unfold its presentation by the government's main IR and foreign policy research centre, the Instituto de Altos Estudios Diplomáticos 'Pedro Gual' (IAEDPG). People's diplomacy not only refers to a doctrine developed by the Venezuelan government that would justify a new kind of international politics, but is also meant to underpin – and thus may be said to be powerfully expressed in – the regional bloc known as the Bolivarian Alliance for the Peoples of Our America – Peoples' Trade Treaty, ALBA-TCP.[2]

In discussing the IAEDPG's thesis on people's diplomacy, I take it I am engaging with a self-avowedly radical and unorthodox project for Latin American IR. Moreover, by revealing what is misplaced in the Venezuelan scheme, I believe I am saying something, however obliquely, that relates to Latin American IR and politics as a whole in both its radical or conservative outfits: a project that expresses the misplaced character of Latin American politics insofar as it fails to account for its colonial conditioning theoretically. In effect, politics and IR remain misplaced as such, because while being charged with thinking about the relations between states and societies, 'nations' whose histories begin in the 16th century of conquest and colonisation, these epistemes of the political fail to visualise their founding *aporia*, that is, the colonial underside of democracy and politics. This failure is revealed by the inability to elaborate and respond to coloniality, clearly expressed in the Venezuelan case in the truth of nature's radical and ruinous subalternity; a truth forcefully dismissed in the fundamental split between radical politics and radical oil 'extractivism'.

Misplaced politics and IR

In 1973, Roberto Schwarz, a Brazilian Marxist literary and cultural scholar, wrote what would become a seminal piece in Latin American cultural and social theory on the theme of 'misplaced ideas'.[3] There are many ways in which Schwarz's thinking on the issue of ideas *fora do lugar* or 'out of place' might be of interest to a critique of political thought and the envisioning of other forms of thinking and engaging with the topologies of the international. Schwarz's own critique was originally concerned with questioning certain truths regarding the role of European ideas and thought in Brazil and peripheral societies. Having picked up on a thread inherent to the perspective advanced by 'dependency' theorists in the 1960s, Schwarz sought to argue that a particular kind of conflict operated at the level of culture and ideology in modern societies at the capitalist system's margins. In fact, Schwarz was specifically concerned in his essay *As idéias fora do lugar*, with the role (European) liberalism played in nineteenth-century Brazilian society.

In his brief and inspired essay the argumentative plot was set up by way of a reading of Machado de Assis and his assessment a propos an 'impolitic and abominable' Brazil for which liberalism, amid the reality of nineteenth-century slavery, could only represent some kind of tasteless joke.[4] Indeed, here was a situation in which, Schwarz writes, by 'its mere presence, slavery indicated the inappropriateness of liberal ideas'.[5] According to Schwarz, and from a broadly Marxist perspective, European liberalism could be shown to be false in its original European context. Nevertheless, within Europe, liberalism's fallacious ideological content was adequate or 'corresponded to the appearances, while covering up the essential: the exploitation of work'.[6] That is, though reprehensible for being a certain kind of falsifying ideology, and not revealing the truth of society's reproduction, liberalism could still be 'in place' within Europe for it corresponded to the ideological self-understanding of a capitalist economy. Still, the question had to be asked, what was the role of liberalism in a society like Brazil, where the truth of slavery as exploitation was there for all to see? What would be the point of an ideology that did not cover up ideologically the truth? Liberalism, understood in this manner, seemed like a set of ideas out of place. Thus Schwarz set himself to describe what he termed an 'ideological comedy'.[7]

This split between economy (or production) and culture (or ideology), though seemingly premised on a somewhat reductive Marxist scheme, reveals in Schwarz's text something of interest about the way thought, culture – but surely also critique – work in peripheral societies. Essentially, what the Brazilian critic argued was that 'while being the fundamental productive relation, slavery, nevertheless, was not the effective link of ideological life'.[8] We may say that what Schwarz had identified was the constitutive split of the modern/colonial – a division of the contemporary persistently represented in spatial and temporal terms – and expressed in the tension between a global epistemology voiced at the centre and the coloniality of the modern pushed out towards the periphery. Liberalism, thus, would remain misplaced, yet functional as an ideological system, as long as it dismissed its contemporaneous colonial conditions, that is, insofar as its mythemes and rationalisations could dispense with the reality of coloniality in slavery as the mere remains of a prehistory assumed to be on its way out. Yet what would happen if liberalism were to thematise slavery as its contemporary and systemic condition of possibility? We may appreciate the fact that at the precise moment that liberalism attempted to do such a thing (to reveal coloniality's slavery as its contemporary condition of possibility), it would no longer be recognisable as such, i.e. as 'liberalism'. In fact, I shall make a similar point as regards 'twenty-first-century socialism' later in this essay.

The point is that 'slavery' and the economic and social world associated with it, should not be seen merely as a set of colonial relations prior to, say, the modernism of liberalism, but, in fact, as pertaining to both a capitalist and colonial venture coherent with the modern as a whole. Slavery is shown in Schwarz's text to be interrelated with a capitalist project and a colonial worldview. According to Schwarz, 'slavery latifundia had from the outset been an enterprise of commercial capital, and thus, its pivot had always been profit'.[9] It is with this thesis that the question of the *fora do lugar* finds its first point of resolution. That is to say, Schwarz argues that capitalism is not linked solely to a history of European modernity, but to colonialism itself. Thus Schwarz maintains, for example, that 'profit as subjective priority is both common to antiquated forms of capital and to its most modern forms'.[10] Indeed, by pointing to profit – and not merely to 'modern' capital – as a capitalist ground for contradictory and uneven relations of production, capitalism and colonialism had been presented as coterminous. Consequently, Schwarz brings back the truth of slavery to bear on the modern present, revealing it to be not simply colonial, but equally (yet improperly) capitalist.

Nonetheless, the truly interesting problem, as wonderfully stated by Schwarz, was not simply that liberalism was false in Latin America (according to the prevalent Marxist argument this had also been the case in Europe), but that 'among us, the same ideas would be false in a different sense, let us say, originally so'.[11] In this manner, Schwarz thought that though the ideological (or temporal) and economic (or spatial) mismatch is essential, it would take different forms in the centre and the periphery. He asserts: 'this misalignment is inevitable', and this would be so for it is a design of colonialism; he continues, 'we were condemned [to it] by the machinery of colonialism'.[12] Thus Schwarz conceived of 'misplaced ideas' as comprehending an inadequacy or 'impropriety of our thinking that is not arbitrary'.[13] It is this duplicitous character in discourse, an ideological disjunction in relation to one's condition, which, following Schwarz, we may render as a 'non-arbitrary impropriety' or an 'original falsity', which concerns me as a way of thinking about recent left-turn politics and IR. In effect, that which ensures that a discourse remains out of place is its determined ignorance or requisite denial of a subaltern other (whose subalternity may be construed in terms of time – slavery is not 'modern' – or space – the 'Third World' is closer to nature, and thus not modern!) as its condition of possibility, that is to say, the denial of the modern/colonial.

As the essay develops, Schwarz's portrayal of the historical relation of Brazil (or Latin America) with Europe (and liberalism) increasingly highlights the importance of colonialism as a master code for understanding the conditions for ideological and cultural exchange and as that which structures different loci of enunciation. Thus he writes that, as Latin Americans, 'we were not to Europe what feudalism had been to capitalism; on the contrary, we were its tributaries in every way, in addition to not having been properly feudal – colonization is a fact of commercial capital'.[14] Being *fora do lugar* requires a kind of consistent and forceful negation of the colonial, which though coherent with and necessitated by global epistemes, ultimately remains untenable on the ground in the periphery and at the level of the everyday. What is striking in Schwarz's concluding remarks is the clarity with which colonialism is understood as a structuring of cultural or social processes producing and requiring the misplacement of ideas and ideology. He writes:

> We began with a common remark, almost a feeling that ideas in Brazil were decentred regarding their European use. And we presented a historical explanation for this dislocation, which encompassed relations of production and parasitic personal relations in the country, our economic dependence, its correlate, and the intellectual hegemony of Europe, as revolutionized by capital. In sum, to discuss a national originality, made manifest in everyday life, we were led to reflect on the process of colonization as a whole, which is international.[15]

It is clear that we may read something other than the particular dynamics of a critique posited on the epistemic scheme of dependency (and its take on political economy) at play in Schwarz's discourse on ideas out of place. Yet it is the fact of colonialism (and coloniality) that, in my reading, is brought back forcefully in Schwarz's Marxist critique. Here the 'machinery of colonialism' appears as that which systematically skews discourse, allowing it to assume an ill-warranted globality or universality, while revealing our subaltern and peripheral status.

I would like to take into account another concept of the misplaced that is to be found in a discussion advanced by Julie Skurski and Fernando Coronil in an essay published 20 years after Schwarz's insightful piece. In their essay, the authors had also looked into a kind of misplacedness proper to Latin American politics while seeking to describe the inner workings of a type of duplicity or, as they termed it, 'double discourse', at work in the 'geopolitics of truth' in Latin America.[16] In the early essay Skurski and Coronil single out the fact that a duplicitous public discourse had become an essential strategy to manage coherently national and international politics given the perennial 'tension between formal national independence and international dependence'.[17]

The difficulty Skurski and Coronil referred to was made manifest in the politics of Latin American states, and, specifically, in the existence of 'a double discourse of national identity that expresses and organizes the split between the appearance of national sovereignty and the continuing hold of international subordination'.[18] That is, a strategy that allows for the subject or the state in this case, to address – or misaddress – colonialism and capitalism. Therefore, we may read in the positing of double discourse as strategy an attempt to solve Schwarz's misplacedness by splitting the truth of the modern/colonial into separate though interrelated discourses on the international and politics.

More recently, in one of Fernando Coronil's very last essays, 'The Future in Question: History and Utopia in Latin America (1989–2010)', the anthropologist would rework the earlier thesis in line with his understanding of the inherent 'split temporality' present in the contemporary politics of the leftward turn in Latin America. In this later piece Coronil writes about 'a peculiar modality of double discourse in which narratives about the present and the future produce accounts that are mutually contradictory but true, since they refer to different temporal horizons'.[19] This contradictory double discourse on the politics of the present and the future 'is constituted by the tension between the two temporal narratives of the short and long term'.[20] In other words, Coronil would like us to appreciate the fact that we face not simply a duplicitous discourse of the present but rather a 'double historical discourse' that Latin American states find it necessary to interweave so as to address both the politics of the immediate (and always pressing!) present and the political transformations promised in the long term. It is crucial to appreciate that the temporal split picks up on the complex relation between capitalism and colonialism that Schwarz's study had analysed earlier. Indeed, we may say that the double discourse Coronil is describing attempts to disassemble the 'machinery of colonialism' by staging two discourses that, on the one hand, address the present of governance (as expressed in capitalist reality or in rent-seeking policies) and, on the other, announce capitalism and colonialism's final overturning.

If in the earlier argument the double discourse of the dependant nation attempted to resolve the issue of formal independence and the sovereignty of a nation facing overwhelming structural economic and political dependency, now Coronil has thought to link the recurrence of this same duplicitous structure in public or state discourse with a different phenomenon. It is not the constraints of dependency that necessitate duplicity in discourse, but the project of social and regional transformation – as imagined by the Left in the region – that currently requires the enactment of double discourse. Coronil summarises the epochal situation as follows:

> while leftist governments proclaim socialist ideals for the long term, they promote capitalism in the short term. And while they promote capitalism in the short term, they regard capitalism as unviable for the long term.

Thus we have capitalism for a present without a future, and socialism for a future without a present.[21]

The point I would stress is that emancipation as presently posited is unable to overcome this duplicity. The promised future may mean in the Venezuelan case, for example, that the Bolivarian Revolution will promote and deepen capitalism, on the ground, in the manner of 'neo-extractivist' practices relating to oil and other natural resources, while 'the long term' is said to belong to the realisation of a socialist imaginary (a 'present-day future imaginary' in Coronil's words) posited daily through government discourse and media,[22] a future that, undeniably, will often seep into government practice and quotidian experiences. What is more, the valorisation of Venezuelan oil as a commodity is necessarily premised on some kind of affinity between the radical government's project and global markets (i.e. capitalism). Yet it is not cynicism that prevails, but rather, to invoke Schwarz's point, twenty-first-century socialism like nineteenth-century liberalism before it, remains misplaced. The disjunction that inheres in a temporality experienced and discursively worked in Latin America is evident.

Though the 'double historical discourse' is a defining characteristic of current left or progressive governments, Coronil also links its existence with the emergence of a 'plural discursive field' that is itself part and parcel of the recent development of contemporary progressive and radical politics.[23] And we may say that the irruption of political plurality within the discursive strictures of duplicity has made it possible to think the future anew. We are confronted, Coronil believes, with 'the possibility of unexpected imaginings and original visions of the future' interrogating and interpolating socialism's future, as the manifold arguments of indigenous actors and visions, popular subjects and demands, nationalist aspirations and governments et al., traverse the formally duplicitous discourse of sovereignty and dependence or independence and subalternity.[24] Accordingly, plurality and duplicity – terms I would normally be happy to oppose! – are brought together in order to describe the contemporary Latin American scene. In fact, for Coronil they converge in order to say something poignant about the present historical moment.

On emancipatory sociality and democracy/politics

Let us now look at two concepts I put forward in order to further the discussion – and I hope, the disruption – of misplaced politics and IR and the interrogation of socialism's future. I mean to say something regarding the notions of 'emancipatory sociality' and 'democracy/politics'; indeed expropriating these formulae from their ('original') context in Latin American political science debates from the mid to late 1990s. I present *emancipatory sociality* as a simple heuristic concept that allows us to better appreciate what is at stake in Latin American counter-examples to European or Eurocentric narratives of emancipation grounded in Enlightenment readings.

Mario Magallón Anaya, a professor of the History of Ideas in Mexico's UNAM, attempted to summarise and push the debate on democracy further in his 'La democracia en América Latina a fin de siglo' ('Democracy in Latin America at the Century's End'), published in Leopoldo Zea and Magallón Anaya's magisterial reading of the Latin American conclusion to the decade and millennium: *Geopolítica de América Latina y el Caribe*.[25] Given democracy's essentially utopian conceptual content, to discuss democracy at the end of the twentieth century, so Magallón Anaya holds, is akin to discussing politics itself: 'Discutir la democracia es discutir sobre la política misma'.[26] Thus I take my cue from Magallón Anaya's claim and proceed to speak in terms of democracy/politics. The simple point is that this identification encapsulates an epochal condensation of politics and democracy (that is itself political!) in Latin America at the closing of the neoliberal decade. Magallón Anaya reasons that 'the theory of democracy comprehends the great general problems of our time, though not necessarily because democracy itself embodies them', but rather because of what democracy can 'reveal within its complexity'.[27]

Yet, what is particularly poignant about the identification is that it allows us to appreciate the fact that 'democracy' is thus itself opened up for questioning. In discussing democracy/politics, that is, by interrogating democracy's 'complexity', we question it by virtue of its own utopian resources. That is to say, we simultaneously posit a series of utopian references that will remain in sight and serve as a horizon for any such discussion itself. Indeed, Magallón Anaya is adamant that 'democracy has a utopian dimension that attaches to aspirations of equality, freedom, sovereignty, equity, justice, participation, solidarity, etc.'.[28] We may say that democracy/politics' 'utopian dimension is the force-idea on the basis of which social struggles aiming to overcome the inconsistencies and contradictions between democracy's normative postulates and its real limitations are premised'.[29] Utopia's force, perhaps as emancipation, lies at the heart of democracy.

In this light, the nation, Magallón Anaya writes, though translating and substituting (European) religiosity and its forms of relatedness or belonging, is from the outset put into crises by utopian thought.[30] The utopian references put in play by the very notion of democracy allow for the instability of the political sphere understood as a national space. And, as already stated, these very same utopian references are incessantly put forward by the very discussion of democracy/politics itself. Following this reading, Magallón Anaya signals towards the urge to challenge the nation as modernity's collaborator in sociality.

> The utopian-political thought of the nineteenth century will posit paradigms of social life, which either aim to overcome the nation-state as is the case with Saint Simon's European Grand Confederation, or represent alternative forms of community, such as Fourier's Phalansterism and the many forms of anarchism and socialism.[31]

That is to say, sociality, and specifically, a form of sociality enjoining emancipation as a way of belonging, is posited throughout, not only in 18th-century Europe, but also in the Latin American situation, in contradistinction to a 'principle of nationality' which by the nineteenth century would clearly become hegemonic. In other words, emancipatory socialities disrupt the imagining of national communities. Therefore, anarchism, socialism, and the social utopias of Fourier et al., may be equally conceived as socialities that compete with the nation as the state's content, i.e. as the meaning of democracy/politics. This is the point that Magallón Anaya's text manages to state, though his excellent discussion moves in another direction. Nevertheless, what I find appealing about this way of expressing the point is the manner in which the underlying globalism of any one of these competing socialities is revealed, given that they respond not to a singular national space but rather to the uneven terrain of modern/colonial politics. That is, socialities understood as particular elaborations and responses to democracy and politics, have not only had an uneasy relationship with the nation, but indeed attempt to displace it as the primary form of belonging, necessarily pushing against the nation in their development of emancipation.

The nation in its commerce with the state, and liberalism/socialism/anarchism in its relation with the state – consider, in this regard, the fraught relationship of communism with the nation as witnessed in Marx's loyal opposition to modernity – as forms of sociality compete with each other. Furthermore, liberalism, socialism and the national, as ways of being and belonging, simultaneously present a non-local, or rather, a kind of global sociality based upon diverse and particular principles of a democratic/political general economy or aesthetic. The latter, we may say, signal to always present cultural and historical possibilities, opened up and developed upon by means of social and popular challenges to the nation (and its state) as hegemonic sociality, and its political and theoretical elaboration.

Yet, we may wish to state the argument once more, and perhaps broaden its epochal reach. It is not uncommon to come across scholars who will state that Latin American modernity has two pivotal moments. That is, scholarship may figure the arch of Latin American peripheral modernity in terms of 'two crucial moments', which are, firstly, the independence period of the early nineteenth century, presented as 'the founding moment of a liberal project of modernity' and, secondly, a key twentieth-century decade spanning the late 1950s and 1960s, the latter being a period characteristically defined as that of socialist triumph or vindication, which, in turn, may also signal the crisis of the liberal epoch and its earlier affirmation.[32]

Once again what I have termed 'emancipatory sociality' shows itself in these two distinct moments: two moments of the state-form, wherein radical democracy/politics bleeds into emancipatory sociality and may momentarily destabilise national belonging. Yet both instances, the revolutionary independence movements of the early nineteenth century and the mid-twentieth-century radical left or socialist movements of Latin America, must be brought back and related to the broader project of colonial modernity. Furthermore, here we may also grasp in what manner a sociality that has come through the transculturation of liberal sociality *as* postcolonial independence and emancipation (in the early nineteenth century), still manages to fail in its opening up of cultural and ethnic difference and the social equality of subaltern groups. That is, a liberalism that remains misplaced despite its local ideological translation and push towards emancipation.

There is, then, a third moment we would have to bring into play, though perhaps not a moment, but rather a foundation to these foundations, a foundation to Latin American 'liberalism' and 'socialism'; indeed, a grounding that would allow for the conditions of any possible liberalism as content for the state-form in the project of modern latinity. Thus the colonial 'invention of America' – to use Edmundo O'Gorman's acute phraseology – marks not simply a third and earlier moment, but a key epistemic binding of (Latin) American colonial ontology, fastening its history for the various centuries that follow.

As regards this particular possibility, that is, the comparison of what must be theorised as the interior moments of a larger modern/colonial latinity, wherein something akin to liberal latinity is first produced for the state, the chronological distance between the liberal and socialist decades may be, to a certain degree, overlooked and both moments may be identified, at least as regards the resources they summon and rework while generating newer forms of sociality, which though challenging the nation ultimately end up restating its centrality. Thus, the nineteenth-century revolutions are responsible for creating the Spanish–American republics, and the Cuban revolution, after having attempted to export the revolution, restated its nationalist components. In summarising the formal structure of this modern Latin discourse of emancipation, both in its earlier liberal sociality and later radical socialist iteration, Gastón Lillo, a contemporary critic, refers to:

> the impossibility of either the liberal or socialist project going beyond the conditions of intelligibility imposed by the universal frame of modernity (and more specifically, posited by the Enlightenment) wherein they are inscribed, without questioning the epistemological order. Thus failing amid the difficulties in establishing the modern project in America.[33]

In this light, the democracy/politics of the Latin American state, whether liberal or socialist, reach a point where the thrust for emancipation presents itself as the *other* of its own sociality – an 'other' that constantly confronts the underside of our modernity as colonial power. That is to say, coloniality understood as a matrix of power – Aníbal Quijano will speak of a 'coloniality of power' according to which epistemic hierarchies are gathered and harnessed in terms of racially inscribed relations – will result in a process whereby 'America' becomes or is 'invented' for its populations and a Western though globalising political economy.[34] In other words, sociality must either settle into the state-form and its national affair or carry on with emancipation. And to continue emancipation in the Latin American context or indeed in the peripheral spaces of the modern/colonial would require confronting the 'grounding' moment (or 'spacing') of coloniality, that is, its continuous temporal and spatial mismatch. In other words, emancipation must turn into decolonisation. Thus, to fully advance some form of emancipatory sociality would require not simply addressing the two or three moments of modern and contemporary democracy/ politics, but taking into view the full arch of its constitution, that is to say, its colonial grounding and aftermath as a more or less singularly coherent political development. In my understanding, to not do such a thing is to commit radical or emancipatory projects to fail and to continue investing in left narratives that misread or misplace the colonial foundations of our democracy/politics. A far-reaching politics of transformation, or indeed 'revolution', requires an understanding of coloniality as traversing modern democracy/politics.

Finally, what is at stake in this reading of the movement of emancipatory sociality and democracy/politics is, to say the least, a kind of wager. The belief that opening up both categories to the plurality of the present – to wit, Coronil's plural field of discourse – in order to listen to and practise novel ways of relating to others and nature, may unearth concepts and practices, i.e. ways of being, with which to respond to the colonial undertow amid the contemporary. In this way we may address ever-greater aspects of the political, a necessary step towards postcolonial futures.

The state against modernity in Latin America

Much of the 1980s and 1990s, what we now identify as a period of hegemonic neoliberalism in Latin America – or of the social legitimacy of 'economic rationalism' in the Australian discourse at the time – signalled and required a colossal delegitimisation and undermining of the nation-state and, specifically, of the democratic state-form as an appropriate structure with which to respond to perceived global transformations and local aspirations for 'progress' and 'development'. What we came to refer to as the 'Washington Consensus', a particular narrative regarding the triumph of Anglo-American liberalism and 'End of History' ideological justifications, has now been challenged in multiple ways throughout the first decade of the twenty-first century.

In Latin America the assertion of the state and its regained legitimacy can easily be contrasted with the previous imagined order of NGOs, and self-sufficient subjectivities against a background of capitalist empire. The truth is rather that whatever was understood as politics, was formally reduced to a kind of depoliticising electoral suffrage, whereby state management would be contested every four or five years – a process monopolised by, and solely focused on, a 'political party system' whose mediation and divested representation of society seemed to constitute the very essence of the political. Furthermore, it is clear that what have once more become crucial categories for politics, were simply unthinkable during the neoliberal ascendancy, i.e. the national, the popular, the poor, but also the indigenous as potential subjects of plurinational societies. This hegemonic understanding of the epoch has now been shattered, and the first decade of the twenty-first century can be read as an initial reconfiguration that has emerged as a forceful response to the neoliberal fragmentation of democracy/politics in the name of markets.

In various countries, such as Venezuela, Brazil and Argentina, but equally in the smaller Andean states of Bolivia and Ecuador, a concerted effort to restore and legitimise the state's centrality has been underway. In fact, the spectacular recovery of the state has been paramount – a step on the way to greater social and political transformation in the region. This transformation 'at the level of the state' – in the words of Coronil – 'has been propelled by new social movements, indigenous communities, and political organizations' whose struggles have converged in the revitalisation of the state.[35] The political shift in the region over the decade has generally meant a renewed emphasis on the state as 'structure', 'actor', and on its democratic 'form', and, furthermore, the resurgence of the state, linked to a politics of emancipation, has been accompanied by significant challenges to previous understandings of the nation and national narratives – without a doubt, and as history would have it, a considerable riposte to twenty or more years of neoliberal globalisation. In this regard, Ecuador and Bolivia's constitutional revolutions – from republics to intercultural plurinational states – signal a key moment in this development.

The paradox, we may say, is to be found in the fact that the derivative discourse and apparatus of the state in Latin America, wholly colonial from the outset, having been set up in the early 16th century against indigenous communities and reconfigured in the nineteenth century in order to direct the destinies of creole and *mestizo* populations, has been appropriated after its forceful dismissal by neoliberal logics, as a necessary structure in the pursuit of greater social and cultural transformation. That is, the state in Latin America is being lined up not only against neoliberalism but also against privileged aspects of political modernity itself.

In an article published on 31 December 2010 in the Mexican newspaper *La Jornada*, the Uruguayan critical intellectual, Raúl Zibechi, referred to three struggles that he believes characterise the political scenario of contemporary Latin America.[36] Zibechi writes about the struggle to overcome US domination, especially political and cultural hegemony; the struggle to overcome capitalism (itself often misguidedly identified with US global hegemony), and finally, a struggle underway to overcome development as the singular narrative with which to think the future in the region.[37] Taken together, Zibechi's three struggles amount, once again, to a challenge *within* modernity *against* modernity.

While reviewing the same article, Edgardo Lander, a Venezuelan sociologist and key thinker in the Latin American decolonial camp, added a fourth process that, in my view, serves to characterise together with Zibechi's three struggles, the onslaught from within modernity against modernity in Latin America. In his essay, Lander refers to the 'national-popular projects' of 'industrialisation, democratisation, inclusion and [wealth] redistribution' as a massive state undertaking – indeed, a social debt relating to the stalled processes of state-formation in the region.[38] Here we may refer, in general terms, to the many 'pending tasks of democratic nation-state construction and its imaginary'.[39] That is, Lander has in mind a kind of democratic deficit accrued since colonial and postcolonial state-formation. Thus we come to appreciate how the state's recovery after neoliberalism interacts with the three highlighted struggles.

Furthermore, with Lander, we may wish to distinguish between two general logics at play in the social and political transformation of Latin America, which not only intersect but also seem to compete in reality. Both logics, it seems to me, run through the three struggles referred to by Zibechi and the process of state affirmation (or formation) underscored by Lander. Firstly, we may speak of a logic of the 'national-popular', identified mainly with the struggles of societies confronting and redefining the states of Venezuela, Argentina, Brazil and, though to a lesser extent and in conjunction with a second logic, Ecuador and Bolivia. The national-popular logic clearly stresses a socialist horizon for democracy/politics and is concerned with issues such as democratisation, wealth redistribution, but also with strengthening the state, national sovereignty, and the felt need to erect a centralising structure with the capacity to carry out policy over the entire national territory, the aim being to benefit the large sectors of the urban poor, *las clases populares*, with national projects in education, employment, poverty reduction, health, and by means of various social subsidies. An emphasis is placed in the growing identification between the state, its government and those it seeks to benefit. But, and I wish to emphasise this point, within this logic of the national – as reconstructed by means of the appropriation of popular understandings and imaginings – questions of cultural, social and ethnic difference are elided, and a rationality of hierarchical or vertical representation, indeed a kind of tutored political participation, has taken precedence.

Lander also refers to a 'logic of decolonisation', which has become a significant force in the politics of countries such as Bolivia and Ecuador, a logic that is also present, though clearly to a lesser extent, in other societies across Latin America and in countries referred to collectively as partaking in the Latin American leftward turn. What is privileged in this case are matters of plurinationalism as opposed to monocultural governance and a previous multiculturalism often appropriate to market-oriented lifestyles; but also rights to difference, and questions regarding the sovereignty of indigenous peoples over land and culture, the preservation of social movements' autonomy, proposals for legal pluralism, and a wealth of critiques aimed at development and extractivism.[40]

The latter discussion, that is, the relation between indigenous peoples and communities, society and nature, as expressed in critiques of development and extractive industries, has become a pressing issue in the last couple of years. Nevertheless, these governments' basic policy towards nature and land remains hegemonised by the demand to value resources in the global market – as is the case with the states in which the national-popular logic predominates. Nevertheless, as Lander remarks: 'The struggle for decolonisation points towards a profound civilizational transformation that questions not only capitalism but the production and knowledge patterns of dominant Western culture, a critique summed up in notions like that of *buen vivir*'.[41] And let us remember that 'buen vivir' is itself the Spanish language translation of the Andean *sumak kawsay*.[42] Here we see that democracy/politics has truly become radical, and in its emancipatory opening up has sought to develop other socialities, in this case, those of indigenous provenance.

It is clear that much of the mid- and long-term politics of the region, as regards progressive politics – that is, newer and better projects for emancipatory socialities – inevitably rests on the manner in which these two logics are coupled and the tensions between them play out.[43] To be sure, acknowledging this tension may allow us to appreciate the contradictory demands one hears from various left political camps regarding the future of the Latin American state. That is, calls for its construction, affirmation and decolonisation respond to the conflicting objectives these two logics encompass. Thus, for example, we should either seek to

> recover the state, strengthen the state, democratise the state, decolonise the state, convert the state into an instrument of transformation or preserve the autonomy of social movements and organisations in relation to the state; to control *common goods* in a sovereign manner utilising these in order to benefit collective well-being, to confront extractivism and the logic of primary product exportation.[44]

We may think of these logics as representing, in the first case, a struggle against modernity from within modernity, and, in the second instance, a rather more complex conflict that engages colonial/modernity. The logic of the national-popular inevitably reproduces a politics of emancipation that though often pushing against its own limits, still, to use Schwarz's turn of phrase, remains misplaced. The decolonial logic, on the other hand, insofar as it is expressed in the political and social processes of Ecuador and Bolivia, suggests that, as regards these societies, a better case could be made in their addressing the misplaced global epistemologies that dispense with the coloniality of the modern world.

Embodied diplomacy and the problem of representation

Let us now consider a recent deployment and particular articulation of Latin American IR in a quasi-official text that is, nevertheless, written under the sign of revolutionary sociality. Accordingly we should find a restating of the inherent globalism of emancipatory sociality as it breaches the national and posits another substance for the state and its politics. As has already been stated, the last decade has as a matter of fact signalled a profound change for Latin America. The euphemisms that capture the shift abound: 'left turn', 'pink tide', etc. In any case, the turn is neither a simple return to left politics nor a simple rehearsal of progressive politics in the region. But rather, we might attempt to think of the geopolitical shift in terms of the projects for international relations, regional politics, and public diplomacy at stake. It is in this light that I have thought it particularly interesting to highlight and critique a text that reads Venezuela's radical diplomacy.

In 2007 the Instituto de Altos Estudios Diplomáticos 'Pedro Gual' (IAEDPG), a higher education and research centre under the umbrella of the Ministerio del Poder Popular para Relaciones Exteriores, published a remarkable text named *Fundamentos filosóficos de la nueva integración del Sur*. We may render the latter title into English as 'Philosophical Foundations for a New Southern Integration'.[45] This is a veritable groundwork for an ambitious and official IR discourse, which, as I outlined above, is part and parcel of the 'Bolivarian Revolution'. The proposal may thus be seen as a recasting of the revolution's understanding of emancipatory sociality, developing the opening up of democracy/politics that was critically asserted against the state's push for neoliberalism in the 1980s and 1990s.[46]

In order to advance its thesis, the text begins by curiously invoking a semantic distinction noted by Edmund Burke as regards the term 'diplomacy'. Though it may be standard practice to note the Burkean coinage of diplomacy to cover the habitual goings-on of ambassadors and government negotiators (while chastising the French Revolution!) throughout IR introductory manuals and other authoritative sources for the study of mainstream IR, it is perhaps equally uncommon to dwell on the supposedly conflicting meanings present in the practice's designation as such. According to the authors of *Philosophical Foundations*, Burke 'diplomacy' could refer to either the relations established among states or the relations developed and assumed among nations or peoples. It would in fact be the liberal and conservative politics of the following century that would disable the latter semantic core, signalling a more organically and authentically popular possibility for international relations, that is, a politics of the international based on the genuine relations among peoples as opposed to a distinctly modern state-centred view of diplomacy for which relations are established through state structures and cultivated from up on high. It is not my intention to disinter the implicitly conservative (or reactionary) genealogy that might inhere in a suspect rehabilitation of the better half of the Burkean reading, for whom it would seem a 'people's diplomacy' could not in any way whatsoever be a venerable project: '...that monstrous evil of governing in concurrence with the opinion of the people'.[47] Though, perhaps, revisiting the site of such a duplicitous affirmation may be worthwhile.

The issue that the thesis in *Philosophical Foundations* aims to outline at the outset before reaching its key affirmation, centres on the 'formalisation' by liberal democracy of the founding expropriation of a people's diplomatic faculty, that is, an expropriation of something akin to 'originary' diplomacy, with nefarious consequences for a truly democratic order. In other words, what is questioned by means of this radical or popular Burkean reading of diplomacy is the failure to recognise a people (or nation) as the 'originary protagonists of diplomatic relations' (*reconocimiento de los pueblos, como originarios protagonistas de las relaciones diplomáticas*).[48] In fact, the text goes on to trace and register other such instances of a cognitive grounding failure. Thus, for example, the authors observe a salient instance of popular diplomatic misrecognition occurring in the preamble to the Vienna Convention of 1961. According to the authors, we learn that

> the Convention itself reminds us that nations [*pueblos*] were originally the trustees of diplomatic relations which – in modern times and under liberal democracy – have been formalised through representatives, that is, states and governments.[49]

There are two points worth commenting on before we take up this interesting construction. The first regards the semantic and conceptual force of the term *pueblo*, which in the Spanish language may, in fact, refer to the nation and its people. But it may equally refer to its poor, particularly the country's economically and symbolically disadvantaged agriculturally based communities and their generational offspring, but also, and as a consequence of various modernising programmes and politics, the urban poor, that is, dwellers resulting from mid-century migration. Thus, for instance, the Mexican-Argentinean 'philosopher of liberation' Enrique Dussel, considers *pueblo* as more than a merely descriptive term with a somewhat vague referential quality, but rather presents it as a foundational political concept and the originating category in an elaborate discourse of Latin American liberation.[50]

The other point we should comment on refers to the thesis's particular and remarkable appropriation of direct democracy. In fact, this is an important point I wish to make that may show in what manner something remains misplaced in the Bolivarian Revolution's proposal of a people's diplomacy. The thesis being put forward by the IAEDPG's researchers has a remarkable palimpsest-like quality, deriving from a particular kind of argumentative transposition that has taken place for this argument to work. That is to say, we may appreciate how it is that a nation's or a *people's diplomacy* could be premised on a certain translation of appeals to the legitimacy of popular or direct democracy within the country's borders. It is this option that is encompassed in the Venezuelan 'revolutionary' political discourse of *participación popular y protagónica* (participatory and popular protagonism), which surfaces in the earlier statement referring to the people as the 'originary protagonists of diplomatic relations'.[51]

Yet, the move away from the nation-state and its earlier abortive liberal sociality towards the people as the true content of democracy/politics, not only requires and posits another sociality within the state, but also towards other *pueblos*. Thus, a 'people's diplomacy' is warranted. Of course, what is evidently problematic and of great significance is the manner in which the people or *pueblo* is conceived; as is equally interesting the guarded attack on contemporary politics' founding arch of modernity, liberalism, democracy and, specifically, political schemes of representation. Yet, what is truly problematic for the authors of *Philosophical Foundations* is, plainly speaking, the nature of the existing bond, or rather, the split between people and diplomacy. The problem can be understood as resulting from a militant denial of representation in the name of self-transparency and emancipation.

Let us paraphrase the basic argument, expressed as it is in the manner of an abstracted and hypothetically stated historical event. The truth of the matter is, we are told, that 'states and governments that should have embodied (*que debieron encarnar*) the interests of the people', increasingly took on an autonomous and ill-conceived independence, which, in fact, would create and broaden the gap between mere forms (and instruments) and the general will of the people. The same problem would then further be compounded by 'liberal democracy', entrenched through the rise of civil society, and the spread of social movements(!) as an alternative to the government and the state.[52] That is to say, according to the reading advanced by the IAEDPG researchers, though there can be no alternative to the state, its undisclosed content would signal the very truth of democracy/politics, construed in terms of direct popular politics or people's participation. Here, it would seem, the narrative of Venezuelan diplomacy has, to a degree, restated the earlier argument we had put forward by discussing Magallón Anaya. But rather, I suggest, embodied diplomacy reveals the limits of an understanding of emancipation conceived mainly as a critique of liberalism and representation (without reference to the persistence of the colonial).

At this point, it is worth noting that there is a particular political and ontological conflation present in the thesis's argument that is of interest to the position I am advancing in this chapter regarding misplaced politics. The text simultaneously identifies yet obscures the necessity of a hiatus between the state's instruments, government *and* the people's general will. That is to say, the fact that states and governments that would and should embody the singular/multiple interests of a people, do not in fact do so. We may assume that they cannot but fail in this task that would see them become more than an instrument – a mere expression of represented interests or their facilitation – and literally become the political body of the people.

The authors attempt to displace what is an inherent characteristic of the state-form and government onto a series of supplements that are made visible by reference to the 'acute crises of representation of liberal democracy'.[53] The rhetorically effective though ultimately politically disingenuous gesture the authors undertake aims at rendering plausible the thesis of an embodied diplomacy by affirming representation as an instrument solely necessary within a liberal democratic frame for politics. The argument then hopes to embarrass a series of further supplements that may be seen as proper to a configuration of IR possible for non-embodied (liberal democratic) states. In this manner, as the authors suggest, 'second-track diplomacy' and 'multi-track diplomacy' or indeed 'non-governmental diplomacy' are understood as further degenerations of a gap that modern political systems and an IR that does not affirm a commitment to an embodied diplomacy – as problematic as that may be – will obediently perform.

A history of the political entropy of the nation's embodied diplomacy has to be presented as a hypothetical construction, and simultaneously affirmed as a historical fact. It becomes necessary to do this in order to allow for a retrieval or some kind of restoration, and the avowal of originary diplomacy's political practicability as a restatement of emancipatory sociality and a novel response to democracy/politics. The Venezuelan researchers at the IAEDPG point to an impossible historical origin wherein representation is revealed as a political supplement facilitating the alienation of an 'original' self-transparency that future emancipation promises:

> insofar as the modern state and representative democracy gradually consolidated itself, beginning in the nineteenth century, the term diplomacy seems to have progressively lost its capacity to designate the links established among peoples, referring thus almost exclusively to relations between states and governments.[54]

The final move the researchers take in the argument I have outlined allows for the identification of embodied diplomacy with the foreign politics currently on track by the Venezuelan Bolivarian government. The thesis's text will claim to present a prominent example of people's diplomacy, stating that 'in the early years of the twenty first century, people's diplomacy has found one of its main referents in the Bolivarian Alternative for the Americas',[55] that is to say, Chávez's (and the Venezuelan government's) affective and embodied alternative to other seemingly more sober regional state groupings.

As the authors of the IAEDPG document reassess in their discussion the concept of diplomacy, they reference the 'diplomatic exchange processes' that have as their basis the 'linking experiences' existing among subjects or inhabitants of the 'same region'.[56] Furthermore, they state that the Latin American peoples (as 'human groupings') have maintained all manner of relations due to the fact that 'they share certain similarities'. In this manner, a certain homogeneity is referenced: an 'identity' to be understood 'racially, geographically, or in any other way'.[57] Likewise, and in its closing pages, the discussion also indicates the reality of ongoing 'internal integration mechanisms' whose 'proper laws' result from the ancestral knowledge held by the continent's originary peoples.[58] To be sure, the thesis I have discussed requires that a definite homogeneity be affirmed in order to forgo representation. For this reason, there are several moments in the argument that seem to militate against representation by invoking natural similarity. If similarity or some kind of near-perfect or natural identity is the case, then representation and mediation are indeed surplus.

Let me say a few words regarding the regional organisations promoted by the Venezuelan government. IR scholars will often pit the ALBA-TCP against UNASUR.[59] As an IR scholar has recently stated, talk of any 'convergence [among these projects] continues to be a mere chimera'.[60] In setting up such an opposition, it is claimed that Venezuela's ALBA-TCP, an essentially political project and long-term model for an inclusive and solidarity-path to 'regional integration', comes into conflict with Brazil's astute regional venture, its wager to 'southamericanise' its global political aspirations by means of UNASUR. It seems to me that to make such an argument is to truly misread the complex movement of left-turn democracy/politics in the region and the coherent shift that both projects – but others too, notably the Community of Latin American and Caribbean States (CELAC) – articulate together against the Washington Consensus.

Still, to make such a claim is not to identify these substantially different projects. In fact, it could be said that for much of the second half of the twentieth century there could be little difference between regional projects given their dependent nature as Washington-approved initiatives. Thus something akin to political difference in the region is paradoxically possible now within Latin America given that the Washington Consensus has been to a great extent displaced. Yet, rather than difference it is convergence that is clearly highlighted at the level of governments and states. Nonetheless, we ought to make a distinction between the ALBA-TCP project and its strong socially oriented economic regional programmes and the UNASUR (itself closer to MERCOSUR and thus, in various ways, an heir to the economic and political realities of the 1980s and 1990s). Yet, if the Venezuelan government is able to participate in what seem to some observers to be fundamentally different regional organisations, this may have much to do with the split between a political economy of the present and the international or regional politics of emancipation. And, of course, such a distinction is premised on the government's relation to nature, that is, the manner in which 'oil wealth' is secured and the social and political use rent and revenue are put to.

But let us now return to our discussion regarding Venezuela's proposal for an embodied diplomacy. One might ask if people's diplomacy and its local or national correlate 'participatory democracy', both find their epistemic force in a repression and destitution of representation in politics, that is, an apprehension towards representation in politics leading to a series of ploys and appeals that would conceive of self-transparency and self-knowledge as the truth of the people. If this were the case, how could any government, ministry or foreign affairs department be understood as avoiding representation? Indeed, can people's diplomacy nevertheless be made coherent with some degree of representation? As a matter of fact, the Venezuelan government has backed the creation of a series of local, national and regional organisations – as is the case of the ALBA-TCP, and locally the 'Community Councils', all defined as of a 'revolutionary' nature – which must, of necessity, be premised on some scheme of 'post-liberal' representation, while conceptually hinging on participation. Therefore, and given this fact, is it possible to truly conceive of people's diplomacy as being in effect something radically different from earlier schemes and understandings of politics, diplomacy or IR? Certainly, though embodied diplomacy fails in its own regard, that is, representation is required, it upholds significantly different hypotheses regarding the role of government and politics in addressing the international. Thus, in the mid-term, this 'revolutionary' deployment in IR has brought about a significant transformation in regional and international politics.

Nevertheless, IR has been misplaced here precisely because the political has been misplaced. The IR of people's diplomacy remains misplaced given that the emancipatory sociality that is being pushed misconstrues colonialism's misalignment as a liberal site of alienation. In the Venezuelan government's analysis, the displacement of liberal representation is portrayed as being the genuine problem, when, in fact, what is truly problematic is the 'machinery of colonialism', whose effects we may see in the radical departure between twenty-first-century socialism (analogous to Schwarz's 'nineteenth-century liberalism') and the economic reality of oil export-led development (Schwarz's 'slavery'). Without a doubt, the material grammar speaks the language of modernity, while a novel global epistemology of emancipation gestures towards the future.

In addition, it is important to stress the fact that despite a decade of 'pink tide' governments, social upheaval, mass mobilisation and politics of a clearly critical bent, Latin American nations fulfil what Coronil had characterised as the Third World predicament. Latin American economies are essentially 'nature exporting societies'.[61] A glance at data presented by the Economic Commission for Latin America and the Caribbean (ECLAC) reveals the fact that the previous decade has seen a sharp rise in the value of 'nature' (or 'primary products') exported as percentage of total exports. If in 2001, according to ECLAC data, we could classify 41.1 per cent of Latin American and Caribbean exports as nature, by mid-decade (2005) this figure had risen to 50.1 per cent. Moreover, in the latest report, by 2010 the figure had risen to 54.1 per cent. Indeed the following countries – clearly crossing the contemporary 'left' and 'right' political divide – according to the same ECLAC document, have nature extraction and exportation as accounting for over 75 per cent of total exports: Belize (98.6 per cent), Bolivia (92.6 per cent), Chile (89.6 per cent), Colombia (77.9 per cent), Ecuador (90.2 per cent), Guyana (93.3 per cent), Honduras (79.9 per cent), Nicaragua (93.7 per cent), Paraguay (89.3 per cent), Peru (89.1 per cent) and Venezuela, which has not disclosed data since 2006 (92.7 per cent).[62]

Furthermore, IR as people's diplomacy, that is, as an embodied practice that is equal to itself and unmediated by representatives (and representation), is held up as the new ideal, while ever more complex schemes of representation are brought back in, which negate being precisely such a thing. Thus, a particular figure has to be posited as that which guarantees that no representation is taking place; a certain figure that guarantees that popular direct self-government or participation and people's diplomacy carry on without mediation – in short, the embodied figure of the head of state – a figure, so now it seems, who holds or knots the threads of democracy/politics and claims to be the figurehead for a novel translation of emancipatory sociality. Thus, with the Bolivarian Revolution we are brought back to Hugo Chávez. IR has been misplaced and a people's diplomacy has been reduced to the embodiment of a singular (though heterogeneous) will or sign. But the negation of representation is also, I would argue, a negation of social difference and the affirmation of an impossible self-transparency and self-knowledge requiring ever-greater spectacles of political participation that attempt to conceal the ever-growing impossibility of embodiment, of non-representation. We may refer to this, though without the extreme pessimism in Agamben's formulation, as a kind of embodied and national-popular 'spectacular-democratic' state, a novel state-form that in the Venezuelan case, after having fostered particular understandings of democracy/ politics, is now set on administering what is left of emancipation.[63]

But the homogenising figurehead whose militancy against representation seeks to spectacularly uphold embodied politics, does not, of course, solely exist and is not merely posited within Venezuela for national enunciation. It is also put forward at the regional level by other governments such as Bolivia, Ecuador and Argentina, and surely others in Latin America beyond the leftward turn. This is partly due to a political discourse that evacuates forms of representation elevating the embodied politics of the head of state (and presidential power) in conjunction with notions of *la patria grande* (the greater fatherland), creating, thereby, new territories of belonging mainly inhabited by the higher echelons of government, which are, once again, offered as a political spectacle to Latin Americans.

The Venezuelan case, intriguing as it is, throws into sharp relief the double discourse Coronil had spoken of regarding peripheral societies, and the misplaced character of socialist emancipation and its political translation as IR. The country billed with constructing twenty-first-century socialism is also the country with one of the largest values for primary product exports as a percentage of total exports in Latin America. It is estimated that over 95 per cent of Venezuelan exports are attributable to one commodity of nature: oil. Simply put, rents on 'nature' finance projects of solidarity and popular inclusion. In fact, whatever Bolivarian socialism may be, as we are aware, it is fundamentally premised on a modern/colonial understanding of a natural world pushed into subalternity. Indeed, we may adapt Timothy Mitchell's coinage and speak of the radicalisation of 'carbon democracy' in Venezuela, and label the country's social and economic reality as 'carbon socialism'.[64]

IR in Venezuela, theoretically grounded in a particular interpretation of popular politics and participation, more or less succeeds in portraying its project as a people's IR. But when it comes to the deep politics of life, nature and oil, Venezuela reproduces capitalism's colonial understanding of nature. In fact, like many other countries wholly foreign to any left turn or discourse of revolution – such as might be the case with contemporary Australia – its government has fully adapted to the Chinese requirement that it fuel its industrial growth and expanding patterns of 'middle-class' consumption. In fact, Venezuela, it seems, will seek to supply China with close to two million barrels of oil per day over the next couple of years and to be extracting from nature close to six million barrels by 2019.[65] The proposed figure simply makes all other Venezuelan IR initiatives seem if not *immaterial*, certainly of lesser consequence. IR, thus, even in the manner of embodied people's diplomacy, remains misplaced. A duplicitous discourse of oil and emancipation carries the day. Schwarz's constitutive split resurfaces and our very own 'non-arbitrary impropriety' or 'original falsity' is offered as a coherent discourse for radical politics and IR.

Notes

1 In this regard, the history of the institutionalisation of IR across Latin America after World War II and specifically in the 1970s would be of particular relevance. For this kind of study see the work of Arlene B. Tickner, *Los estudios internacionales en América Latina, ¿subordinación intelectual o pensamiento emancipatorio?* (Bogotá: Alfaomega, 2002) and more recently her co-edited volume *Global Scholarship in International Relations* (London: Routledge, 2009).

2 The *Alianza Bolivariana para los Pueblos de Nuestra América – Tratado de Comercio de los Pueblos*, initially presented as an 'alternative' to the US-backed Free Trade Area of the Americas (or ALCA in Spanish), was established in December 2004 by Venezuela and Cuba. As Thomas Muhr has stated recently 'the ALBA-TCP can be understood as a counter-hegemonic globalization project', that is, 'a geostrategic project governed by the principles of solidarity, cooperation, complementarity, reciprocity, and sustainability'. The latter being 'principles that economic theory regards as distinctly different from market exchange'. See Thomas Muhr, 'Bolivarian Globalization? The New Left's Struggle in Latin America and the Caribbean to Negotiate a Revolutionary Approach to Humanitarian Militarism and International Intervention', *Globalizations* 9 (2012) 145–159, pp. 146–147.

3 See Roberto Schwarz 'As idéias fora do lugar' in *Ao Vencedor as Batatas: Forma literária e processo social nos inícios do romance brasileiro* (São Paulo: Duas Cidades, 1981), pp. 13–28. For a good critique of Schwarz's essay that also manages to summarise the later Brazilian debates, see Elías J. Palti, 'Lugares y no lugares de las ideas en América Latina', *El tiempo de la política* (Buenos Aires: Siglo XXI, 2007), pp. 259–308.

4 Schwarz, 'As idéias fora do lugar', p. 13. All translations from Schwarz's Portuguese are my own.

5 Schwarz, 'As idéias fora do lugar', p. 15.

6 Ibid., p. 14.

7 Schwarz, 'As idéias fora do lugar', p. 13.

8 Ibid., pp. 15–16.

9 Ibid., p. 15.

10 Ibid.

11 Ibid., p. 14.

12 Ibid., p. 22.

13 Ibid., p. 14.

14 Ibid., pp. 16–17.

15 Ibid., p. 24.

16 Julie Skurski and Fernando Coronil, 'Country and City in a Colonial Landscape: Double Discourse and the Geopolitics of Truth in Latin America,' in *View from the Border: Essays in Honor of Raymond Williams*, ed. Dennis Dworkin and Leslie Roman (New York: Routledge, 1993), p. 25, quoted in Fernando Coronil, 'The Future in Question: History and Utopia in Latin America (1989–2010)' in Craig Calhoun

and Georgi Derluguian, editors, *Business as Usual: The Roots of the Global Financial Meltdown* (New York, NYU Press, 2011), p. 256.
17 Fernando Coronil, 'The Future in Question: History and Utopia in Latin America (1989–2010)', p. 256.
18 Skurski and Coronil, 'Country and City in a Colonial Landscape', p. 25.
19 Coronil, 'The Future in Question', p. 256.
20 Ibid.
21 Ibid., p. 250.
22 Ibid., p. 232.
23 Ibid., 'The Future in Question', p. 258.
24 Ibid.
25 This book itself forms part of a three-volume project coordinated by Mario Magallón Anaya and Leopoldo Zea, the latter being perhaps the best known of all twentieth-century Latin American philosophers and thinkers of 'identity'. See Zea and Magallón Anaya, *Geopolítica de América Latina y el Caribe* (Mexico: Fondo de Cultura Económica/Instituto Panamericano de Geografía e Historia, 1999).
26 Mario Magallón Anaya, 'La democracia en América Latina a fin de siglo', *Geopolítica de América Latina y el Caribe* (Mexico: Fondo de Cultura Económica/Instituto Panamericano de Geografía e Historia, 1999), p 73.
27 Mario Magallón Anaya, 'La democracia en América Latina a fin de siglo', p. 73.
28 Ibid.
29 Ibid.
30 The nation 'as a culturally defined community is modernity's most important symbolic value, and insofar as it possesses an almost sacred value – we might even say, religious – it became a modern and secular substitute for religion, or one of its most important allies'. Ibid., p. 74.
31 Ibid., p. 75.
32 Gastón Lillo, 'Las formas discursivas de la Independencia (siglo XIX) y la Revolución (siglo XX)' in *De Independencias y Revoluciones: Avatares de la modernidad en América Latina* (Santiago de Chile: LOM / University of Ottawa / Ediciones Universidad Alberto Hurtado, 2010), p. 7.
33 Gastón Lillo, 'Las formas discursivas de la Independencia (siglo XIX) y la Revolución (siglo XX)', p. 10.
34 See Aníbal Quijano's early essay 'Americanity as a concept or the Americas in the modern world-system', *International Social Science Journal* 134 (1992); and, more recently, his 'Coloniality and Modernity/Rationality', *Cultural Studies* 21 (2007) 168–178. See my discussion of 'coloniality of power' in 'Construcción y deconstrucción de la colonialidad del poder', *Actualidades* 21 (2010) 210–224.
35 Coronil, 'The Future in Question', p. 232.
36 Raúl Zibechi, 'Luces y sombras de la década progresista', *La Jornada* (31 December 2010). Retrieved from http://www.jornada.unam.mx/2010/12/31/opinion/017a2pol
37 Ibid. As regards the struggle to 'overcome capitalism' Zibechi states that 'things have not gone well'. Indeed, the 'expansion of monocultures, opencast mining and livestock, has transformed the region into a major exporter of commodities, representing a deepening of capitalism in its extractivist approach'. See Zibechi, 'Luces y sombras de la década progresista'.
38 Edgardo Lander, 'El Estado en los actuales procesos de cambio en América Latina: Proyectos complementarios/divergentes en sociedades heterogéneas', in Miriam Lang and Dunia Mokrani, editors, *Más allá del desarrollo* (Quito: Fundación Rosa Luxemburg/Abya Yala, 2011), p. 125.
39 Edgardo Lander, 'El Estado en los actuales procesos de cambio en América Latina', p. 125.
40 Lander, p. 127.
41 Ibid.

42 Much has been written recently on Quechuan 'sumak kawsay', roughly translating as 'good life'. The formula refers to ways of existence that promote harmony between human life, community and nature, and the regeneration of nature or 'Pachamama'. Its espousal has been instrumental in the translation of an indigenous political outlook for the non-indigenous peoples of the Andean region and Latin America. See the special issue published by the well-known Latin American social movements' communications network *América Latina en movimiento*: 'Sumak Kawsay: Recuperar el sentido de vida', *América Latina en movimiento* 452 (February 2010). Available from http://www.alainet.org/publica/452.phtml

43 John Beverley has also attempted to theorise the various political logics that constitute the current progression of the Left in Latin America. In one of his latest contributions he has written about the need to think about 'post-subaltern' politics. The latter, in his view, captures a new horizon for politics in Latin America and, in particular, the kind of position that Marxist sociologist and Bolivian vice-president Alvaro García Linera has developed by backing a national-popular strategy as regards the Bolivian political process. Thus in the 'post-subaltern' we may have an attempt to think a synthesis of the logic of decolonisation and the national-popular. See *Políticas de la teoría. Ensayos sobre subalternidad y hegemonía* (Caracas: CELARG, 2011). I discuss this turn in the politics of subaltern theory in 'El "post-subalternismo" o la teoría de las políticas de la teoría de John Beverley', *SUR/version* 2 (2012).

44 Lander, 'El Estado en los actuales procesos de cambio en América Latina', pp. 128–129.

45 The institution that would become the current 'Pedro Gual' Institute for Higher Diplomatic Studies was originally set up in 1977; Chávez's government restructured it in 2006 as part of an overhaul of the Ministry of Popular Power for Foreign Affairs. The thesis on people's diplomacy I discuss represents one of the very first theoretical elaborations of an IR project coherent with the institution's new role.

46 The text is effectively the collaboration of various senior and younger researchers working at the IAEDPG. In what follows, I offer a close reading of its fourth chapter or thesis: 'Diplomacia de los Pueblos', that is to say, 'People's Diplomacy'. IAEDPG, *Fundamentos filosóficos de la nueva integración del Sur* (Caracas: Instituto de Altos Estudios Diplomáticos 'Pedro Gual'/Asamblea Nacional–Dirección General de Investigación y Desarrollo Legislativo, 2007) p. 44.

47 See Edmund Burke, 'Thoughts on the Cause of the Present Discontents', *Pre-Revolutionary Writings* (Cambridge: Cambridge University Press, 1993).

48 IAEDPG, *Fundamentos filosóficos*, p. 45.

49 Ibid.

50 See Dussel's *Cinco tesis sobre el populismo* (2007). Available from enriquedussel.com/txt/Populismo.5%20tesis.pdf

51 IAEDPG, *Fundamentos filosóficos*, p. 45.

52 This key sentence in the document is phrased as following: 'the states and governments that should have embodied the interests of the people, gradually gained greater autonomy and independence from the popular will, generating liberal democracy's acute crisis of representation, which had become visible by the 1960s'. Ibid., p. 46.

53 IAEDPG, *Fundamentos filosóficos*, p. 46.

54 Ibid., p. 45.

55 Ibid., p. 49.

56 Ibid., p. 48.

57 Ibid.

58 Ibid.

59 On the supposed clash between projects see, for instance, Sebastián Santander, 'El giro a la izquierda en América Latina, Fragmentación y recomposición de la geopolítica regional', *Cuadernos sobre Relaciones Internacionales, Regionalismo y Desarrollo* 7, 4, (January–June, 2009), pp. 17–38.

60 See Gian Luca Gardini, 'Proyectos de integración regional sudamericana hacia una teoría de convergencia regional', *Relaciones Internacionales* 15 (October 2010), 11–31, p. 26.

61 See Fernando Coronil, *The Magical State: Nature, Money, and Modernity in Venezuela* (Chicago: University of Chicago Press, 1997).

62 The lowest figure in 2001 referred to Mexico, with 14.9%, but by 2010, this figure had risen to 25.3%. Likewise, Brazil presented a figure of 46% in 2001 and 63.6% in 2010. That is, close to 15 years after NAFTA came into effect, Mexico's ability to extract and export nature has deepened, and it may be said that Brazil's BRIC status and muscle is premised on exporting commodity-nature. For all data see 'Exports of primary products as percentage of total exports' in the *Statistical Yearbook for Latin America and the Caribbean* (Santiago de Chile: ECLAC, 2011) p. 97, and 'Exports of primary products as percentage of total exports' in the *Statistical Yearbook for Latin America and the Caribbean* (Santiago de Chile: ECLAC, 2009), p. 105.

63 'One cannot be sure, however, that the spectacle's attempt to maintain control over the process it contributed to putting in motion in the first place will actually succeed. The state of the spectacle, after all, is still a state that bases itself (as Badiou has shown every state to base itself) not on social bonds, of which it purportedly is the expression, but rather on their dissolution, which it forbids.' Giorgio Agamben, 'Tiananmen', in *Marginal Notes on Comments on the Society of the Spectacle 2*, p. 10.

64 Mitchell's opening line: 'Fossil fuels helped create both the possibility of twentieth-century democracy and its limits'. See Timothy Mitchell, 'Carbon Democracy', *Economy and Society*, 38 (2009) 399–432. 'Carbon democracy' and – its radical Latin American version – 'carbon socialism' might be part and parcel of an epoch, spanning nineteenth- and twenty first-century modernity, which we may refer to as carbon or 'oil modernity'.

65 At present Venezuela exports close to 640,000 barrels per day to China. Chávez's government had established a Venezuelan–Chinese joint venture aiming to extract and export to China in the mid-term (2015) an additional 1,000,000 barrels per day. Such an export volume would represent over 10% of China's current oil needs. See 'Venezuela eleva a 640.000 barriles de petróleo su venta diaria a China', *El Mundo, Economía y Negocios* (12 August 2012). Retrieved from http://www.elmundo.com.ve/ noticias/petroleo/pdvsa/venezuela-eleva-a-640-000-barriles-de-petroleo-su-.aspx; 'Ramírez: Producción petrolera llegará a 4 millones de barriles diarios en 2014', *El Mundo, Economía y Negocios* (4 November 2012). Retrieved from http://www. elmundo.com.ve/noticias/petroleo/pdvsa/ramirez--produccion-petrolera-llegara-a-4-millones.aspx and Carlos Romero, 'Venezuela y China: Múltiples caminos', *Diploos. Política Exterior Venezolana* (11 February 2012). Retrieved from http://www. diploos.com/opinion/item/1519-venezuela-y-china-múltiples-caminos.html

7

PERFORMING PEDAGOGY

Memory and the aesthetic turn

David L. Martin

This chapter represents an experiment in writing. It is a chapter about memory, aesthetics and pedagogy. More specifically, it is an attempt to write back against a mode of pedagogic practice in International Relations which uncritically replicates particular core methodological concerns of the discipline. In doing so these pedagogic practices not only help reinforce a particularly narrow and restrictive interpretive view of the world, they also have an ontological disciplinary effect through the training and policing of IR graduates to be this way in the world (whether that being in the world is working in development, government or replicating their own kind in institutions of teaching). In this regard I will be taking my cue from Sankaran Krishna's overtly politicised and discursive reading of the discipline as tending toward acts of containment and domestication.[1] In highlighting the structurally amnesic moments of IR discourse as they pertain to matters of race, Krishna does much to open up the discipline to both an internal gaze (a kind of participatory ethnography of its pedagogic practices)[2] as well as to broader reflections on the patterns and systems of its knowledge formations, and their resultant power effects in terms of the discipline's "positional superiority" in matters relating to the International.[3] In Krishna's case it was the device of amnesia which enabled him to mount his critique; in mine it will be amnesia's flip-side in the act of remembering.

I say this chapter is an experiment in writing as it will use the act of remembering and remembrance as ways of making manifest this self-reinforcing relationship between certain methodologies valorised by IR (like abstraction, problem-solving theory, hyper-masculine, realist interpretations of a supposedly "interpretable" world, etc.) and its teaching practices. It will do this through a specific reclamation (and hence inherent critique) of the potential, but ultimately thwarted, disruptive effect that lay (or that should have laid) at the heart of the recent, so-called "aesthetic turn" in the discipline, as espoused by the likes of Roland Bleiker, Gerald Holden and Christine Sylvester.[4] In doing so it will attempt to show that if the aesthetic is to have any hope of making the intervention in the discipline which it aspired to then it will necessarily need to break free of the discipline's methodological forms which are, following Krishna, openly designed to domesticate other ways of knowing and being which the aesthetic call upon (affect, shock, empathy and excess). In essence then, I say this chapter is an experiment in writing as I firmly believe that form can be as important as content, and that if we are to take seriously the task of addressing the stranglehold certain methodologies (and their resultant subject positions) have over a discipline then we must be more expansive in our approaches. More to the point, this expansiveness needs to occur at a level far in excess of merely incorporating new materials for analysis.[5] How we enact and perform our disciplines mark them and the knowledges they produce. Through a particular experimentation in remembering, then, I wish to show that if we are to avoid curtailing the power of the aesthetic then it is something which must be performed, and not just theorised.

$\star\star\star$

It is enough to say that the following narrative unfolded at an annual conference of no small significance; one known for its critical edge, its championing of alternative views and for fostering a generation of post-positivist scholars.

Despite the newness of its fittings and its recently installed bank of multimedia facilities, the room was typical of its kind: barren – the kind of opulent unimaginativeness which is now as much a mainstay of the new academy as it is anywhere else; the kind of barrenness which has a name: "client focused". A line of tables was arranged at the front of the room with four chairs neatly tucked behind them, each facing back out toward the room. There was no mistaking where one belonged or what one's role was to be. The barrenness of the room was thus mirrored in, and reinforced by, a kind of staid predictability of form: I would not be speaking, nor would I be an active participant in knowledge production; I would merely be a recipient. Dutifully I played my part: I sat down, I fished around in my bag for my notebook and a pen, and I sat in wait. The only little act of rebellion I took was not to unfurl the arm-rest of the chair designed for note-taking; instead I rested my notebook in my lap.

Immediately something seemed out of place with this otherwise most familiar of academic scenes. As the rest of the panel entered and sat in two of the seats at the front of the room, an assistant scurried around helping the person I presumed to be the first speaker prop-up a make-shift lectern off to the side somewhere near the multimedia control panel. Meanwhile, the session chair entered. He took his place at the end of the table, craned his neck to read the slide projected on the screen behind him, and turned to the speaker who was now straightening some notes on the impromptu lectern. The chair received a nod from the speaker, and so promptly introduced the session.

I barely raised an eyebrow at the lack of response by the speaker to their introduction; I merely took it as matter-of-factness and a desire on their behalf to get underway that they did not utter the customary thanks to the chair for granting licence to speak. But speak they did not. Is this a nervous pause I thought? It was not. Instead the black screen behind the panellists jumped to life with a series of alternating images of religious idols and symbols of state, as the room filled with the sound of pealing bells. It took me a while to recognise the fragment being played. It was from Eisenstein's film *October*; the segment was called "In the name of God…". Conceptually stunning for its literal egalitarianism – where each frame is as long as the next so as not to prioritise one visual moment over another – Eisenstein's depiction of the overthrowing of the Tsarist state by Bolshevik revolutionaries stands to this day as a striking study of visual tempo; the segment, "In the name of God…" a clear call to the conjoined nature of state and church in the suppression of the proletariat.

For over a minute we sat somewhat uneasily in the fact that we were present at an academic conference session where one of the three panellists who had been selected to read a paper was actively denying themselves precisely that enunciative modality: no speech, no text… but something else. Then the speaker continued (and it is only with hindsight that I can say "continued" rather than "started"):

> *From the outset, let me make my allegiances clear. I am not here to engage in an iconoclastic dual with any of the authors who would see themselves as part of the so-called 'aesthetic turn', trading blows over which image, which text, which idol should be included within the pantheon of interpretive gods, and which should be cast to the ground. That is, I am not here to fight over the value of the aesthetic as a way of opening up different sensibilities and different ways of understanding politics in general, and the International more specifically – far from it in fact…*

The speaker followed this up with an almost staccato-like precision of elaborating statements showing an understanding of, and allegiance to, the general project of an aesthetic turn, claiming in agreement: that our comprehension of facts cannot be separated from our relationship with them; that signification itself is an inherently incomplete and problematic process; that the notion of a "common sense" or a reasonable and rational middle ground has been hijacked by a failure to remember that the interpretation is not actually the event itself; that this has in turn allowed the social sciences to claim an interpretive higher ground through a call to the supposed transparency of their techniques; and that the practice of interpreting the world thus is, in fact, itself a highly political act. The manner and tempo in which these statements were delivered suggested that these were not matters of contention or debate for the speaker, but rather things to be taken as givens. At the point where some people might finish, this speaker was merely beginning.

It was at this point that I allowed myself the opportunity to scan the room to see if I was the only one with a slightly amused look on my face. It was then that I saw the scowls. Anyone who has taught in a classroom before will know the type: typical acts of masculine aggression normally aimed at intimidation – backs slouched, arms crossed, legs spread wide, and a sulkiness which occupies space palpably. I started to wonder what it was, specifically, that would engender such a display this early on in proceedings… but the speaker interrupted my thoughts:

> *However, this does not mean that I stand as one with those academic participants of this latest of so-called 'turns', and I would go so far as to say that I fear that this particular 'turn' will end up following a similar path to those which have gone before. Yes, they might broaden the scope of what might be admitted as objects of study of International Relations, but in doing so they are likely to be subsumed within the folds of the discipline as just another coloured pot from which the brush of IR can continue to paint its fairly naive picture of the world.*

Almost as if in answer to the immediate, slightly defensive questions which leapt to mind, the speaker went on to paint a picture of their own, one of reversion to disciplinary type; at precisely the time when the potential of the aesthetic to change our understandings of the International was being considered, there was a curious lack of dialogue with those disciplines from which these materials were being gleaned. Film, literature and art may well now be seen as fertile ground for the investigation of the politics of the International, but reference to the debates which had long raged in English, cultural studies, art history and critical theory, were surprisingly absent, as if the outcomes of the history and culture wars (of decades ago now) did not matter and needed reinvention. As the speaker elaborated upon these accusations I got the impression, however, that this was almost an incidental point; on the one hand a subtle swipe at the kinds of knowledge silos which tend to accompany most disciplinary exchange; and on the other, a not-so-subtle swipe at those who profit from appearing fresh and invigorating by presenting material acquired from outside the discipline as if new back within their home discipline.

My hunch was proven correct when, with an economy of style, the speaker continued toward what was obviously their more sustained explanation of this charge of reversion to disciplinary type, doing so with only the slightest of movements: a single keystroke made an image of a statue flick across the screen at the front of the room. Without pause, speech resumed:

> *This paper is a call to arms; it is an attempt to implore those who loosely identify with the aesthetic turn to take to heart the lessons of their investigations into the aesthetic and to apply those lessons to their own tasks; it is a call, in essence, not to make aesthetics the object of one's inquiries but the method or style of them – it is a call to affect and embodiment, to occupy the space opened up by the aesthetic and inhabit that space, to allow one's self to be thrown off centre, and to take the spirit of the aesthetic as a method and style of academic practice. To do anything less is merely to plunder other disciplines for treasures to lay at the feet of realist gods…*

In principle, as I understood it at the time, the charge being laid was not so much about the (now infamous) disciplinary introspection of IR that would see matters fundamental to the international deemed outside its purview (development, gender, race, culture), nor even the subtle analogy being made to a kind of family resemblance between IR's disciplinary practices of riding roughshod into other disciplinary terrains in search of academic loot and the image of politics it is so exclusively wedded to describing (power politics). No, what I took this charge to refer to was what happens even when those things once outside this disciplinary purview are finally brought within it.

Distractedly I noticed that the image of the statue had changed; it was now one frame into a state of being toppled. Without pause or reference the speaker continued.

Roland Bleiker's *Aesthetics and World Politics* – the publication of which marked a decade since its author coined the phrase "the aesthetic turn" – enabled the speaker to press on. We were reminded that a central theoretical tenant of Bleiker's work was that through the sheer weight of time IR had forgotten that the interpretation of a political event was not the event itself, and that it was actually in the gap *between* reality and representation that politics truly lay: "This is Bleiker at his most suggestive best," our speaker intoned. As with all phrases of this kind, you couldn't help but expect a "but..." to come in somewhere. And when it did, it made clear what the speaker was referring to in calling for scholars to inhabit the space of the aesthetic:

> As much as Bleiker wants to undermine the ground upon which traditional IR has proclaimed its interpretive superiority, Bleiker invariably keeps giving that ground back by suggesting that a focus on the aesthetic should not take away from the importance of social science understandings of the world; that the aesthetic should, in fact, be seen on par with theory, with evidence and with quantitative data.

Another image of the statue flashed up on the projector screen, this time even further into fall. Again, the speaker took no notice:

> ...In doing so, the aesthetic is methodologically reduced to a text, to an object of analysis removed from the positionality, the embodiment and temporality of the analyst. And Bleiker is not at all alone in this endeavour. For nearly all proponents of this aesthetic turn the aesthetic object produces affect because it is aesthetic, failing to see the production or bringing into being of the aesthetic. Yes, they acknowledge there are practices of the aesthetic (painting, writing literature or poetry), but always in a very textual way rather than in an embodied way. For all this talk about politics being found in the messy gap between representation and event, the post-positive IR practitioner of the aesthetic turn is still the same Cartesian observer upon a world from which it is largely divorced that characterises the realist scholar – representation, like politics, remains something 'out there'.

The statue toppled a little further. Again, the speaker took no notice. I grimaced; slightly annoyed at the amount of work the speaker was asking me to do in juggling their different modes, but most of all I grimaced at myself for thinking this.

> Put another way, the disciplinary training of social science evidence, of cause and effect, of abstraction, of knowability, and of the detachment of the scholar from the object of their study, reduces disciplinary wanderings into other domains to little more than efforts to seek bigger and better sticks

with which to beat disciplinary forefathers. In doing so, such sorties have amounted to little more than active acts of domestication. The powers of the aesthetic to throw us, to produce affect, to disrupt our logics and to trouble us, are all actively neutered and denied; translated into the familiar with all barbs removed.

The speaker was deliberate and impassioned; their performance explicitly highlighting the point they were making. It was precisely this kind of reflexivity they were asking the audience to make in their own scholarship. It made me recall the number of times I have been left strangely disappointed by borrowings from the Frankfurt School and critical theory in recent IR scholarship; more specifically at the perfunctory renditions of interpretive devices such as "the sublime", Benjamin's *flâneur* or de Certeau's act of "walking in the city". Until now I had merely thought that what had disappointed me about them was just that they were fairly flat or dry renditions of the topic, not quite up to the written flair of the original authors or even of practitioners in other disciplines who seemed to "get into" the spirit of the original and employ it to much greater effect. But now what I was beginning to wonder was whether these texts felt this way not because they were examples of poor IR scholarship, but because they were actually examples of good, or at least *effective*, IR scholarship – the pedestrian nature of the texts a sure sign that domestication had occurred.

I'm not sure why, but at that moment I looked down at the notebook in my lap. Rather than the page being full of notes, as is my way, it was covered instead by a huge ink blot welling out from the tip my pen still lightly touching the page, poised ready to write. Shit! In a flurry of activity I burrowed into my bag for a tissue.

I had missed the end of the paper. As I watched the following two speakers read their papers seated at the front of the room I wondered what had become of the falling statue. But immediately I had a slight twinge... not of guilt, but almost of shame. Perhaps the point for me today was to let go of the notion of closure; to allow myself to be unsettled by the fate and meaning of the statue.

Then I began wondering what I would be feeling right now if I were one of the two speakers following on from the first. Would I feel unsettled by either the content or the manner in which it was delivered, or would I have realised that the point was that the two cannot actually be separated and hence be unsettled by both? Would I be actively or unwittingly defensive in the presentation of my own material, or would I feign calmness so as not to appear to be defensive? Would I say something about my colleague's performance, or would I forge on as if nothing out of the ordinary had taken place, or as if what they had said couldn't possibly pertain to me and *my* disciplinary performance? I cast yet another glance around the room. A relaxed calm had settled in; we had returned to something more familiar and knowable.

Soon enough the last of the three panellists had finished their papers and as if in answer to the question which now began to form in my mind – what will they make of this? – the Chair of the panel cleared his throat and began his opening remarks: "Well, thank you. We have heard two excellent papers and a presentation today...".

★ ★ ★

If there is a postscript to our narrative of the conference paper it lies in a strangely telling final scene of enforced ostracision; a quite literal disciplinary closing of ranks.

Our speaker stands in the conference coffee room surrounded, not by the usual receptive and congratulatory noises, or even the all-too-frequent consolatory (or is it nervously polite?) gesture of "Hello, I *really* enjoyed your paper", but rather by a wall of silence; a kind of disciplinary banding together and a clear showing of force. But as these bodies of the discipline clump and arrange themselves in palpable opposition to our speaker, leaving the latter marooned, somewhat forlornly clutching a crumpled paper cup in the middle of the room, what occurs to the casual observer of this scene is that this final statement is not an assured showing of force at all, but rather of its opposite: of insecurity and unknowingness, a condemnation born of pure symptoms.

One might well imagine what is going through our speaker's mind in this moment of social isolation, when colleagues (almost as if to prove the point yet again) close ranks on one now deemed an outsider. Is it the rapidness or the violence of the audience's reaction which sticks our speaker to the spot? Or do they continue to stand there out of a kind of stubbornness in the face of such crude sand-pit diplomacy? It's hard to tell. One thing is for certain though, there is definitely something unnerved or unsettled about the speaker's post-performance performance. It is certainly not an act of defiant arrogance, chin raised triumphantly at the victory secured minutes earlier. Rather, in the shakiness of how our speaker holds their body, it is almost as if there is a strange mirroring of performance going on between crowd and victim. It is barely perceivable but it's there: the eyes which lock onto no other, the foot which nervously scuffs the carpet, and the ever-so-slightly hunched shoulders all speak to a different register of performance. Rattled, insecure and probably holding out as long as pride will allow before beating a hasty retreat to the corridor or toilet, our speaker strangely manifests and reflects back all the symptoms of insecurity wrought upon them by the agents of the discipline.

Finally when enough becomes enough and our speaker does indeed leave the room, it is interesting to pause and linger to consider the crowd. Are they aware that their own performance is just that, a performance? Are they aware that this performance is one which speaks to their disciplinary training so well? Do they even realise that what this person has done for them today is provide them with a fool-proof script by which they may come to be aware of their own positionality as agents of a discipline so geared toward epistemic and even bodily violence?

Unfortunately, such self-reflection is absent today; there is mirroring, yes, but reflection, no. And why? Because in many ways the speaker was right. This is a discipline which, for all its post-positivist claims, and throwing open of the gates to new materials, new approaches and new methodologies, is still dominated by a way of knowing and replicating itself which fails to take these lessons to heart. And this charge is in no way to be equated with the suggestion that the problem lies with a current crop of IR practitioners; that they are somehow not up to standard and if only we trained them more rigorously this problem would go away – far from it, in fact, as it is actually the latter which is the problem: training.

★ ★ ★

From: David L Martin <dr.davidlmartin@gmail.com>
To: Institute of Postcolonial Studies <postcol@netspace.net.au>
Date: 13 August 2010 16:57
Subject: Re: Devika memorial collection

Dear Phillip

Yes, I'm very keen to contribute to the Devika memorial
collection, and assume it will take a similar form and
intellectual trajectory to your last book – an engagement
at the intersections of IR and postcolonialism. But I am
wondering if it is to be structured or framed around Devika or
her work in any way, or whether it will merely be dedicated to
her? Why I ask is because my contribution might be different
depending on logic of the book. Perhaps I should tell you one
of my Devika stories…

Often Devika and I would share a late lunch on a Thursday
after three or four hours of tutorials following on from your
morning lecture of *IR (and its Others)*. Usually we would
compare notes on how the students fared with this author
or that, or exchange ideas about getting students to open
up a little more: the usual kind of tutor-talk. However, I
have a very vivid memory of this one particular lunch as it
was one of the few occasions that I got to see Devika talk
passionately about something that wasn't her work. I can't
remember how it started, but Devika took the conch and for
the next half an hour or so related to me the most intricate
details of her passion for watching science fiction. I knew she
was partial to the occasional escape of Bollywood, but this
was something else – it was intricate, it was personal, and
it was escapism, yet it was also thoughtful and, typical of
her, theorised. What I found particularly interesting about
this discovered passion was that it was primarily visual – she
watched TV series and films but didn't necessarily read that
much, which seemed strange considering her voracious appetite
for reading. I was careful not to interject or ask for
explanations lest it silence; preferring instead to just keep
nodding as she went on about this episode or that, showing how
popular culture was trying to work through issues of race,
sexuality, territoriality or any number of other current,
pressing social concerns.

This conversation stuck with me for a particular reason: when
I asked her why she hadn't tried incorporating this kind of
material into her doctoral work she said without hesitation:
"Well… it's just not literature".

Immediately upon uttering it, the statement caught in her
throat. Devika started blushing, perhaps because she knew I
was so keen on theorising the visual, or more likely because

she had just revealed to herself a tension; a tension she
clearly resolved unwittingly each time she indulged in her
world of the visual as "escape" from the "serious" world of
literature. This sparked off what, for me, has been one of the
most sustained engagements I have had with anyone on the topic
of why the visual is absent from postcolonial discourse. It
was a conversation about disciplinary and cultural politics,
aesthetic hierarchies, and the centrality of literature to the
formation of certain Indian identities.

Nearly a decade later this conversation came back to me in my
position as the managing editor of the journal [*Postcolonial
Studies*]. It's a position which has given me remarkable
insight into how the discipline is shaping up, how it is
surviving in an age of funding cuts, and what it thinks
its primary tasks to be. What's most interesting in this
regard is that there seems to be something of a reversion
to disciplinary origins going on; a return to the practices
of commonwealth literature studies and, later, literary
criticism. Each year the number of submissions from people
in English departments teaching what could be called postcolonial literature (the hyphen here indicating a largely
temporal consideration, not so much a theoretical set of
concerns) increases. Dwindling away is the political potential
or sense of a shared reclamative endeavour which first marked
the discipline's formation. What we're being left with instead
is a strange, slightly self-consuming, short-hand image of
itself.

Now of course this is all very loose and fast, and one day
I should write about it properly, but for now the point for
me about this lunch with Devika was that in this moment of
her revealing a passion, but immediately realising that that
passion was disallowed (by herself and more importantly by
the discipline she was so passionate about), a disciplinary
politics (or a disciplining of the discipline if you will)
seemed to be at play. And it is this politics which,
ironically, brings postcolonial studies into close orbit
with that other shared discipline of ours: IR. As remarkably
far apart as the content of these two fields may appear at
times there is a kindred logo-centrism at play which is
deeply distrustful of the aesthetic as an analytical device
or mode of practice, outside of high literature. It has been
interesting re-reading Roland Bleiker's *Aesthetics and World
Politics* in this regard for there is a clear, unacknowledged,
hierarchy of aesthetics at work: it is poetry and poetics
that is most valorised, followed by literature (and here it
is the canon, not graphic novels or fanzines), followed by
music (and here it is Handel and Vivaldi, not rap, reggae or
Bangala music); next there is art (and here it is the high art
of Impressionism, not manga or flashmobs), and finally there is
the somewhat ambiguous category of popular culture. It begs

the question of whether this so-called "aesthetic turn" might
not be better described as a "cultural turn" thirty years too
late.

But what I keep coming back to year after year is this
conversation with a colleague I still miss, and how in that
conversation and in those feelings seems to reside something
which has the power to throw into sharp relief the way in
which certain disciplinary trainings tend to replicate very
specific hierarchies and modes of being; ways of not only
performing the discipline, but also ways of taking that
discipline (and its logics) out into the world.

It would be nice, I guess, if I could write back to Devika of
the outcome of those conversations we had nearly a decade ago
now.

Much love
David

★ ★ ★

The act of academic writing has always been akin to performing obituary; the daily memorialisations and genuflections we perform going strangely unrecognised for what they are. But as much as memory has been profoundly responsible for shaping Western discourses of the International – one need only think of the role witnessing played in this regard – memory has also borne the brunt of social science ire as being not rigorous enough and too open to the vagaries of individual cognition. In response to these perceived inadequacies, social science has tended to codify and discipline memory in the form of legal stricture: the pain of witnessing being reduced to transcript; the creative and affective qualities of memory curtailed as mere evidence.

The matter of memory has recently come to the fore in the work of a number of scholars of the International concerned with issues of witnessing in an age of the image's ubiquity. A recent special issue in *Security Dialogue* on "securitisation, militarisation and visual culture" has been matched by various submissions in *Review of International Studies*, each dealing with the ethics of viewing/not viewing the kinds of images coming out of places like Abu Ghraib and Saddam Hussein's execution chamber.[6] Two things are worth (incidental) note here: first, it is telling that the issue of seeing such images has centred mainly on questions of ethics; and second, that of the two sites of image production mentioned, it is the former (Abu Ghraib) and not the latter which is largely seen as most problematic. In both instances one cannot help but feel the comfort provided by the law's proscriptions on how to deal with these events: as intricate as they may be, ethics and justice are rarely invoked when messiness and ambivalence are desired.

One thing this return of interest in the act of witnessing (and how it is enacted so as to avoid attracting disciplinary ire) can do, however, is alert us to the possibilities of pushing the equation back the other way; of starting with a particular manifestation of disciplinary domestication and seeing if it is possible to dwell instead in its more messy aspects which are otherwise so requiring of disciplinary censure: in the case of memory, its ability to undo the rationality which keeps safely at arm's length the subject of our studies as an object, at the same time as traversing the temporal and spatial divides which occlude an embodied, feeling and vulnerable disciplinary practitioner.[7] What if we were to dally then in the messiness of memory and memorialisation (which, as I have said, have always been there even in the social sciences), and allowed them their creative associations with the aesthetic rather than curtailing them as inappropriate? That is, what if we were to take the aesthetic not as an object of study, but rather as a method, and *perform* memory as something other than evidence? What we might do, I would suggest, is find a mode of scholarship which resists this impulse toward domestication, at the same time as making forcefully present to ourselves the centrality of our modes of performing "disciplinarily" and the pedagogies we employ for its uncritical replication.

The power of the aesthetic to throw us, to make us feel, to make us remember gives it great licence. If the "aesthetic turn" is to be a "turn" it must revel in this licence.

★ ★ ★

I remember the day I presented my paper on the aesthetic turn. I remember the sense of vulnerability my performance brought crashing down upon me. I remember the sympathetic looks I received from one woman in the audience who stained her notebook with a large ink-blot. And I remember the opening remarks of the session Chair, cordoning off my paper from the others as if it were illegitimate or dangerous. Yet as much as the Chair's comments carried with them a certain sting at the time, they did, and still do, point to something worth noting: that disciplines have a way of manifesting and mirroring certain methodological assumptions in the training of their graduates and in their daily performances (whether those be in the classroom, the conference hall or the wider arena of vocations which carry these lessons out into the world). International Relations, while not alone in this, is a discipline now quite infamous for its closures and domestications: one need only think of feminism's vast array of interpretive and analytical offerings reduced to the "gender variable" to get a sense of the violence of such reductions, not to mention the deeply masculinist public performances of them.[8]

Memory and the act of remembrance have within them the ability to resist our discipline's impulses toward domestication. But in many ways it is also about how we perform memory. The memories I have indulged in in this chapter are not meant to be (and in fact could not be) codified as evidence; they are not presented to show the weight of argumentation which might swing the reader one way or another; they are not meant to offer closure. Instead, I have kept them as they appear to me: necessarily fragmentary and personal. Yet through their recollection in different performances of genre writing I hope that something of both their messiness and potentiality has filtered through.

Notes

1 S Krishna, 'Race, Amnesia, and the Education of International Relations', in B Gruffydd Jones (ed.), *Decolonising International Relations* (Plymouth: Rowman & Littlefield 2006), pp. 89–108.

2 An interesting parallel can be found in Kim Nossal's work on IR textbooks, wherein the author rightly starts from the premise that textbooks take their place alongside the broader issue of what happens in seminars, lectures and tutorials as training vehicles for bringing graduates into a disciplinary fold, at the same time as influencing how that field will manifest in the world. See KR Nossal, 'Tales That Textbooks Tell: Ethnocentricity and Diversity in American Introductions to International Relations,' in R Crawford & D Jarvis (eds.), *International Relations – Still an American Social Science? Toward Diversity in International Thought* (Albany: State University of New York Press 2001), pp. 167–186.

3 PGC Darby [riffing on Edward Said], 'Reworking Knowledge Conventions', in PGC Darby (ed.), *Postcolonizing the International: Working to Change the Way We Are* (Honolulu: University of Hawai'i Press 2006), pp. 15–39 at p. 22.

4 R Bleiker, 'The Aesthetic Turn in International Political Theory', *Millennium: Journal of International Studies* 30/3 (2001) 509–533. R Bleiker, *Aesthetics and World Politics* (Basingstoke: Palgrave Macmillan 2009). R Bleiker, 'Learning from Art: A Reply to Holden's World Literature and World Politics', *Global Society* 17/4 (2003) 415–428. G Holden, 'Cinematic IR, the Sublime, and the Indistinctness of Art', *Millennium: Journal of International Studies* 34/3 (2006) 793–818. G Holden, 'World Literature and World Politics: In Search of a Research Agenda', *Global Society* 17/3 (2003) 229–252. C Sylvester, 'Art, Abstraction, and International Relations', *Millennium: Journal of International Studies* 30/3 (2001) 535–554. C Sylvester, *Art/ Museums: International Relations Where We Least Expect It* (Boulder: Paradigm 2009) and curiously predating them: PGC Darby, *The Fiction of Imperialism: Reading Between International Relations and Postcolonialism* (London: Continuum International Publishing 1998).

5 This is perhaps the only criticism I would have of recent efforts to decolonise the discipline through the incorporation of Postcolonial or Southern perspectives. Often these efforts have a tendency to seek equivalence; to grant such material (be it the agency of gods and spirits, alternative understandings of exchange, or indigenous notions of territoriality), an equal footing to Western material. The problem with this is that the structures and methodologies of how the discipline processes this material remain largely unaltered by such moves; the resultant domestication reducing these other ways of knowing and being to "variables" within an otherwise largely unaltered field.

6 In the spirit of memorialisation I offer the following: L Amoore, 'Vigilant Visualities: the Watchful Politics of the War on Terror', *Security Dialogue* 38/2 (2007) 215–232; E Dauphinée, 'The Politics of the Body in Pain: Reading the Ethics of Imagery', *Security Dialogue* 38/2 (2007) 139–155; F Möller, 'The Looking/Not Looking dilemma', *Review of International Studies* 35 (2009) 781–794.

7 Memory – or to be more precise, how memory manifests as evidence – is, of course, just one among many aspects of a discipline we might choose to perform differently as part of an aesthetic turn. It is the one I have chosen today to perform. But equally

I might have chosen to start with any of the methodologies IR valorises most, working back toward their more destabilising flipsides: abstraction/embodiment, closure/fragmentation, rationality/enchantment, and so on.

8 G Youngs, 'Feminist International Relations: A Contradiction in Terms? Or: Why Women and Gender are Essential to Understand the World "We" Live in', *International Affairs* 80/1 (2004) 75–87.

8

THE NEGLECTED SHADOW SELF

Christine Deftereos

International Relations theory is not an area of knowledge traditionally recognised for its attentiveness to human subjectivity. It is also not an area of knowledge typically concerned with different accounts of selfhood. This is somewhat curious given that self and other relations underpin all human relations, irrespective of whether these relationships are domestic or international. To speak of an 'international self' or to 'act internationally' though seems to move us away from the complexities that define human relations. To enter the domain of the 'international' is to enter a world seemingly governed by a singular and universal concept, where our differences and complexities are both contained and sanitised through the discourse of the nation state or, more commonly, eliminated. As a theoretical device this abstraction in defining the 'self' is understandable. After all, how can we begin to understand international relations and its rules of engagement and human rights without consensus of what it means to act 'internationally'? However, in accepting this consensus we are also accepting a falsification of the self and of self and other relations – at once a simplification and a misrepresentation. While a certain reductionism of this nature is perhaps part and parcel of most disciplinary structures of knowledge, we need to be mindful that efforts to understand the complexities of selfhood within international relations are driven by desires to contain our irrational polymorphous selves.

Alongside these desires to contain the 'unknowable' and irrational parts of our selves, international relations theory affirms its predictive and explanatory powers. Consequently, the 'self' and 'other' become clearly definable and knowable, as 'citizen' and 'non-citizen', as 'friend' or 'enemy' of the state, for instance, or as 'victim' and 'perpetrator' in the fight against terrorism. These identifiable roles provide a degree of certainty and predictability within an anarchic world system. They provide a sense of security, albeit elusive and illusionary, that a collective logic or a collective self will prevail in the battle between 'us' and 'them'. International organisations and leaders take on this rhetoric of claiming to know the 'other', in ways that are simultaneously reductive and reassuring. An extension of a colonising logic, the ability to divide and conquer by defining and representing the self and other in particular ways becomes the prerogative of the nation state. In recent years, these inclusive and exclusionary mechanisms have been the primary filter through which to analyse issues of national security. In Australia, recent debates demonstrate how the nation state can 'de-authorise' inclusion in the nation state by potentially stripping Australian nationals of their citizenship if deemed to be a national threat. Such extreme instances of 'othering' raise a myriad of concerns, though they can be seen to be part of a continuing logic for intervention, despite potential human rights abuses. These dominant representations are also mirrored in all aspects of international relations, especially in the discourses of development where the under-developed and under-civilised 'other' can justify interventionist strategies.

Despite its widely contested significance, the terrorist attacks on America on September 11 were a sobering reminder of the limits of this kind of 'knowing,' or assuming to know the other. The attacks on the Twin Towers and the Pentagon pointed to an act of international terrorism that was itself not entirely 'international'. It was also part of a 'home-grown' story that demonstrated just how close to home the enemy could be. George Bush's response of 'either being with us or against us' in the fight against terrorism was an attempt to re-affirm a familiar geographic and psychological boundary between 'us and them'. Terrorism across the globe in all its forms, however, whether statist or transnational, continues to prove that the enemy is not always external to the self, and is increasingly lurking within. Many have gone so far as to even suggest that it is a part of an individual or collective self that has been repressed to its abject limits. Alternatively, it can be considered to be a part of our selves that has been disavowed. An aggressive and violent affirmation of anti-modernism in many terrorists organisations around the world for instance cannot be understood as an aberration or as outside of modern life, but must be viewed as symptomatic of modernity. This is an enemy that can be difficult to locate or identify, that can be international and foreign, local and familiar. Here the predictive powers of international relations theory in 'knowing the other', especially in knowing its enemy, reach its limits. There is a need for international relations to seriously engage with political phenomenon and aspects of selfhood that it did not take too seriously before. As one commentator suggests, using a sporting analogy,

> [international relations] should go fishing a bit more in the waters of the periphery and bring back to port those scaly items – such as international terrorism, messianic religion and pre-modern forms of opposition to modernity – that it tended to throw back or ignore in the past.[1]

In this chapter, I argue that there is a need for international relations to engage with other selves traditionally excluded from the purview of the political and psychological boundaries of the state. In the process international relations needs to recover its 'other' neglected selves. If we are to address the epistemic violence that marks the discipline's blind spots and exclusions, then 'other' selves must be included in the building of humane futures. The first section of this chapter questions the account of selfhood that international relations privileges and advances as universal. It goes on to show how the long intellectual alliance between psychology and international relations has contributed to the privileging of this self and the disavowal of 'other' selves. Here the discourses of psychology and psychoanalysis function as tools of 'knowing', as tools of normalisation and validation of a specific concept of self, rather than as critical tools of 'unknowing', used to interrogate these certitudes. The second section explores how a recovery of other selves within international relations also requires a recovery of these analytical tools – that the possibility of 'knowing' must necessarily contain an element of self-destruction and 'unknowing'. What is needed is an understanding of the psychology of politics alongside the politics of psychology. This creates an intellectual space where the recovery of other selves becomes possible as well as a dialogue between international relations and its others.

The politics of psychology and the rational international self

The intellectual alliance between psychology and international relations takes many forms.[2] These include, though are not limited to, rational actor theories, behaviourist or cognitive psychology, depth psychology in what is referred to as the constructivist turn in international relations. These theories differ in their scope and methods, but confirm a long-standing interest within disciplinary international relations in the collective psychology of large groups (a theory of a collective self), the nature of political culture, and the motives and behaviours of rational international actors and organisations. With the exception of constructivist critiques of identity, which have sought to inject the importance of socially constituted identities in determining international outcomes into the debates, the linkage between psychology and the development of international relations theory has led to a privileging of a specific concept of selfhood.

In 1932, Albert Einstein wrote to Sigmund Freud asking him if psychoanalysis could provide insights into how to end war and violence. At that time Freud, in responding to Einstein, expressed very little hope for an end to war and in the role of psychoanalysis in altering human behaviours beyond the individual.[3] Despite Freud's initial reservations, psychoanalysis via his work into individual and group psychology provided a groundbreaking challenge to the Enlightenment vision of an integrated rational self. Psychoanalysis with the Freudian discovery of the unconscious recognised from the outset the precariousness of a rational self, or a rational collective self for that matter. Psychoanalysis as a theory of selfhood brought into play a more complex understanding of how individual and collective selves are formed. The concepts of the unconscious, repression, identification, projection and splitting offered a more sophisticated language to understand human behaviour and interactions. Freud, via his civilisation and its discontents thesis and analysis of group dynamics, also offered a radically different understanding of the relationship between human agency and social structures, challenging the rationality of social structures and ideologies. Yet despite these potentialities, the extension of psychoanalysis as a therapeutic practice and as social criticism to the colonies resulted in a different experience. This history is well documented, including the ways in which psychoanalytic tools of demystification were utilised in service of the making over of the colonised in the image of the coloniser. Postcolonial theorists such as Frantz Fanon, Edward Said and Homi K. Bhabha have critiqued these processes of identification extensively. Such work points to ways in which psychoanalysis carries within its legacy this double-edged desire to 'know' and of knowing alongside a more critical interpretation and as a radical politics of unknowing.

What lingers as part of this legacy is an idealised trope of selfhood, predicated on a Eurocentric understanding of rational and strategic actions. This collective self can take on different guises. Whether referencing the nation state, the international system, or international organisations, this account of selfhood foregrounds the modus operandi of instrumental rationality. Consequently, this reified rational self has produced a number of elaborate theories quantifying and qualifying rational behaviour and actions. Inherent within this body of knowledge is the epistemological assumption that this self is both 'knowable' and 'known'. Moreover, it assumes that interactions with others, based on the rationality of collective behaviours, can be predicted and controlled. In Neorealist accounts the abstract idealised collective self is evident in the assumption that the state is a unitary actor, subject to a series of measurable rational policy decisions and calculable strategic foreign policy decisions. This collective self, one that is known and predictable, is idealised within the state-centric rationality that is privileged and domesticated within the citadels of international relations theory.

Even the 'self-' in self-interest that underpins international politics has very little to do with the complexities of human subjectivity and selfhood. Littered with the abstract aphorisms of 'state self-interest', 'the public interest' and the 'national interest', international relations both assumes and idealises a specific account of the self. This has led to the formation of a dominant collective self that is symptomatic of the discipline's tendency towards acts of containment and domestication. Even in responses to a 'humanitarian crisis', where human experiences and perspectives are often curiously missing, the international self that is 'ethically' obligated to respond and define the 'crisis' on behalf of its 'other', does so by reinforcing the ontological pre-eminence of this integrated self as rational actor and decision-maker. Arguably, it is this ability to act rationally as opposed to the images of an irrational, helpless, chaotic 'other' that also justifies interventionist policies.

International relations theory has largely turned to psychology for both its explanatory and predictive powers. Taking their cues from individual psychology, theorists of group psychology have sought to identify the characteristics, motives and actions of a collective self. Applying the principles of individual psychology to group psychology has attracted its fair share of criticism, especially with respect to whether a single 'consciousness' can be attributed to a political entity. Can we speak of a collective consciousness of the nation state? Can we speak of a collective consciousness within international politics? Further still, whose interests is this consciousness claiming to represent? These questions are not simply matters of scholarly debate when we remember that foreign policy is driven by elite attitudes, bureaucratic politics and interest group activities. We may then ask, what does this collective self and collective consciousness enacted within foreign policy decisions include? And simultaneously what does it exclude? Foreign policy decisions, especially those pertaining to classified national security interests, highlight the disjuncture in different expressions of 'consciousness' that exist within a society. This is heightened when the state engages in policies affirming a specific collective consciousness that does not accord with the visions, or impinges on the civil liberties, of its democratic citizens. Whilst multiple collective selves and multiple collective fantasies may exist, each competes for recognition and validation. This is evident in the competing tensions between being, for instance, an 'entitled domestic citizen of the state' and an 'international citizen of the world.' The high-profile cases of whistle-blowing in America against national security policies and homeland security are akin to treason, and the ensuing debates over tighter legislation to prevent these events from happening again exemplify these tensions in conflicted selfhood and belonging. In Australia, recent debates about stripping Australian nationals of their citizenship and denying them safe return to Australia if deemed in breach of national security, also point to the way the nation state can potentially 'de-authorize' the entitled subject. The willing surrendering of our civil liberties for a collective 'greater good' takes place in exchange for the security and protection of the nation state and, in turn, securing our status within the 'international.'

The impetus to characterise the 'consciousness' of a collective self, along with its explanatory and predictive powers is evident in the discipline's engagement with a number of psychological perspectives. International relations has consistently turned to rational choice and rational actor theories, although it has also given some coverage to alternative perspectives challenging rational understandings of self-interest, actions and behaviours. The prevalence of rationalist thought mirrored intellectual trends and developments in the social sciences more broadly. Rational actor theories and models were used to advance a specific kind of group consciousness. The appropriation of psychological theories into the discipline of international relations are embedded in the imperatives of 'knowing' and 'predicting' how nation states and state actors will think and act.

Alternative theories sought to undermine the ontological role that rationality played in selfhood. This history, along with the successes and failures of these theories, is part of the development of the discipline of international relations. Despite the 'intellectual alliance' Realism and Neorealism share with positivist psychology, the privileging of a collective rational self has been critiqued from a range of different perspectives. Cognitive psychology, depth psychology, political psychology and psychoanalysis stand out here along with the critical voices of Marxism, pluralism and international society theory, social constructivism, postcolonial studies, critical theory, including the aesthetic turn and feminism.[4]

A major contribution to the literature is the work of Alexander Mitscherlich and Margarete Mitscherlich whose contributions to social psychology and trauma point to the constructive interventions in understanding international relations. In particular, their ground-breaking writing on German post-war trauma and guilt expanded concepts of trauma beyond traumatised individuals and individual psychology to large-group psychology and societal processes. The study of trauma was the entry point for much of this research with William Neiderland's work on the Holocaust and his diagnosis of survivors' syndrome and 'survival guilt' in the late 1960s. This paved the way for other interventions into the application of psychoanalysis in understanding international conflict, terrorism and trauma. Robert J. Lifton's contributions stand out here, especially his meticulous work in documenting the behaviours and motives of the Nazi doctors.

Psychoanalysis has opened up theoretical spaces to explore the psychic worlds of individuals embedded in specific political systems and cultures. Taking the individual as a product of social and political forces, allows for a deeper appreciation of individual and collective processes of identification. This is demonstrated in the intersection of psychoanalysis with political psychology, resulting in psychohistories and psychobiographies of individual leaders. Such research predominantly drew on the political history of a person and had much to reveal about social reality. Depth analysis of how the self is constituted and constitutive of political, social and cultural realities broadened definitions of a collective self and enhanced our understanding of how a collective consciousness is mobilised. Erik. H. Erikson's study of Mahatma Gandhi compellingly shows the way such perspectives can illuminate the relationship between self and society.[5] Starting with the historical, political and psychic specificity of the narrative of the self can open up new horizons in what this means for the 'international'. Understanding how human subjectivity is constituted says something important about how social reality (and collective consciousness) is constituted. Interpreting and re-interpreting the relationship between self and society is a way to re-engage the 'personal as political', thus expanding our understanding of politics. In doing so, it is also an appeal to reclaim and recover 'other' selves that remain outside of 'international relations' and which tell a very different story.

The dynamism of psychic processes, including the role of the unconscious, has traditionally been down-played, with the ego integrative features of selfhood hauled into service of the rational self. This is in part explainable by the way that international relations theory has constituted itself as a discipline grounded in scientific rationality, and alongside positivist and largely quantitative developments in sociological and economic thought. Cognitive psychology or the rise of behaviouralism in the 1960s overtook psychoanalytic theory as the principle challenger to rational models of behaviour. Cognitive psychology was used to 'improve' the way international relations addresses theories of identity. This interest in identity was largely mediated by the need to quantify and qualify international action and behaviours. The roles of emotions and re-modelling emotions in decision-making, have also been absorbed into this logic of 'knowability'. The emphasis on identity has given theoretical support for the idea of an international self. Alongside the utility of such a reading is the concern of whether we can speak of universal primordial archetypes across civilisations.

Appealing as such generalisations might be in their ability to establish certitudes, order and classifiable selves in a violent and anarchic world, they repeat distinct epistemic structures. The desire to know and domesticate the other, including the widespread appeal of such work, is evident, for example, in the success Samuel Huntington's clash of civilisations thesis received. Despite the scholarly debate that the thesis received, its influence in informing American foreign policy has been well documented. Recent interpretations of an international self, such as that found in Mira Sucharov's analysis of the Israeli–Palestinian conflict, suggest a more nuanced reading. For Sucharov each state does possess a distinct identity, a personality and character that is classifiable, but this identity is not established in isolation. It develops out of a state's relationship with other international actors.[6] Drawing on a relational model she suggests that this is where the clues are to understanding state behaviour and action. Modifying state identity whilst possible is, however, contingent on changing relationships with 'other' international actors.

The reification of a specific kind of collective self that dominates our understandings of the 'international' has led to the proliferation of knowledge experts, qualified to speak for and on behalf of the 'international'. The rise of this corporatisation and managerial approach in negotiating the psychological boundaries of the international reinforces the division between theory and praxis. As the logic runs, it is knowledge experts who understand the true nature of the international system who also establish the raison d'être of international discourse. These experts are to be found within international relations theory, psychology, security studies and, as Paul Virilio has argued, in the rise of logistic experts. In short, global security, national security and threat are now expertly managed and, paradoxically, increasingly outsourced to the private sector. While the desire for security, in all its forms, has become more acute, the processes of protection, how these are defined and achieved have become increasingly abstract. Paul Virilio suggests that we are now living in 'the age of logistics' through which the very concept of danger is now scripted by logistical experts. As Virilio puts it, civilians find they are discriminated against in favour of a kind of crystallisation of the scientific and military.[7] This mimicking of scientific practice within international relations by policy makers has been described as 'theory-driven behaviour'.[8]

The privileging of this mode of military intelligence amounts to a depoliticisation of international danger, insofar as it downplays anything but a scientific/military standpoint as valid knowledge. Virilio's classic illustration of how the politics play out is evident in his discussion of the policy of deterrence. It is because deterrence preoccupies itself with the avoidance of nuclear war, that other forms of war and violence are approached in basically the same terms. The result is what Virilio has termed 'acts of war without war'. Writing from within the Indian postcolonial experience, Ashis Nandy argues that the abstraction and reification of violence 'have become an elaborate, ornate play against recognizing only some kinds of violence and denying or de-recognizing others'.[9] The abstraction and reification of violence takes place alongside the epistemic violence of privileging a particular rational enlightened self over others. This denies the historical, cultural and psychological dimensions of violence. Moreover, it denies an appreciation of the violation that takes place within the self–other relation. What is missing from debates of the 'international' is how psychoanalysis as a tool of 'unknowing' can function as a radical critique of these very processes.

The psychology of politics and the recovery of other selves

I have suggested that the alliance between international relations theory and psychology has advanced an essentially Eurocentric rational account of selfhood. This account of self has been intimately tied to a sovereign self with its foundations in the protective boundaries of the nation state. This has led to a distinct politics of 'knowing', in which psychological theories and psychoanalysis have been used to theorise, affirm and domesticate a very specific collective self. Psychoanalysis thus becomes utilised as theory of knowing and of closure, in establishing the entitled subject. The claim to know 'the self and the other' in absolute terms is, however, an illusion or rather a fantasy. It is a fantasy of mastery over the self which as psychoanalysis reminds us with the Freudian discovery of the unconscious, is not entirely possible. There are not only other selves, but also other selves within, that undermine the rationality of the self and the certainty of mastery. Psychoanalysis as a theory of how the self is constituted, has within it an element of self-criticism and self-destruction, a politics of 'unknowing', that equally needs to be acknowledged. Just as psychoanalysis can be domesticated as a tool of normalisation in service of an 'ideal' self, it can also be used as a tool of radical social critique and of 'unknowing'. Critiquing how self and other relations are formed and privileged within political ideologies of entitlement has much to reveal about how our political cultures, both local and international, take shape.

Writing in the aftermath of the September 11 terrorist attacks, the American philosopher and social commentator Judith Butler suggests that collective trauma, or the scene of trauma where established self and other relationships collapse, provides an opportunity to reconstitute these relationships differently. More specifically, she argues that it's at the very scene of trauma itself that the boundaries that separate self and other collapse and can potentially be reconstituted. It is also through the collective trauma and processes of collective grieving that our relationships with others and our sense of self and belonging are questioned. Moreover, trauma and grief provide an opportunity to radically question how the American self is embedded within ideologies of entitlement and self-mastery that govern international politics. Exploring the precariousness of life in the context of the collective violence and national outpouring of mourning post 9-11, Butler asks the provocative question 'who counts as human?' The politics of mourning for Butler has much to reveal about how human life itself and its value is framed by concepts of the international. Butler establishes that 'if certain lives do not qualify as lives or are from the start, not conceived as lives within certain epistemological frames, then these lives are never lived and not lost in the full sense'.[10] Butler revisits psychoanalysis and the precariousness of the psychoanalytic self as a means of critiquing the hierarchy of selfhood that forms. This opens up the question of how to understand the erasure or disavowal of certain lives and accounts of self. In Butler's analysis 'war is framed in certain ways to control and heighten affect in relation to the differential grievability of lives'.[11] It is then the entitled subject whose life is grieved, and as Butler notes this is also reinforced by the processes of international politics. Thus we are faced with a compromised collective form of grieving or a distorted form of healing, one based on a regressive reiteration of an existing self (the grievable self) and other (the non-grievable self). It is necessarily distorted because it legitimises the defensive protection of selfhood, in effect closing off the opportunity to collectively reflect on those relations. For Butler, returning to the precariousness of subjectivity is a reminder that the boundaries of self, and the boundary separating self and other are by definition dynamic and changeable. Grief and melancholia are radically disruptive states that can challenge our very foundations, and in that sense useful analytical categories for reconstituting the boundaries of self.

This potential for a rethinking of a collective American self, both domestic and international, in the wake of the terrorist attacks was limited by the political response to trauma and grief. The offensive attacks and defensive attitudes within American foreign policy to heighten security, whilst understandable, were for commentators like Butler, a missed opportunity to regenerate our understanding of this privileged collective self. Rather, what the last decade of American foreign policy has demonstrated is an over-determined reinforcement of this entitled collective self. As Nancy Hollander argues, what September 11 actively justified, at least within international relations, is that 'American exceptionalism' was a force to contend with. The reiteration of ideologies of entitlement and exceptionalism does little to challenge historically embedded self and other relations that are symptomatically reproduced. What is needed is a deeper engagement with how these ideologies take shape. As the discourses of exceptionalism now expand to include 'states of exception', this becomes a more urgent political task. For theorists like Hollander, psychoanalysis and psychoanalytic theory can function as social and political critique here, providing the tools needed for understanding how these 'states' are formed and reproduced as ideology at the level of individuals and societies. How such ideologies of entitlement inform our collective selves and identities within our political cultures is equally revealing. These ideologies are instituted in policy and gain legitimacy through the reproduction and reification of distinct and privileged accounts of selfhood. Psychoanalysis, in its critical and disruptive mode, then can significantly contribute to social struggles in the name of human rights and redistributive justice.

As a form of social and political criticism, psychoanalysis offers more than just a theory to explore the boundaries of selfhood and how the political (international) subject is formed. It also allows for a reading of the 'politics of imagery' at play.[12] These ideologies of entitlement are legitimised and reinforced, at least for public consumption, through a visible register. The fight against 'the axis of evil' or the affirmation of 'American exceptionalism' is, for example, reinforced through a performative dimension. The distorted efforts to heal the fragility of the American ego, or a diminished sense of self, produced by the attack, were publically consumed through the imagery of aggressive warfare, and the re-affirmation of the paternal state in the global fight against terrorism. Even the terminology of engaging the 'coalition of the willing' reinforces this imagery of entitlement. This collective sense of entitlement is also maintained by collective fantasies of insecurity, 'high alert', 'states of emergency' and the 'states of exception', that erupt symptomatically within international relations. According to Andrew Samuels, 'the politics of imagery now operates, in the external world, at a pace that often precludes rational debate. If we are to avoid being permanently after-the-event – the unending social Nachtraglichkeit – then we have to try to engage not only with the politics of psychological imagery but also with the politics of depth psychology itself.'[13] International relations theory must search for new ways to understand how the politics of imagery and collective consciousness now functions to justify these states of exception. The state of constant emergency and high alert as norm, threatens to annihilate self and other relations. Rather, these discourses of entitlement, of states of exception and states of emergency, mediated and managed by security expects, foreclose alternative political imaginaries and other experiences of the 'international.'

In this sense, I am suggesting that psychoanalysis opens up debate to explore the attachments, projections and fantasies that underpin these performances of self. The Indian political psychologist Ashis Nandy argues that the identifications formed by individuals and societies are intimate, in the sense that distinct psychic investments are made in political processes. In writing on the politics of statehood and the perceived security offered by the state he notes that,

> the kind of agency and coherence often imputed to these impersonal entities (the State) is usually a projection of our inner needs and anthropomorphic fantasies of a parental state; such feel good attributions are a tribute to our trusting nature rather than to political acumen.[14]

In opening up discussion in this way, critical psychoanalysis can challenge rational based explanations as to why nation states take on, as it were, a life of their own. Reclaiming the critical impetus within depth psychology and psychoanalysis is needed to recover other concepts of collective consciousness and other selves, excluded from the international. This necessitates disrupting the politics of knowing or the fantasy structures that underpin the entitlement of claiming to know the other that informs international relations theory. In doing so, psychoanalysis as a tool of social and political criticism can recover its own radical politics of unknowing and dissent. As Samuels argues, the pervasive presence of doubt, even 'radical doubt', as a feature of modern critical reason points us to a 'psychology of not knowing, of unknowing, of interpretation and reinterpretation'.[15] Essential to such a task is the recognition that a psychology of politics needs to include a self-critical dimension, if the politics of psychology are to be taken seriously.

In writing about the dissenting possibilities of psychoanalysis, Nandy explores how disciplinary politics and certain schools of thought have compromised the Freudian analytic attitude, radical in its inception. Freudian psychoanalysis in its various disciplinary manifestations, and the dissenting Freudian 'analytic attitude', has in effect been truncated and reinscribed as conformity. As a critic of western modernity, Nandy locates this issue firmly within modernity. In critiquing psychoanalysis' own fantasies of mastery, Nandy builds a case against this style of demystification. For, as he warns, to assume that in rupturing and demystifying manifest reality one constructs a new reality closer to the truth, and that this is the primary goal of psychoanalysis, is a dangerous seduction. This conformity takes effect because these 'stalwarts who contributed to the Enlightenment vision, tended to nurture one particular kind of critical attitude'.[16] Privileging one kind of critical attitude, namely the promise of demystification as a mastery of one's reality, is therefore problematic. That historically the application of this critical attitude has been used in service of ideologies of entitlement has been successfully demonstrated by postcolonial scholarship. In the case of British colonialism, the Indian 'civilizing mission' was heavily dependent on the archetype of an idealised western civilised self, that was central to a colonialist mindset. It was also central in providing a trope through which the other could identify, aspire and perform selfhood in accord with being an entitled subject. For theorists like Nandy, the use of psychoanalysis theory as a tool of demystification for mastery leads to the establishment of a second order reality specific to the postcolony. This provides the conditions for a new set of certitudes, through which 'a new society, a new social vision and even a new human personality could be built based on this new hermeneutics'.[17] Simply uncovering the certitudes that underpin collective consciousness and collective fantasies of entitlement does not take us far enough. What is needed is an element of self-destruction and self-critique within this politics of unknowing.

In its current manifestation these certitudes are now expressed through a global culture of commonsense that prevails, and as 'status quo' within international politics. Again the danger here is that demystification as an end point can justify ideologies of entitlement and in the process maintain existing 'self and other' relations. Clearly a more radical and dissenting analytical attitude is needed if we are to seriously engage with the politics of psychology and the psychology of politics. The dialogue and intellectual alliance between international relations and psychoanalysis would then take a distinctive turn. Here we might argue that psychoanalysis and its potentials for 'knowing' and 'unknowing' move us into a radically disruptive but also therapeutic register. This therapeutic register provides us with the analytical space to recover alternatives, including alternative understandings of the self and other relationship. These critical interventions, mindful of the politics of demystification, also lead to a recovery of alternatives not only for the self, but always and necessarily in tandem with recognition of our own radical alterity and otherness. This reflexivity and awareness of otherness (including our own radical otherness) can lead to a regeneration of the self–other relationship. In recognising that our discourses of 'knowing the other', and our discourses of entitlement are as precarious as claiming to 'know the self', moves us into very different intellectual terrain. More importantly, it leads to a new understanding of politics itself, including the conceptual and psychological spaces of the international. As Nandy reminds us, '...openness to voices, familiar or strange, may well have to be the first criterion of the shared self which transcends nation-states, communities, perhaps even cultures themselves'.[18] In addressing politics and the politics of selfhood as an ontological condition, theorising possible and retrievable selves becomes essential to establishing alternative political realities. This may need to begin with recognising the inadequacy of our theoretical models that fail to embrace the neglected shadow self of international relations.

Postscript

In writing this chapter in memory of my friend and colleague Devika Goonewardene, I have been thinking about the importance ideas and knowledge hold for our own representations of self. Ideas and knowledge become more than just intellectual pursuits, courses taught at university, degrees or writing projects. They can be a kind of performative armour intimately connected to how we see ourselves, how we want ourselves to be and what we allow others to see of us. Devika was someone who in many ways defined herself and understood herself through her intellectual interests and research. When she spoke of postcolonial identities and South Asian politics, of other selves of cultures and communities, she would come alive in a fresh way. It was as if the fragments of her identity would momentarily take shape within a singular focus. I always felt that in those moments she was speaking of herself. The personal was necessarily political. Energised and transformed from her usual guarded self, she found another voice. When she was defending why the relationship between self and other was the foundation for understanding the international, she was revealing something of herself. The 'international' did not belong 'out there', it was within, carried with our partitioned selves.

In other moments I was privy to a more vulnerable private self, always lingering close to the surface. There were talks of working late into the night, Devika coy in revealing the full extent of her discipline and dedication to her studies. Talks littered with romantic escapist fantasies of Bollywood heroes rescuing us from libraries. These secret revelations were fleeting interruptions to an otherwise consistent intensity. The joy these conversations about film would elicit was matched by her belief in the transformative powers of knowledge. This was driven by a fascination with the politics of knowledge and its ethical potentialities. Different knowledges could provide us with different ways of seeing the world. Devika was a serious and measured thinker whose intellectual journeys remain unknown. It is the proud and courageous woman that memory preserves in the present.

Notes

1 Michael Cox, (2002) 'Paradigm Shifts and 9/11: International Relations and the Twin Towers', *Security Dialogue,* 33(2).
2 See for instance Rose McDermott, (2004) *Political Psychology in International Relations,* Michigan, University of Michigan. Jonathan Mercer, (2005) 'Rationality and Psychology in International Politics', *International Organization,* 59(1): 77–106. Alexander Wendt, (1999) *Social Theory of International Politics,* New York, Cambridge University Press.
3 See Sigmund Freud, (1932) *Why War?* Standard Edition, 22: 1997–2215.
4 These include: Alexander Wendt, (1999) *Social Theory of International Politics,* New York, Cambridge University Press. Christine Sylvester, (1994) *Feminist Theory and International Relations in a Postmodern Era,* New York, Cambridge University Press. Christine Sylvester, (2002) *Feminist International Relations: An Unfinished Journey,* New York, Cambridge University Press. Geeta Chowdhry and Sheila Nair, (2002) *Power, Postcolonialism and International Relations: Reading Race, Gender and Class,* London, Routledge. Phillip Darby ed., (1997) *At the Edge of International Relations: Postcolonialism, Gender and Dependency,* London: Continuum.
5 See Erik H. Erikson, (1969) *Gandhi's Truth: On the Origins of Militant Nonviolence,* New York: W.W. Norton.
6 Mira Sucharov, (2005) *The International Self: Psychoanalysis and the Search for Israeli–Palestinian Peace,* Albany: State University of New York Press.
7 Paul Virilio and Sylvere Lotringer, ([1983]2008) *Pure War,* Los Angeles, Semiotext(e).
8 P.E. Tetlock, C. McGuire, & P.G. Mitchell, (1991) 'Psychological Perspectives on Nuclear Deterrence', *Annual Review of Psychology,* 42, 239–276. Palo Alto: Annual Reviews.
9 Ashis Nandy, (2002) *Time Warps: Silent and Evasive Pasts in Indian Politics and Religion,* New Brunswick: Rutgers University Press.
10 Judith Butler, (2009) *Frames of War: When Is Life Grievable?* London, Verso: p.1.
11 Judith Butler, (2004) *Precarious Life: The Powers of Mourning and Violence,* London, Verso: p.26.
12 Andrew Samuels, (1993) *The Political Psyche,* London, Routledge.
13 Andrew Samuels, (1993) *The Political Psyche,* London, Routledge: p.64.
14 Ashis Nandy, (2003) 'Unclaimed Baggage', http://www.littlemag.com/looking/ashisnandy.html. 4(5&6): p.2.
15 Andrew Samuels, (1993) *The Political Psyche,* London, Routledge: p.8.
16 Ashis Nandy, (2005)'Freud Modernity and Postcolonial Violence: Analytic dissent and the boundaries of Self', *The Little Magazine,* Vol. IV (5&6): p.1.
17 Ashis Nandy, (2005) 'Freud Modernity and Postcolonial Violence: Analytic dissent and the boundaries of Self', *The Little Magazine,* Vol. IV (5&6): p.1.
18 Ashis Nandy, (2004) *Bonfire of the Creeds: The Essential Ashis Nandy,* Delhi: Oxford University Press: p.481.

9

SEA LEVEL

Towards a poetic geography

Paul Carter

To write in the wake of one who died young is to imagine the world she might have inhabited. It is to develop her first seedling insights on her behalf, to assist them to find their fertile landing places. By a bitter paradox, in which the Romantics discovered a poetic wisdom preceding exhaustive scholarship, the one who dies young remains closer to the essential situation than those, more learned, who settle for the minor coastal solace of amending scholarship. The authorities on which she relied for her first sailings into the deep come after her; or, in relation to her idealism, which compelled her to question what had been given, the entrenched injustices which, in the privilege of her decade, she could imagine shifting, they were, and remain, consciously landbound, their authority vested in the disappointment of having lived too long. But she, by virtue of her advance mortality, plunged into the deep. We know this because, despite all her accomplishments, the echo of her voice does not come back – to answer her critics, to supply better maps, to admonish our purblindness. Or, to put it another way, the premature loss of a scholar forces scholarship to confront the mortality of its own interests. It asks us to confront the unnameable at the heart of the project of mapping the unknown (determining the names of its parts).

In this context, and particularly in the context of rethinking the foundations of international relations, the oceanic figure is far from gratuitous. For, in a sense, the oceanic is the repressed term in orthodox discourses about the conditions for the adjustment of inequalities between nations in their access to the world's resources. The ocean signifies the dissolution of identity, the suspension of certainties – and perhaps the limits of a certain kind of logic, one that Foucault indicated when he suggested, in *Madness and Civilisation,* that western definitions of knowledge have a distinctly *landed* quality.[1] By the same token, the ocean obviously connects, supplying the one geographical universal – the sea level –

that no amount of territorial (or engineering or militaristic) brinkmanship can eliminate. At the same time, to acknowledge this bias is not to correct it. On the contrary, it may perpetuate the habit dry or landed thinking has of treating the landless portions of the globe as deficient in reason.[2] It is a commonplace that emancipated colonies become neo-colonialist: a comparable phenomenon can afflict the new oceanic scholarship, for of what use will it be to rehabilitate oceanic cultures, to understand ways in which seascapes have been inscribed with memory, myth and language,[3] if the consequence is to assimilate them to terrestrial conceptions of these terms?

It is essential to right the lean of western scholarship, 'to recognise that the seas are spaces on which history has been enacted: places where conflict, possession and dispossession, exile and enforced migration has occurred … to recognise the sea as a contact zone, a place of exchange',[4] but to bring about recognition means something more than normalising oceanic relations, assimilating them to habits of legally-adjusted association suited to social life on land. Thomas de Quincey made a nice point about the ocean when he imagined writing its history: in comparison with writing a history of England, it would, he said, be like trying to compass infinity, a task, he implied, more suited to poets than historians. In the wake of these reflections, the object of this essay is to suggest that a valuable insight into the preconditions of a new international order predicated on the ontological priority and epistemological significance of the oceans is afforded by what the Neapolitan philosopher, Giambattista Vico, called poetic geography – broadly, the poetic logic informing the invention of place names that have served historically to bring other places into the orbit of imperial discourse and power. The analogical application of names is a heuristic device for opening up new regions; it can be, in fact, a device for marking presently unconfirmed connections, and in this context adumbrate an open figure, rather than a closed territory.[5] At the very least, poetic place-naming practices grapple with the problem of containing infinity in the absence of the power to legislate for it.

To adapt these general propositions to the present theme, the renegotiation of the conceptual foundations of past and present dialogues between Indian and Australian world views and senses of place, let me begin with a case of inner colonisation in which a new Australia was imagined on the analogy of an ideally improved Bengal – a case where, in the first instance, the proposed resemblance was argued on poetic grounds. For, simply looking at the names Australia and India, there is prima facie a case for arguing that the two countries are, if nothing else, *stylistically* related, the name given to the austral continent having apparently been influenced by the precedent of the Anglo name for Bharat: India. If this formal (and phonic) analogy is valid, it no doubt embodied and exploited a geo-political ambition focused on the importance of maintaining maritime supremacy across the oceans between Bengal and Australia's north-west coasts. But there is no need to speculate about this as in *The Friend of Australia*, a little known (but substantial) publication dating from 1827, an ex-British army officer, T.J. Maslen, who had served in India, visualised exactly this imperial desideratum. Maslen had never visited Australia but this did not inhibit him from printing in his book a remarkable cartographical fantasy, or 'Sketch of the Coasts of Australia and of the supposed Entrance of The Great River', in which he denominated the country north of the river (roughly the present Northern Territory) 'Australindia'. The 'Great River of the Desired Blessing', as Maslen christened it, appeared to flow purposefully from the centre of the country towards an outlet somewhere near the present town of Broome, a disembogement devoutly to be wished because it was located as near as could be *opposite* the delta of the Ganges and its capital Kolkota (Calcutta): not literally but geo-figuratively opposite, as the imagined mirroring of the mighty Ganges in Australia provided a new military and commercial region, a rationale for patrolling the otherwise directionless oceanic flats to the south of the great East Indies trade routes.

In poetic logic the right naming of things is directly associated with the law governing them: 'In Roman law *nomen* signifies right. Similarly, in Greek *nomos* signifies law, and from *nomos* comes *nomisma*, money, as Aristotle notes.'[6] Applied to geographical entities at least, poetic logic and the logic of strict 'sequential continuity' may be one and the same thing. Entities such as India, Indonesia and Australia share 'a relationship of adjacency' that is prior to any imperial line of communication that might be drawn through them. This is not to say that the form of the names may not be imperial: the original of names like Australia is the Roman imperial form found, for example, in Arabia. Apparently, the suffix '-ia', meaning 'state of' comes from the Greek; in any case it is absorbed into English and normalised as the way of turning a word stem into the name of a country. However, such formal etymologies do not get us very far; that is, simply to trace back the form to a putative origin is not to penetrate its poetic character, the semantic constellation that generates it. It may be debatable how far a recovery of the poetic logic of names such as India and Australia can go – at least as the basis of a persuasive critique of present conceptualisations of international relations – but any value it has will clearly depend in the first instance on grasping what the name properly named. Without an idea of what we are referring to, a discussion of the law proper to its legislation is premature.

The first, thought-provoking observation is that the names in question originate in efforts to characterise open geographical figures rather than closed ones. The Greek India, referring to Indus region, may have been applied by the British (from the mid-17th century) to parts or all of the terra firma 'subcontinent', but it primarily refers to a flowing water body. The name of Australia may have been confirmed as the name of a continentally-large island (as Australians paradoxically like to imagine where they live)[7] when its circumnavigator, Matthew Flinders, adopted the name in his *Voyage to Terra Australis*; however, when Alexander Dalrymple used the term in *An Historical Collection of Voyages and Discoveries in the South Pacific Ocean*, published in 1771, he referred to the entire South Pacific region. Such names regionalised a multitude of geographical objects, locating them within an oceanic matrix, a semantic tendency more vividly illustrated by the term

The term Indonesia was first used in 1850 by the British anthropologist J.R. Logan to designate islands called the 'Indian Archipelago' by other Western writers.[8] The term Indonesia is a good example of poetic geography; formed, one supposes, by analogy with Australia, it is also a clever hybrid of India and Asia, mediated through the Greek word for island ('nesos'): Polynesia, Micronesia, etc., utilise the same regionalising technique.[9] The corollary of respecting the poetic geography implied by such terms is that places or regions named after them will also be open, flowing and interconnected, a suggestion strikingly illustrated by Maslen's map, where, in effect, the Australian land mass is turned inside out, and rendered as a kind of gigantic atoll directly connected to, and irrigated by, the sea.

Nowhere is the nexus between *nomen*, *nomos* and *nomisma* more obvious than in the East Indies, a region synonymous in Europe with the spice trade.[10] Early Portuguese charts of the East Indies are interesting in this regard because they preserve the idea of the open figure, representing an imperial presence and interest that was commercial rather than territorial. In the most elaborate and delicious chart of all, Lope Homem's Atlas of 1519, now in the Bibliothèque Nationale in Paris, where it is known as the 'Miller Atlas',[11] the pelagic gaps in the approximately known geography of the East Indies are filled with jewel-like shoals of islands that for all the world resemble polychromatic doubloons and other tokens of exchange and wealth. The map historian Christian Jacob detects a logical constraint behind this style of visualisation. 'For lack of being named – indeed nameable – these islands (which for the most part appear on a map for the first and last time) find their identity only in their colour.'[12] It is a nice thought that the aspect of maps that resists imperial creep – the territorial homogenisation of the globe – survives in the differential colouring of the surface. However, the important point in the present context is that the unnameable do not necessarily lie outside the law; they are simply subject to a different poetic (and commercial) logic, one that desires to connect (to multiply the opportunities for connection) rather than to surround and bound.

More telling, though, in the context of renegotiating land–sea relations – and, through the reclamation of the porous boundary, a new imagination of international relations – is the way that charts coming out of the Manueline cartographical schools treat coastlines as tooth-like sequences of openings that correspond to river mouths, passages, ports and other opportunities for interconnection. In terms of the Platonic myth about Eros (he mingles the characteristics of Lack (Penia) and Plenty (Poros)), these discontinuous figures, amoebic, or diatomic, suspended between the insular and the peninsular, represent an erotic geography. Composed of apertures or discontinuous capes, they are figures of porosity. They maximise the opportunities for trade, associating this with the lack of a distinct form of their own. Constitutionally open, ready to be entered, they are not islands at all but parts of a larger mart, elements of an archipelago that is many-mouthed, hungry to suck in and to spit out, a gigantic multiple orifice: the orient as osculation. This conception myth finds support in the *Suma Oriental* of Tomé Pires, whose account of Malacca is roughly contemporary with the production of the Miller Atlas. 'Men cannot estimate the worth of Malacca, on account of its greatness and profit. Malacca is a city that was made for merchandise, fitter than any other in the world.' As the particular location of geography's open mouth, Malacca *personifies* the erotic projection of the Miller Atlas: 'Malacca is surrounded and lies in the middle, and the trade and commerce between the different nations for a thousand leagues on every hand must come to Malacca.'[13]

In other words, from an erotic and commercial point of view, the interest of Malacca resides in the *inter esse*, in the multiplication of opportunities for passage, for meeting, exchange and profit. This inclination to disclosure or risk-taking is constantly susceptible to militaristic overthrow or imperialistic centralisation. According to a recent account, 'despite its apparent aim of disclosure, the *Atlas Miller* hides more than it reveals'.[14] The proposition is that the Atlas was 'an instrument of geographic and geopolitical counter-information ... the graphic expression of the Portuguese strategic vision of the globe intended to counter the vision upheld by Castile'. The argument is that 'the peculiar "neo-Ptolemaic" concept it features, with the sea as *stagnon* (the oceans surrounded by land, the New World as a continent, the mythical Austral Land, etc.), suited the Portuguese in c. 1519 because it suggested that it was not possible to sail westwards across to the other side of the planet, i.e. to do what was attempted first by Columbus and subsequently achieved by Ferdinand Magellan.'[15] In this case, the jewel-like isles of plenty represent a regional economy of concrete situations and transactions that not only operates at a different geographical scale but depends for its stability on a different reflexive system of adjusting differences, one in which the law is locally and contextually adjudicated.

Evidently the sea is, geo-politically speaking, as likely to be territorialised as the land. As a conceptually opaque geographical term like Oceania suggests, the dry thinking of normative territorialising cultures strains to imagine an association of island societies except as a kind of archipelagic Atlantis sinking under the waves. As regards the politics of representation, what psychologist J.J. Gibson says about perception also applies environmentally: all the action is at the surface, meaning in a geographical context, the coast. In the context of international relations predicated on the integrity of the nation state, a recognition that the coast might be constitutionally permeable is already something. For one thing it brings into play an entirely new natural as well as human region: the tidal environment inhabited by the Yawuru, for example, who occupy the 'sea country' zealously imagined by Maslen as the mouth of a second Ganges, is a region where, in fact, 'At times the sea itself is dry as the tide recedes almost to the horizon.'[16] Perhaps not surprisingly customary law, the protocols governing access to resources and their maintenance, is also amphibious: 'Use of the land is not distinct from use of the sea: in other words Yawuru people hunt and forage in the sea and the assertion of rights in the sea is essentially the same as assertion of rights in the land.'[17] To be clear, this is not a claim of extended sovereignty, comparable perhaps to the intention of the Australian Federal government's recent proposal to create 'the world's largest network of marine parks'. It implies instead an amplified sociability where 'gaining rights in land and sea' entails a diplomatic 'flexibility' that is not ancillary to senses of belonging but, in effect, constitutes 'the system'.[18]

It is interesting that India is described as a 'subcontinent', as if it were a kind of subaltern continent. Imperial qua administrative geography finds it hard to conceptualise a promontory, a vast angular deviation that occupies an ambiguous zone between Asiatic highland and landless oceanic extension. It cannot be a continent because it cannot be isolated and contained. India resists what might be called cartographic *mediterreanismo*, the habit of presenting the oceans of the world as contained by land – a continuous coastline here and there growing promontories and intermittently incubating little theatres of turbulence. It may be noted that geo-political *mediterreanismo* is quite consistent with the existence of an island continent like Australia, which is after all the empirical residue of the old land of the not yet known (*terra nondum cognitorum*), a hearsay amalgam of Antarctica and other antipodean outcrops. And, as Maslen's wish-fulfilment map reminds us, Australia is quite capable of breeding its own inland seas.

These inversions of environmental hierarchy reflect deeply embedded habits of dry or land oriented thinking that have analogies in the way the legislation of the *nomos* is conceived. In southern (south of the Alps) cultural studies, *mediterreanismo* refers to the revival of the environmental determinist idea (now poetically interpreted) that a relationship exists between the character of the Mediterranean's founding cultures and their geography. In *L'Arcipelago*, for example, Massimo Cacciari argues that Athenian democracy was the political expression of the archipelagic distribution of Athens's allies (and enemies) in the wake of the Persian War. Democracy's polyvocal approach to resolution conflict is a translation to the agora of the arrangement of, say, the Cyclades. In a sense Greece works as the home of democracy because of the number of its promontories and its mountainous internal self-division. Once again, the elephantine India comes off second best, while slovenly Australia, far too large to be another Sicily, simply does what it can to market its surf.

At issue here is not simply the subordination of the ocean to landbound interests but the challenge of imagining the governance of the world differently. The geographical habit of presenting the oceans of the world as a blue void disguises the fact that they consist of interflowing internal regions, which not only have a determining impact on the global climate but also leave their trace in the distribution, migrations and inter-relationship of human and non-human populations. The Yolngu people in Arnhem Land understand that the vitality of places resides in their humid potential to interconnect, in their possessing a track that embodies their vitality, so that places come alive through the spirit that moves across and through them. 'The two names for the open sea are the names of multiple ancestral spirits that flow along the coast to join with the waters of the open sea.' The Manybuynga and Rulyapa currents are forms of connectivity, not so much in between places as stretches of vitality. They cannot be defined in terms of hard-and-fast boundaries; they cross salt- and fresh-water edges, walls with interiors like snakes. Moving inside themselves, the currents are the jointure of the sea, the darker colour suggesting muscular depth. To recognise Yolngu understandings of the sea is to find the Australian government's maritime park network proposal culturally as well as ecologically dubious. The corollary seems obvious: 'to recognise that the seas are spaces on which history has been enacted: places where conflict, possession and dispossession, exile and enforced migration has occurred ... to recognise the sea as a contact zone, a place of exchange.'[19]

But how is this to be done? One approach – already hinted at in the allusions to Yawuru and Yolngu cultures – is to regionalise 'sea country' and to embrace the pluralisation of its understanding. It is (once again) to recruit non-capitalistic social, economic and environmental practices that emerge from concrete situations to the task of detoxifying western (democratic) capitalism, whose out-of-control Eros threatens to destroy the very thing it loves. Certainly, locally-attached or regionally-distinct moiety-based cultures, which define social identity dialectically through the other, seem coastal in constitution: for them it is coasts all the way down; and where empires erect walls – some as mighty as entire continents – they proliferate contact zones. In her book about the Vezo, a group of people who live on the western coast of Madagascar, R. Astuti states that being Vezo is the outcome of an activity (not an independent, timeless state of being): 'Vezo-ness is intermittent rather than continuous. It "happens" in a succession of minute incidents – eating fish, tricking Spanish mackerel into biting the line, sailing in a strong wind.'[20] Vezo-ness is bound to the present because only in the present can it be performed – 'and performed it must be in order for people to "be" Vezo.'[21] As for learning, it does not occur via a plodding progress over well-trodden ground: it is conceived 'as a sharp transition (a "jump" rather than a process) from a state of not-yet-knowing to a state of full knowledge'.[22] Astuti argues that the capacity to live with the unpredictability of the sea (which, interestingly, 'is sometimes referred to as a *vazaha*, white man; this is because the sea is not only the Vezo's boss (*patron*), but is also, as whites are, quick-tempered and violent, unpredictable and unreliable')[23] embodies a performative conception of self-identification and social identity practically as well as metaphorically derived from their transformation of the ocean-edge into a zone of exchange, the margin into the realm of blue nativeness.

When the Sakalava kings came to the western regions of Madagascar, the Vezo say that they fled – avoided becoming attached. The Vezo's flight asserted an 'alternative mode of defining identity, a mode in which people "are" what they do in the present rather than being determined by their own and someone else's "history"'.[24] The name 'Vezo' means 'paddle': 'people who struggle with the sea and live on the coast'.[25] The Vezo never '"come to have the land in themselves" ... when they move, they do not take their old ways with them'.[26]

A similar philosophy of living in the present influences the Vezo notion of kinship (*filongoa*) which 'preserves and enhances the transparency (the lack of residues from the past) of the Vezo person, who knows and is made aware of who and what she is through what she does contextually in the present'.[27] Relatedness is created in the present, a belief that means in effect that the social grammar of everyday life is composed entirely of accidence. As for the past, it is not remembered genealogically but archipelagically, 'as the source of many alternative histories (paths of ascendancy) through which people come to be related to one another in the present. In *filongoa*, all these histories are equally important, for they serve to establish to whom one is related, rather than to determine what kind of person one is. The past … does not fix the person into an identity that lasts through time; rather, it provides the person with relations that expand and branch out in all directions, and which can all be enacted in different contexts and at different times.'[28]

The story of the Vezo poignantly illustrates an alternative jurisdiction of the sea (and self) that opposes western notions of sovereignty and identity so utterly, symmetrically and at every point as to possess an almost Borgesian or Swiftian quality. The problem with such instances, though, apart from that of intercultural translation in general, is that they resist generalisation. It appears that in legislating for the truly global commons (the oceanic water body), different systems operate at different scales, and it is doubtful whether they are commensurable. Just as the Malaccan trade (and its maps of shoal-like islands) was nested inside the imperial ambitions of Portugal, so the cultural practices of the Vezo exist within a network of state-sanctioned law that is scarcely able to recognise, let alone capture, their way of managing things. In Moore's phrase, they represent a 'semi-autonomous social field', where social units 'can generate rules and customs internally, but [are also] vulnerable to rules and decisions and other forces emanating from the larger world by which [they are] surrounded'.[29] Applying this concept to a Tamil Nadu case study, where the regional Fisheries Department intervened in a dispute between neighbouring fishing communities, Maarten Bavinck concluded that 'the two legal systems lead a largely separate existence'.[30] While 'Economic concerns, which include notions of ecological harm, play an important role in fishermen regulations', the state 'approaches the disputes which come to its notice mainly from the viewpoint of conflict resolution'.[31]

A poetic geography that sought to combat what Foucault calls the *landed* quality of western knowledge would not look to anthropological counter-examples for inspiration; it would stay within its own discursive terrain, making the case for the critical value of analogical thinking, particularly in the context of narrating international relations in terms of oceanically-mediated interconnections. Elaborating on what Vico meant by *poetic*, Said explains that it is a quality of complementarity where different branches of knowledge co-exist: 'the sinews between different branches bind these branches together despite an appearance of dispersion'. Enlarging on the figure of speech, Said adds that 'a perfect analogy' for this 'relationship of adjacency' is 'the set of relationships obtaining between parts of the human body'.[32] Now consider this figure in the context of speaking of a 'body of water', a geographical entity adumbrated, as we saw, in the name India. A poetic geography of the sea would replace the imperial image of an ocean whose model is the Pacific, nominally liberated of obstacles to passage and rendered level even in advance of its navigation, with one conceived in terms of adjacencies.

Without straining the parallel too far, the focus would be on the jointure of the sea rather than its skeletal apparatus of scattered islands and reefs. Maurice Merleau-Ponty frequently used a bodily image to explain the nature of his philosophical interrogation. He compared his focus of interest to the joints in the body. 'The joints of our bodies, as distinguished from the bones, are themselves hollows of a specific kind.' That is, they operate in, they articulate, the spaces between substances (bones): focusing on these, 'philosophy seeks to allow the way the world works to display itself by first subtracting from it the stuff of which it is made'.[33] The hydrological (and rhetorical) term anastomosis is used to describe the occasional, lacework distributary water systems of the Australian interior, but in another guise it describes the sort of knowledge associated with ships, where it is impossible to say whether the ship is a pool or a channel, for it is, in reality, a lake or reflective space that moves and a channel (the course it sets) that is where it always is. In a similar spirit islands, the sea's other, wear a double aspect. The association of island with isolation is well known, but etymologists tell us that the Greek term for island (*nesos*) comes from an Indo-European root referring to that which navigates. The Croat *otok* (island) comes from a root meaning to flow, to escape; the term *ostrvo* ('more Serb than Croat') comes from a word meaning 'current'.[34] Islands are not only a reason to move but themselves move. To be truly among islands is not to arrive anywhere; it is to experience an absolute perspectivism where the islands slide past one another and everything is subject to parallax except for the steersman.

Such Odyssean scenarios may sound like the stuff of literature. In fact, they render concrete, or *poetical*, a way of formulating relationships that is distinctively unlanded. It is sobering to find that Antony Anghie's recent *Imperialism, Sovereignty and the Making of International Law* unfolds its argument that colonialism was central to the constitution of international law and sovereignty doctrine without a single page of discussion of sea rights or maritime law. Perhaps this is in deference to Grotius's argument in *Mare liberum* that the sea cannot become private property, 'because nature not only allows but enjoins its common use'.[35] However, this argument is clearly self-interested. Anghie argues that the colonial focus of international law is clear in the distinction it makes between 'the civilized and the uncivilized'.[36] It is the same distinction that Grotius makes. Quoting Johannes Faber, he explains that the sea 'remains in the primitive condition where all things were common. If it were otherwise there would be no difference between the things which are "common to all", and those which are strictly termed "public"; no difference, that is, between the sea and a river. A nation can take possession of a river, as it is inclosed within their boundaries, with the sea, they cannot do so.'[37] Interestingly, in Grotius's scheme, the coast occupies an ambiguous legal position. While the shore can be occupied, the offing cannot 'because the sea, except for a very restricted space, can neither easily be built upon, nor inclosed'.[38]

In short, if the sea *could* be enclosed, it *would* be enclosed. The only reason for keeping it open is to facilitate commercial expansion, a development that in the modern period always carries with it a colonising inflection; after all to trade is to connect and what society can develop its full potential in isolation? Hence William Strachey's defence of English activities in North America – 'the Law of Nations ... admits yt lawfull, to trade with any manner of people ... the Salvages themselves may not impugne, or forbid the same in respect of Common fellowship and Community betwixt man and man'.[39] But the aim is never to cultivate a commercial cosmopolitanism of the kind Pires found at Malacca. The goal is pelagic protectionism underwritten by naval supremacy. In the late eighteenth century British naval dominance meant that it could fantasise the sea as a wooden gang plank extending the girth of the globe. The downside of this perilous dream was a growing need to manage risk, from which emerges the modern nation state's obsession with security – a symptom of the insecurity it visits on itself because of its extra-territorial ambitions (and dependency). In the contemporary period, concerns about environmental security display the same neurotic symptoms – as Simon Dalby points out, environmental security debates are embedded within 'larger discursive economies where some identities have more value than others'.[40] This echoes Anghie's argument; in this scenario the paddle psyche of the Vezo would receive short shrift. As Dalby says, the sharpness of real and potential conflicts over resources – and the habit of government agencies of responding to these in terms of conflict resolution and risk minimisation – depends on forgetting the prior history of imperial resource capture that precipitates them – 'the dominant development and security narratives are premised on geopolitical specifications that obscure histories of ecology and resource appropriation'.[41] Among the most obscured of those histories are those to do with the contact zone, or place of exchange, known as the sea.

A revisionist poetic geography designed to throw light on the character of a maritime law that resisted enclosure might begin by questioning the efficacy of Cacciari's geographical figure of speech. After all, few archipelagos conform to the distribution of islands across the Aegean Sea. It is debatable, in fact, that the various island chains and groupings associated with the vicissitudes of Athens' naval rise and fall are an archipelago in any strong sense of the term. Enclosed by the coastlines of the Mediterranean, they are at the very least a relatively passive flock[42] with little or no collective political identity. It is telling in this regard that a *mediterreanista* like Cassano suggests that, prior to the Mediterranean, the Greek sea was the Aegean, a microcosm of the Mediterranean as a whole, and he derives the name from Aegeus (or 'out of the earth').[43] The Greek archipelago is conceived as a fragmentation, or Orphic dismemberment, of the three continents that contain it. Although in relation to the continental sensibility the Greek temperament is open, dialectical, pluralistic and in a state of becoming, this does not mean a genuinely maritime or oceanic culture. In contrast with the limited liberation of passage afforded by the *pontos*, the network of exchanges that the sea enforces but the adjacent lands contain and limit, the ocean beyond the Pillars of Hercules remains limitless.

Hölderlin's heroic response to this conceptual and imaginative enclosure is to revive Poseidon's claim to sovereignty over the Mediterranean. The ousted co-ruler of Athens identifies, according to Hölderlin, with the experience of Athenian exile. In contrast with the landed law of Pallas Athene, Poseidon rules over change; his Aegean scattered with islands is what remains of vanquished Atlantis. In Hölderlin's myth, Poseidon is geography as poetry. 'Immortal, even though not now celebrated by Greek song,' he models the poetic adventure; 'out of your waves with music infuse my soul, that over your waters fearlessly active my mind, like the swimmer, may practise the quickening joy of the strong, and learn the divine language of Chance and Becoming'.[44] This is a far cry from Vezo dexterity and its channelling of Proteus offers little guidance to the ordinary archipelago dweller – the outer archipelago fishermen and inner archipelago farmers of south-west Finland, for example. Here, we are told, 'communication defines the archipelago' and a word even exists to describe 'an area with many archipelagos'! What would this be unless a fractal scaling up and down of regions that resisted the top-down containment of the other practised by empires? Apropos of empires, the same study explains that for these Finns 'close connection to the sea is the minimum condition of an archipelago'. As one resident explains, 'I know myself that you must have the feeling that you can take a rowboat and row even to China from your own seashore.'[45]

This Columbus reverie brings us poetically (and geographically) back to the East Indies, to an archipelago that exhibits different physical, cultural – and even logical – features from anything to be found in the home territories of western democracy, property-based law and the geopolitical normalisation of imperialism. Indonesia – which, in its 1850 formulation, also included the Philippines – is obviously an area of archipelagos. It is neither a geometrically unified arrangement of islands (like the Cyclades) nor a trailing away into isolation of formerly related communities (like the Sporades – where, remote from society, the poet Shelley fancied he could establish a utopia for two). It is, instead, a region that displays the unusual quality of being innumerable.[46] There is no end of the connections that can be made, of the permutations of passages imaginable between the endlessly appearing islands. From the point of view of the Romantic poet bravely swimming out into the midst of these, it is a formula for despair; however, from the point of view of the multiplicity of singularities (here Jean-Luc Nancy's attempt to express the character of a post-communitarian community also applies to the regionality of the islands in the archipelago), the fact that the possible communication in the system always exceeds what can be actualised offers a political and economic principle of growth (becoming, change) that does not lead to colonisation, subordination and enclosure.

A different political logic is at work here. Archipelago consciousness is not the product of environmental determinism; it reflects a different way of imagining geopolitical reality, one that factors in the sea or, rather, predicates the negotiation of just exchange rates between societies and nations on the archipelagic character of the shared commons. Instances of what might be called *malayalismo*[47] in the organisation of relationships may come from different traditions. Ian Keen, for example, discusses 'many religious beliefs and practices [involving] supra-local relations and cooperation' in Aboriginal Australia that offer examples of 'the way in which more or less local modes of social relationships and ways of doing things depended on regional interconnections'.[48] In this 'regional system' Australia is an archipelago of inter-related (inter-regional) practices; when early white explorers fantasised a lost Malay people marooned in the heart of Australia, they overlooked the Indigenous malayalismo all around them! At issue here (not least from an administrative point of view) is the theory and practice of division. The origins of the word tide go back to Indo-European terms referring to divisions of time; cuts in time come to be applied to cuts in people and land, Sanskrit *dati* being connected to the Greek *demos*. In this case, while the European Cartesians invested in hard and fast divisions, Aboriginal peoples like the Yawuru, the Yolngu and many others opted to be tidal people, understanding the regular fluctuations in time and space as an analogue of human vitality.

Recessive lines of thought within the European intellectual tradition prove that similar topologies of people and place were imaginable even in the Mediterranean. The great cosmographer of the Republic of Venice, Vincenzo Coronelli, proposed organising his *Atlante Veneto* like an archipelago, the history, economy, politics and culture of the Venetians being found in the narration of the network, the rules of inter-island navigation. Coronelli's contemporary, the Venetian writer on art, Marco Boschini, similarly conceived his account of Venetian painters as the chart of a voyage (*La carta del navegar pittoresco*). In fact, the history of the Lagoon, and more broadly of Venice, offers a remarkable example of a culture developed around non-linear modes of organisation and communication. The anastomosing character of the rivers of the Paduan pianura, the meandering distributary systems of the Lagoon, and their commercial corollary, the proud boast that Venice was 'everywhere a port', represent a remarkable counterpoint, and alternative, to the landed Cartesian logic that has driven processes of territorialisation and colonisation elsewhere within and outside Europe.[49] At the same time, it is intriguing (and symptomatic of land-focused, territorialist values) that Portuguese and Spanish navigators coasting South America and the East Indies habitually referred to the coastal pile villages encountered as 'little Venices',[50] as if, even within Europe, Venice was considered a type of the anomalous, the primitive and the tidally unstable.

Can one build on these shifting foundations a different approach to international relations? What resources exist within the poetic logic of other traditions and within the counter or recessive traditions of western thought to design a regional system of legal relations that relocates the negotiation of interests in the communications between peoples who recognise they share a commons? One thing is clear: a discourse that took the sea level seriously, as an environmental contract to co-exist rather than contain, would do away with the fear tactics of nation apologists, whose rhetoric conjures up a sea imagined as an abyss dotted with shipwrecks. It would replace the reasoning that 'perpetuates the patterns of development thinking and the geo-political assumptions of separate competing polities that are the cause of so much difficulty in the first place',[51] with an environmental (or, perhaps more precisely, archipelagic) understanding of human relations, non-human relations (and the inter-relationship between these) more adequate to the anthropocene epoch. The term 'anthropocene', referring to the idea that humans have achieved a power over nature that renders humanity something like a geological force, is adapted by Dipesh Chakrabarty to advocate a new historical consciousness. He points out that the age-old identification of 'History' with progress towards human emancipation no longer holds: 'whatever the rights we wish to celebrate as our freedom, we cannot afford to destabilise conditions (such as the temperature zone in which the planet exists) that work like boundary parameters of human existence'.[52] The prospect of imminent catastrophe demands we rethink 'the history of the world since the Enlightenment'.[53] Overcoming the false distinction humanists have made between natural history and human history, we need 'a general history of life'.[54]

A regional starting point for such an endeavour might be the language theories of Wilhelm von Humboldt, who located the *beau ideal* of language, the language that most closely resembled the ideal *Ursprache* from which languages evolved, in Java and the differentiated but closely related island cultures in its proximity. In his 1836 publication *The Heterogeneity of Language and its Influence on the Intellectual Development of Mankind*, he supposes that the existence of a Malayan–Polynesian language culture reflects the 'stronger connection' that Malayans have with different cultures, due to the fact that 'They inhabit merely islands and archipelagos, which are spread so far and wide, however, as to furnish irrefutable testimony of their early skills as navigators.' It is this archipelagic distribution that, in his view, stimulates the growth of language. The archipelago is not a stable polyglot set of islands; it is an evolving interlingual discourse, where tongues are constantly morphing, innovating and migrating. The key point here is that languages will be favoured that relate easily, which *travel*. Good travelling means in this context having a formal or intellectual impulse that lends them a sense of direction (or self-regulation) and a freedom to self-modify. Humboldt detected this aptness for growth and development in the sophisticated *accidence* of the Malayan–Polynesian language culture. A capacity to mark speaking positions, to differentiate different temporal states and degrees of probability, is obviously critical to building a consensus when peoples from different places meet and attempt to find common ground. The affixes and suffixes that signified self and other, singular and plural, subject and object, agency, ownership of the past and design on the future were the hinges of sociability that enabled language to create a common place where differences could be discursively inscribed and regulated. Accordingly, Humboldt identified the capability of languages to foster human progress with the flexibility of their inflections, a phenomenon that embodied, he thought, 'a pure principle in lawful freedom'.[55]

What would the 'lawful freedom' found in inflected languages look like transposed to the arena of international relations? It would suggest, for instance, the interpersonal praxis necessary to bring into being Dalby's 'ecological politics', for, while it is true in the anthropocene period that 'under an ecological security approach there is no Other, no hierarchy, no utility for reductionism and little motivation for subjective valuing of danger, time, history and geographic space', the new regional system governed by the setting of relational exchange rates cannot, and should not, eliminate subjectivities. Speaking positions, like birth and death, are constantly coming into view and disappearing. Who, exactly, is going to be the agent of the new *nomos* that reflects the 'historiography demanded by anthropogenic theories of climate change' and locates the 'narrative of capitalism' within 'the history of life on this planet'?

The answer is unlikely to be sociological. Roberts states that 'The constitution of imperial power along naval lines gave special importance to sailors, a class that included many of the truly poor.'[56] However, this has not translated into laws to protect their interests; while sailors make the mobilisation of the state possible, they have been, like slaves, treated as outsiders, accidental in relation to the citizens whom the laws protect. Structurally, in relation to the mindset that identifies sovereignty with enclosure, these seafaring poor are like the pre-Enclosure peasants who derive benefit from the wastelands. They occupy a space and time that precedes the split allegorised in the Atlantis myth, a pre-dialectical realm which is autochthonous not because it is cut off but because its analogue state of flows and catchments resists digitisation. It is attractive to imagine a new hybrid subject who is the beneficiary of, say, Glissant's poetics of relation, where diversity (or creolismo) is at the source of history. In this spirit Ikas and Wagner quote the lines, 'I'm just a red nigger who love the sea,/ I had a sound colonial education,/ I have Dutch, nigger, and English in me,/ And either I'm a nobody, or I'm a nation', suggesting that Derek Walcott's 'semi-grammatical Patois of the Caribbean' enunciates a 'third space', hybrid or *something else besides*'.[57]

It is unclear how this Whitmanesque many-in-one figure of the future attains power. It is more likely that a systems approach will yield influential results. Translated into a dynamic theory of systems, 'the relationship between nature, geopolitics and ourselves' that Dalby explores, finds expression in Michel Serres' notion of syrrhesis – 'Living syrrhesis combines sea and islands. In a completely new sense, the organism is synchronous for meanings and directions, for the continuous and discontinuous, for the local and the global; it combines memory, invariance, plan, message, loss, redundancy, and so forth.'[58] The context of this is a poetic (and scientific) reverie on the nature of information and knowledge: 'From this moment on, I do not need to know who or what the first dispatcher is: whatever it is, it is an island in an ocean of noise, just like me, no matter where I am. It is the genetic information, the molecules or crystals of the world, the interior, as one used to say, or the exterior – none of this is important any longer. A macro-molecule, or any given crystallised solid, or the system of the world, or ultimately what I call "me" –we are all in the same boat.' Serres' new knowledge is anthropocene in the sense that its geography or environment is both figurative and real, both a representation of the world derived from the real and a real-time immersion in it: 'All dispatchers and all receivers are structured similarly. It is no longer incomprehensible that the world is comprehensible. The real produces the conditions and the means for its self-knowledge. The "rational" is a tiny island of reality, a rare summit, exceptional, as miraculous as the complex system that produces it, by a slow conquest of the surf's randomness along the coast. All knowledge is bordered by that about which we have no information.'[59]

My inclination is to say that whatever the content of the new law it will be poetic in form; the idea is that in the new discourse of international relations the two aspects are inseparable. A law of accidents depends for its power on a preparedness in the convening parties to be flexible. It assumes a sensibility attuned to change, a cultural inclination towards decision-making. Decision-making is at the heart of poetry, whose figurative pronouncements demand interpretation because they always embed other possibilities; India lies nested in Australia in more ways than one. The rise of modern technocratic discourse has had the paradoxical effect of making us less, not more, ready for change. Ironically, the identification of progress with a growing control over the future – characterised by the whole anticipatory armature of master planning – undermines our ability to be decisive. It is interesting that when French philosopher Chantal Delsol argues that techno-politics' 'reluctance to make decisions' derives from the absence of a concrete 'situation' – the denser the situation, the more complex it is, and the greater the frequency of decisions – she recalls us to the particular vocation of mythic thought which, as Paul Ricoeur taught, is always a philosophy of occasions. Myth, story as such, is a figurative discourse of densely situated decision-making; without the deviations of choice, narrative would lack its complex labyrinth; freed of error, it would resemble a policy review or any other government document that treats the future as the present extended by planning. To prepare us for a future noticeably different from this, we need to incorporate disaster into the here and now. Following Jung's lead, we need to prepare ourselves for plummeting into the abyss – whereupon we become remarkably like Delsol's 'prudent man' – 'While the competent man finds a solution that he imagines as almost tautologically leaping out of the problem itself, the prudent man proposes an answer that is more like a suggestion and imposes itself only because a decision must be made … It is precisely the uncertainty – the veritable leap into the unknown – of the prudent man that so terrifies our contemporaries.'[60]

Notes

1 Bernhard Klein and Gesa Mackenthun (eds), *Sea Changes: Historicising the Ocean*, Routledge, 2004, 2.
2 On 'dry thinking', see Paul Carter, 'Trockenes Denken: vom Verlust des Wasserbewustseins und von der Poesie des Fluiden' ['Dry Thinking: on praying for rain'], *Lettre International*, Winter 2008, 76–81.
3 See for example, Greg Dening's discussion of Oceania, 'Deep Times, Deep Spaces: Civilising the Sea', in Gesa MacKenthun and Bernhard Klein, *Sea Changes: Historicizing the Ocean*, Routledge: London, 2004, 14.
4 Ruth Balint, 'The Yellow Sea', in David Walker and Agnieszka Sobocinka (ed.), *Australia's Asia: From Yellow Peril to Asian Century*, UWA Publishing, Perth, Western Australia, 2012, 345–366.
5 See Paul Carter, *The Road to Botany Bay*, Minneapolis, University of Minnesota Press, 2010, 328, index entry 'Naming'.
6 Quoting this passage, Edward Said notes that associative logic is poetic rather than strictly etymological: 'it appears to Vico that all knowledge during every historical moment is poetic … [signifying] a relationship of adjacency asserted against logical, sequential continuity' (Edward Said, *Beginnings: Intention and Method*, 351).
7 In 1793, George Shaw and Sir James Smith published *Zoology and Botany of New Holland*, in which they wrote of 'the vast island, or rather continent, of Australia, Australasia or New Holland'.
8 Logan's attempt to regionalise a diversity of localities scaled up an older European tendency: thus, 'most of Indonesia's islands derive their names from European labeling. Early European traders at the port of Samudera named the entire island Sumatra, and visitors to the sultanate of Brunei called the whole island Borneo.'
9 An older geographical neologism, 'Insulindia', yokes Latin forms.
10 Wikipedia states that the name Maluku (Moluccas) is derived from the Arab traders' name for the region.
11 The Atlas consists of 8 maps 41.5 ´ 59 cm and 2 maps, 61 ´ 117 cm on parchment leaves. It was made by Pedro and Jorge Reinel, Lopo Homem (cartographers) and António de Holanda (miniaturist). The geographical areas depicted in the atlas are the North Atlantic Ocean, Northern Europe, the Azores Archipelago, Madagascar, the Indian Ocean, Insulindia, the China Sea, the Moluccas, Brazil, the Atlantic Ocean and the Mediterranean.
12 Christian Jacob, *The Sovereign Map*, 150.
13 Tomé Pires, *The Suma Oriental of Tomé Pires and The Book of Francisco Rodrigues*, Hakluyt Society, London, 1944, 2 vols, vol. 2, 286.
14 Joaquim Ferreira do Amaral, see www.moleiro.com/infoplus.php?p=AM/en
15 Alfredo Pinheiro Marques, see www.moleiro.com/infoplus.php?p=AM/en
16 Patrick Sullivan, 'Salt Water, Fresh Water and Yawuru Social Organization', in *Customary Marine Tenure in Australia*, Oceania Monograph, 48, eds, N. Peterson and B. Rigby, University of Sydney, 1998, 96–108, at 97.
17 Ibid., 97.
18 Ibid., 105.
19 Ruth Balint, 'The Yellow Sea'.
20 Rita Astuti, *People of the Sea*, Cambridge University Press, Cambridge, 1995, 34.
21 Ibid., 34.
22 Ibid., 35.
23 Ibid., 51.
24 Ibid., 75.
25 Ibid., 1.
26 Ibid., 40.
27 Ibid., 104.
28 Ibid., 158.

29 Sally Falk Moore, 'Law and social change: the semi-autonomous social field as an appropriate subject of study,' *Law & Society Review* 7 (1973), 719–746, at 720.

30 Maarten Bavinck, '"A Matter of Maintaining Peace": State accommodation to subordinate legal systems: the case of fisheries along the Coromandel Coast of Tamil Nadu, India,' *Journal of Legal Pluralism*, 40 (1998), 151–170, at 165.

31 Ibid., 166. Bavinck argues for a 'middle ground' (167) but the danger of a tragedy of the commons occurring because the fishing communities could not resolve their differences, while real, overlooks the origins of the dispute in pressures on the physical environment in 'resource capture', 'the degradation and depletion of a renewable resource', associated in this case with the coming of industrial trawling to the Coromandel coast. (See Tom Deligiannis, 'The Evolution of Environment-Conflict Research,' in *Critical Environmental Security*, eds. M.A. Schnurr & L.A. Swatuk, New Issues in Security, #5, Centre for Foreign Policy Studies: Dalhousie University, 2010, 1–28, at 3.)

32 Said, *Beginnings and Intentions*, 351.

33 Jerry H. Gill, *Merleau-Ponty and Metaphor*, Humanities Press, New Jersey, 1991, 66.

34 Predrag Matvejevic, *Mediterranean, a Cultural Landscape*, trans. M.H. Heim, University of California Press, Berkeley, 1999, 162–163.

35 Hugo Grotius, *The Free Sea*, trans. R. Hakluyt, see chapter 5, accessed at http://oll.libertyfund.org/?option=com_staticxt&staticfile=show.php%3Ftitle=859&chapter=66169&layout=html&Itemid=27

36 Antony Anghie, *Imperialism, Sovereignty and the Making of International Law*, Cambridge University Press, Cambridge, 2005, ch.2.

37 Hugo Grotius, *The Free Sea*, op.cit.

38 Ibid.

39 Quoted by A. Dirk Moses (ed.), *Empire, Colony, Genocide: Conquest, Occupation, and Subaltern Resistance*, Berghahn Books, New York, 2008, 63.

40 Katrina Lee Koo, review of Simon Dalby, *Complex in Nature*, *Borderlands ejournal*, vol. 2, no.1.

41 Ibid.

42 Varro says: 'The Aegean is named from the islands, because in this sea the craggy islands in the open water are called aeges "goats", from their likeness to she-goats' (Varro, Marcus Terentius, *Varro on the Latin Language*, trans. R.G. Kent, 2 vols, Cambridge, MA, 1938, vol. 1, 291).

43 Franco Cassano, *Il Pensiero meridiano*, Laterza, Roma-Bari, 1998, 22.

44 Hölderlin, 'Der Archipelagus', *Selected Verse*, trans. Michael Hamburger, Penguin, London, 1961, 96.

45 All quotations in this paragraph are from http://balticstudies.utu.fi/nondegree/courses/academicyr08–09/archipelago.pdf, accessed 7 August 2012.

46 A paradox anticipated by Marco Polo when he remarked that beyond the China Sea there were 7,448 islands, all of which no one had seen.

47 In contrast with *mediterreanismo* and coined with the former dominance of Malay as the *lingua franca* of trade from the Malacca Straits to Canton.

48 Ian Keen, 'A continent of foragers: Aboriginal Australia as a "regional system"', 261–273, p.269 in *Archaeology and Linguistics: Aboriginal Australia in a Global Perspective*, eds. P. MacConvell & N. Evans, OUP: Melbourne, 1997.

49 In *The Lie of the Land* (1996) I make the case for a poetic analogy between Venetian painting and work emerging from the Papunya Tula or Western Desert Painting Movement. Both involve processual, relational, non-linear accumulations of marks to create spatio-temporal traces that are mimetic as well as representational in their appeal.

50 Most famously 'Venezuela'.

51 Dalby, 100. All quotations are taken from a review article: Katrina Lee Koo, 'Complex in Nature: Reading Environmental Security Debates,' *Borderlands*

ejournal, vol 2, no. 1, 2003 accessed at www.borderlands.net.au/vol2no1/leekoo_dalby.html, accessed 12 August 2012.

52 Dipesh Chakrabarty, 'The Climate of History: Four Theses', *Critical Inquiry*, Winter 2009, 218.

53 Ibid., 219.

54 Ibid., 219.

55 Critics who accuse Humboldt of an ethnocentric or even racist bias against Chinese writing, because it fails to mark speaking positions, lacking any equivalent of the inflections found in Malayan-Polynesian and Indo-European languages, would be better advised to detect a geo-political preference for open evolving networks of communities organised archipelagically, joined by their ability to communicate differences, over the massively centralised, unitary and oppressive powers of the empire.

56 Roberts, 29.

57 Karin Ikas & Gerhard Wagner, 'Postcolonial Subjectivity and the Transcendental Logic of the Third', 96–103, in *Communicating in the Third Space*, Routledge, 2009, 101.

58 Michel Serres, 'The Origin of Language: Biology, Information Theory, & Thermodynamics,' from ed. Josue V. Harari & David F. Bell, *Hermes; Literature, Science, Philosophy*, Johns Hopkins University Press, Baltimore, 1982. Accessed at www.apomechanes.com/readings/TheOriginOfLanguageMichelSerres.pdf

59 Ibid.

60 Chantal DelSol, *Icarus Fallen*, trans. R. Dick, ISI Books, Wilmington, DE, 2004, 117.

INDEX